Certified OpenStack Administrator Study Guide

■ ■ ■

Andrey Markelov

Apress®

Certified OpenStack Administrator Study Guide

Andrey Markelov
Stockholm, Sweden

ISBN-13 (pbk): 978-1-4842-2124-2   ISBN-13 (electronic): 978-1-4842-2125-9
DOI 10.1007/978-1-4842-2125-9

Library of Congress Control Number: 2016958120

Managing Director: Welmoed Spahr
Acquisitions Editor: Louise Corrigan
Development Editor: Corbin Collins
Technical Reviewer: Anton Arapov
Editorial Board: Steve Anglin, Pramila Balan, Laura Berendson, Aaron Black, Louise Corrigan, Jonathan Gennick, Todd Green, Robert Hutchinson, Celestin Suresh John, Nikhil Karkal, James Markham, Susan McDermott, Matthew Moodie, Natalie Pao, Gwenan Spearing
Coordinating Editor: Nancy Chen
Copy Editor: Mary Bearden
Compositor: SPi Global
Indexer: SPi Global
Cover Image: Courtesy of Freepik.com

Distributed to the book trade worldwide by Springer Science+Business Media New York, 233 Spring Street, 6th Floor, New York, NY 10013. Phone 1-800-SPRINGER, fax (201) 348-4505, e-mail orders-ny@springer-sbm.com, or visit www.springer.com. Apress Media, LLC is a California LLC and the sole member (owner) is Springer Science + Business Media Finance Inc (SSBM Finance Inc). SSBM Finance Inc is a **Delaware** corporation.

For information on translations, please e-mail rights@apress.com, or visit www.apress.com.

Apress and friends of ED books may be purchased in bulk for academic, corporate, or promotional use. eBook versions and licenses are also available for most titles. For more information, reference our Special Bulk Sales–eBook Licensing web page at www.apress.com/bulk-sales.

Any source code or other supplementary materials referenced by the author in this text are available to readers at www.apress.com. For detailed information about how to locate your book's source code, go to www.apress.com/source-code/. Readers can also access source code at SpringerLink in the Supplementary Material section for each chapter.

Printed on acid-free paper

To my wife, Elena, for her love and support.

Contents at a Glance

Contents

About the Author

Andrey Markelov is an experienced Linux and cloud architect who currently works as a Senior Solution Architect at Ericsson in Sweden. Before Ericsson, Andrey worked as the first ever Red Hat Solution Architect in Russia and with various large system integrators. He has written more than 50 articles about Linux and Unix systems services, virtual systems, and OpenSource, published in the Russian IT Press (*Linux Format RE*, *Computerra*, *PCWeek/RE*, and others). Andrey is the author of the only Russian OpenStack book at the moment. He also has experience in teaching Microsoft and Red Hat authorized courses over the past ten years. Andrey has been a Red Hat Certified Architect since 2009. He has the following certifications: Microsoft Certified System Engineer, Sun Certified System Administrator, Novell Certified Linux Professional, Mirantis Certified OpenStack Administrator, and Certified OpenStack Administrator by The OpenStack Foundation. His LinkedIn profile can be found at http://ru.linkedin.com/in/amarkelov.

About the Technical Reviewer

Anton Arapov leads the team responsible for infrastructure projects in Xura, which help customers unlock and protect the full potential of their mobile communication channels, while supporting the evolution to LTE 4G services and accelerating return on investment. Nowadays, virtualization is crucial for achieving the goals. Prior to Xura, Anton held a role of Engineering Manager at Red Hat, responsible for development of virtualization technologies in Linux Kernel.

Introduction

The Certified OpenStack Administrator (COA) is the first professional certification offered by the OpenStack Foundation. As OpenStack's web site states, it's designed to help companies identify top talent in the industry, and help job seekers demonstrate their skills.

The COA certification is available to anyone who passes the exam. No mandatory learning is required. However, the Certified OpenStack Administrator is a professional, typically with at least six months' OpenStack experience. It is very important to gain practical skills of work with OpenStack before taking the exam. If you read this or any other books or if you watch any video courses with no practice, you will likely fail your exam. Practice, practice, practice is the only way to successfully reach the exam goals.

Quick facts about the exam:

- The duration is 2.5 hours.

- The price (at the time of writing) to take the exam is $300. One free retake per exam purchase will be granted in the event that a passing score is not achieved.

- The exam is performance-based. You may use a graphical interface or the command line.

- The exam is available anywhere in the world through the Internet.

- Candidates are monitored virtually by a proctor during the exam session via streaming audio, video, and screensharing.

This book is organized to cover all COA exam requirements, publicly available at www.openstack.org/coa/requirements. They are also shown at Figure I-1 in short form. Exam objectives are subject to change. Please visit the COA exam web site for the most current listing of exam objectives. Even if you don't plan to take the COA exam, this book can be a useful tutorial for OpenStack operators.

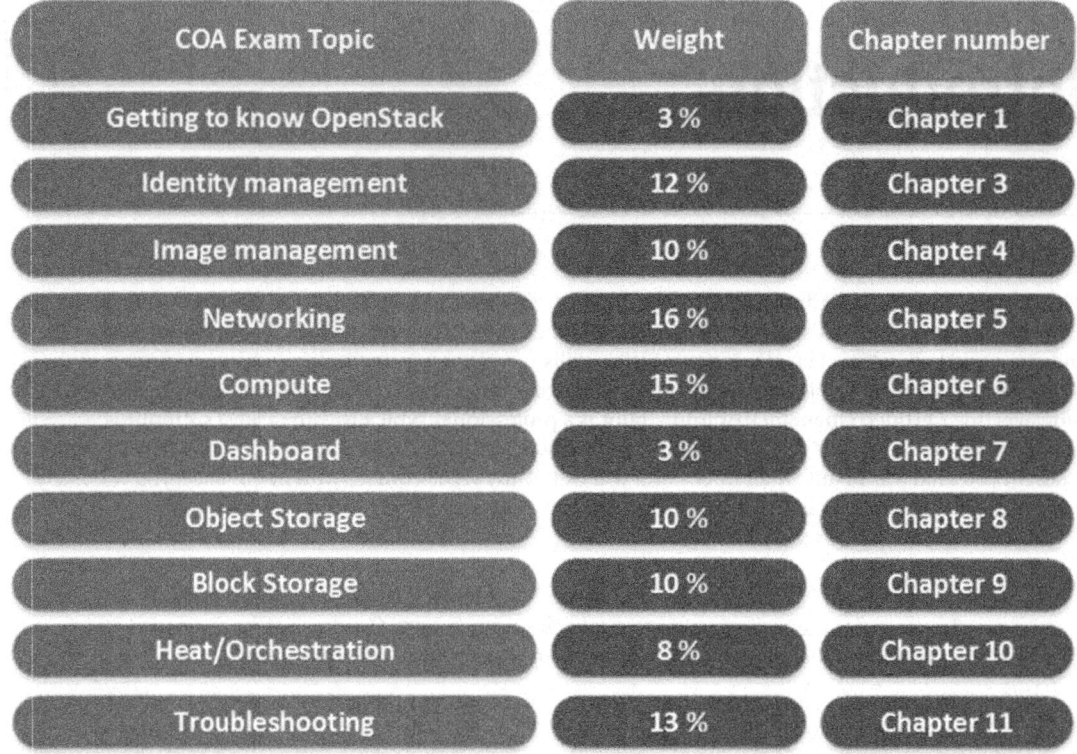

COA Exam Topic	Weight	Chapter number
Getting to know OpenStack	3 %	Chapter 1
Identity management	12 %	Chapter 3
Image management	10 %	Chapter 4
Networking	16 %	Chapter 5
Compute	15 %	Chapter 6
Dashboard	3 %	Chapter 7
Object Storage	10 %	Chapter 8
Block Storage	10 %	Chapter 9
Heat/Orchestration	8 %	Chapter 10
Troubleshooting	13 %	Chapter 11

Figure I-1. *OpenStack COA exam requirements*

Tips for COA Exam Preparation

If you successfully run through all of the book's contents and think you are ready for exam, you should start by reading the OpenStack Foundation Certification Candidate Handbook for OpenStack Foundation Certified OpenStack Administrator (COA). This guide is available from the COA web site at www.openstack. org/coa/. It contains all the instructions and conditions you need to know before taking the exam.

A day before the exam, it is better to rest and not to study until into the late evening. Try to schedule the exam for the first part of the day when your brain is fresh.

It's very important to test your PC to make sure it meets the minimal requirements with the exam provider's web site. Figure I-2 shows the requirements (at the time of this writing). Pay attention to the screen resolution. At the time of writing, the minimum was set to 1280x800. It is really a minimum value and it will probably be uncomfortable to work with exam consoles with this resolution. I would recommend you use a monitor as big as possible.

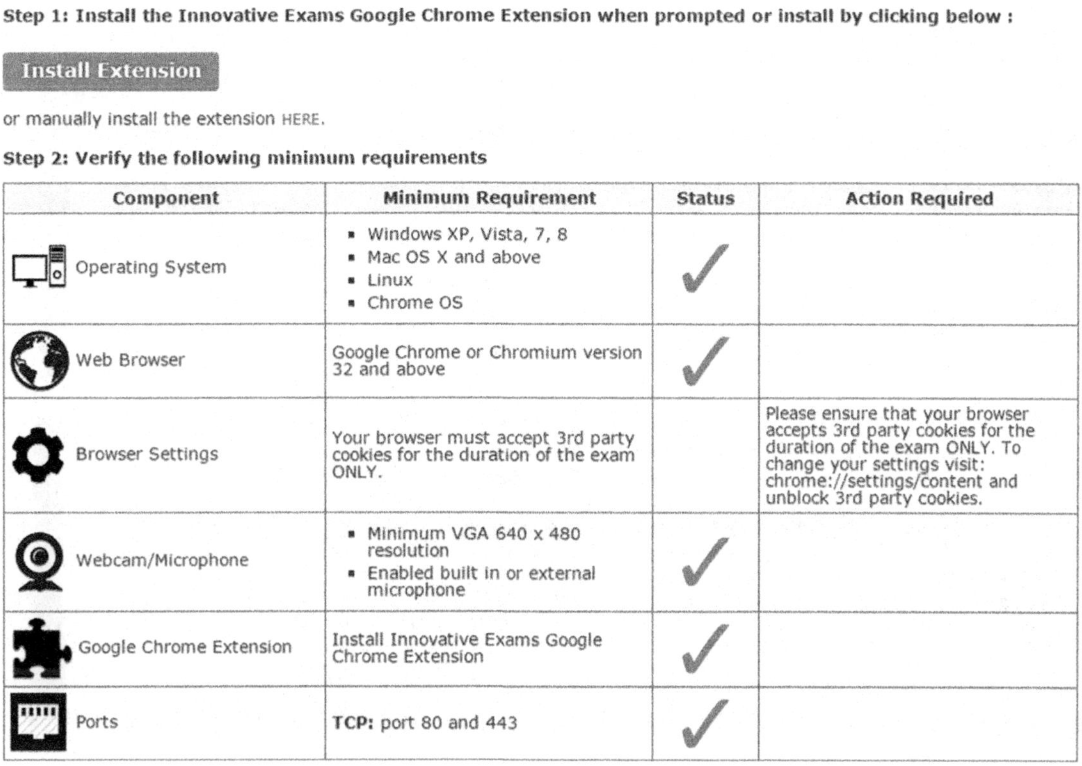

Step 1: Install the Innovative Exams Google Chrome Extension when prompted or install by clicking below :

Install Extension

or manually install the extension HERE.

Step 2: Verify the following minimum requirements

Component	Minimum Requirement	Status	Action Required
Operating System	• Windows XP, Vista, 7, 8 • Mac OS X and above • Linux • Chrome OS	✓	
Web Browser	Google Chrome or Chromium version 32 and above	✓	
Browser Settings	Your browser must accept 3rd party cookies for the duration of the exam ONLY.		Please ensure that your browser accepts 3rd party cookies for the duration of the exam ONLY. To change your settings visit: chrome://settings/content and unblock 3rd party cookies.
Webcam/Microphone	• Minimum VGA 640 x 480 resolution • Enabled built in or external microphone	✓	
Google Chrome Extension	Install Innovative Exams Google Chrome Extension	✓	
Ports	**TCP:** port 80 and 443	✓	

Figure I-2. *Screenshot of compatibility checklist at exam provider web site*

The handbook tells you to launch http://docs.openstack.org/ to access the technical documentation. Take some time to investigate the information. You do not need to memorize everything, but it is good to know what the documentation web site contains.

It is probably better not to type long names of projects, volumes, directories, and so forth but rather to copy them from the exam task list to the command line during the exam. You can avoid mistypes and errors if you do so. Use Ctrl+Insert to copy and Shift+Insert to paste in Microsoft Windows operating systems. Shortcuts Ctrl+C and Ctrl+V are not currently supported in the exam terminal.

It is highly recommended to use one of the terminal multiplexers because the exam terminal has a single console. You can use the screen command or the more advanced tmux. Take your time to practice with one of them. If you choose to use tmux you can start a new session with the command:

```
# tmux new
```

If the connection is lost, you can rejoin a session with the command:

```
# tmux attach
```

In Figure I-3 you can see what the tmux display looks like. Table I-1 lists the most common shortcuts for tmux commands.

```
PROJECT_DOMAIN_ID=default
2016-05-09 10:22:21.871 | ++userrc_early:source:10                          OS_PROJECT
_DOMAIN_ID=default
2016-05-09 10:22:21.881 | ++userrc_early:source:11                          export OS_
REGION_NAME=RegionOne
2016-05-09 10:22:21.891 | ++userrc_early:source:11                          OS_REGION_
NAME=RegionOne
2016-05-09 10:22:21.901 | +./stack.sh:main:1033                             create_keys
tone_accounts
2016-05-09 10:22:21.907 | +lib/keystone:create_keystone_accounts:368   local admi
n_project
2016-05-09 10:22:21.918 | ++lib/keystone:create_keystone_accounts:369   openstack
 project show admin -f value -c id
```

```
top - 13:22:28 up 17 min,  1 user,  load average: 1.07, 0.58, 0.27
Tasks: 149 total,   1 running, 148 sleeping,   0 stopped,   0 zombie
%Cpu(s): 93.0 us,  6.3 sy,  0.0 ni,  0.0 id,  0.3 wa,  0.0 hi,  0.3 si,  0.0 st
KiB Mem:   4047420 total,  1330368 used,  2717052 free,    96740 buffers
KiB Swap:  2093052 total,        0 used,  2093052 free.   618684 cached Mem

  PID USER      PR  NI    VIRT    RES    SHR S %CPU %MEM     TIME+ COMMAND
13510 stack     20   0  334612  62656   9592 S 61.9  1.5   0:01.87 apache2
13509 stack     20   0  337444  67256   9592 S 31.9  1.7   0:03.16 apache2
12903 stack     20   0   34048   9504   4860 S  1.3  0.2   0:00.37 dstat
14448 stack     20   0  106172  40748   9540 S  0.7  1.0   0:01.41 openstack
    7 root      20   0       0      0      0 S  0.3  0.0   0:00.77 rcu_sched
    9 root      20   0       0      0      0 S  0.3  0.0   0:00.82 rcuos/0
  191 root      20   0       0      0      0 S  0.3  0.0   0:00.05 jbd2/dm-0-8
[0] 0:bash- 1:bash  2:top*                            "ubuntu" 13:22 09-May-16
```

Screen 2

Screen 1

Screen 0

Figure I-3. *The tmux screen multiplexer*

Table I-1. *Some of tmux Command Key Bindings*

Command Key Bindings	Action
Ctrl-B ?	Show screen with help.
Ctrl-B d	Detach from session.
Ctrl-B s	List sessions.
Ctrl-B c	Create a new window.
Ctrl-B n	Change to the next window.
Ctrl-B p	Change to the previous window.
Ctrl-B 0...9	Select windows 0 through 9.
Ctrl-B %	Create a horizontal pane.
Ctrl-B "	Create a vertical pane.
Ctrl-B ↑↓→←	Move to pane.

Other OpenStack Certifications

Although I have the other two OpenStack certificates, there will not be any discussion of other vendors' OpenStack exams in this book. This book may help for their preparation, but it does not contain any specific information other than for the COA exam. Exam objectives can be different. The comparison in Table I-2 is purely for information purposes only. It is accurate at the time of writing but is always subject to change.

Table I-2. *Comparison of OpenStack Certifications*

Vendor	COA	Mirantis	Red Hat
Certification name	Certified OpenStack Administrator	Mirantis Certified Administrator for OpenStack	Red Hat Certified System Administrator in Red Hat OpenStack
Exam availability	Worldwide (through Internet connection)	Restricted (vendor and partners facility)	Restricted (vendor and partners facility)
Performance-based	Yes	Yes (MCA200)	Yes
Vendor neutral	Yes	Yes	No
Free retake per purchase	One	No	No
Certification validity	3 years	--	3 years
Passing score	78%	--	210 out of 300
Exam price	$300	$600	$600
Source of information	https://www.openstack.org/coa/	https://training.mirantis.com/certification	https://www.redhat.com/en/services/certification

CHAPTER 1

Getting to Know OpenStack

Before we delve into a discussion of OpenStack, let's determine what we mean when we refer to cloud computing. The National Institute of Standards and Technology's (NIST) definition is considered the established definition in the industry:

> *Cloud computing is a model of providing widely accessible and convenient access via the network to the common set of adjustable computational resources on demand (such as networks, servers, data storages, applications and services). These resources can be promptly allocated and released with minimum customer efforts spent for management and interactions with service provider.*

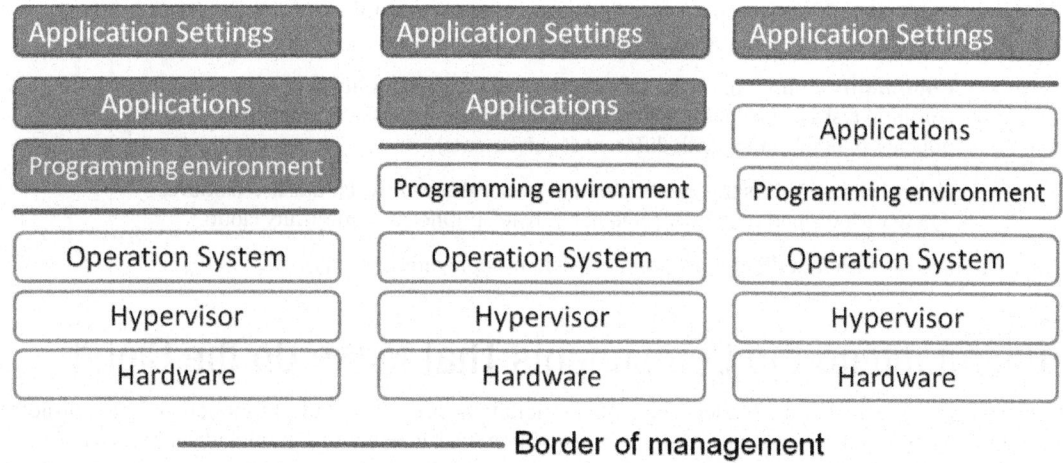

Figure 1-1. *Cloud service models*

© Andrey Markelov 2016

A. Markelov, *Certified OpenStack Administrator Study Guide*, DOI 10.1007/978-1-4842-2125-9_1

The service models shown in Figure 1-1 are defined by five essential characteristics, three service models, and four deployment models. It includes self-service, general access to the network, a common set of resources, flexibility, and calculation of use. Service models differ by the level of customer control of the provided infrastructure and include:

- **Infrastructure as a service (IaaS):** In this case, the user gets control over all levels of the software stack above the cloud platform—virtual machines, networks, space volume at data storage system—given to the user. The user is an administrator of the operation system and all the work above it to the applications. OpenStack is an example of IaaS.

- **Platform as a service (PaaS):** The cloud of this model can exist "inside" the cloud of the IaaS model. In this case, the user gets control on the level of the platform applications built, for example, applications server, libraries, programming environment, and database. The user does not control and does not administer virtual machines and operational systems deployed on them, data storage systems, and networks. Ericsson Apcea and Red Hat OpenShift would be examples of PaaS.

- **Software as a service (SaaS):** In this case, the user level of control is for only the application itself. The user would be unaware of what the virtual machine or the operational system is and would only work with the application. Examples of such products are Google Docs or Microsoft Office 365.

Four deployment models of the cloud platform implementations include:

- **Private cloud**: All the infrastructure is deployed in the data center and defined as a division of one company or a group of companies.

- **Public cloud**: Any company or even a person can be a customer of cloud services. This is the integration model the cloud service providers use.

- **Community cloud**: This is the model used when a community of companies with common tasks is the customer (common tasks can be missions, safety requirements, policies, or compliance with different requirements).

- **Hybrid cloud**: This is the combination of two or three of the clouds listed above, where various loads can be located at a private, public, or community cloud.

OpenStack can be a foundation for Clouds of all four deployment models.

Understanding the Components That Make Up the Cloud

OpenStack project, which is also called a cloud operational system, consists of a number of different projects developing separate subsystems (see Figure 1-2). Any OpenStack installation can include only a part of them. Some subsystems can even be used separately or as part of any other OpenSource project. Their number is increasing from version to version of OpenStack project, both through the appearance of new ones and the functionality split of the existing ones. For example, nova-volume service was extracted as a separate Cinder project.

Each project has its own documented set of Representational State Transfer Application Program Interfaces (REST APIs), command raw utilities, and "native" Python interfaces, providing a set of functions that are similar to the command raw utilities.

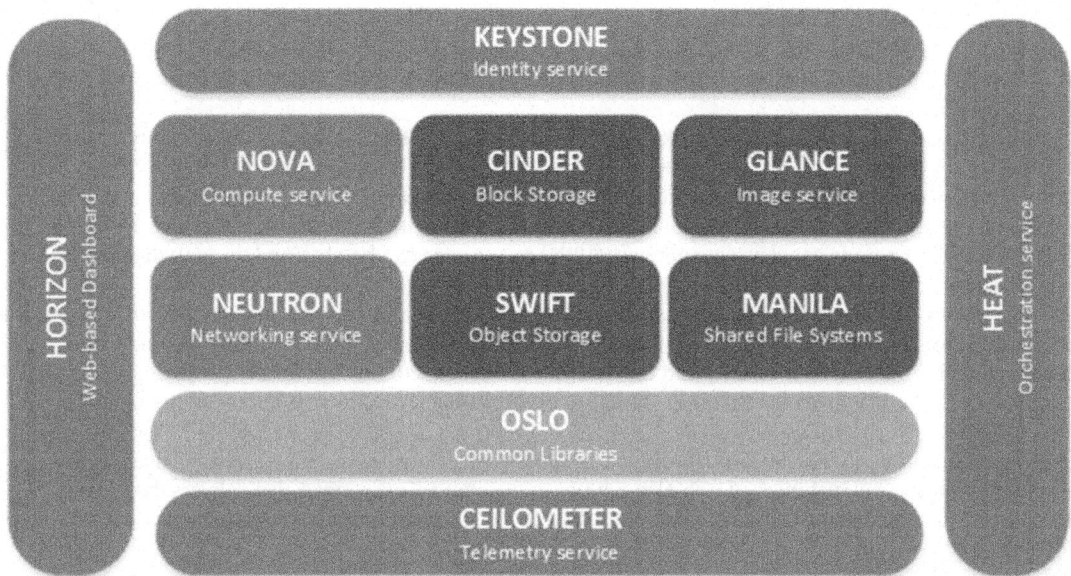

Figure 1-2. *OpenStack architecture and components*

One of the basic services is OpenStack Compute (Nova). This service is installed on all cluster computer nodes. It manages the level of abstraction of virtual equipment (processors, memory, block devices, network adapters). Nova provides the management of instances of virtual machines addressing the hypervisor and giving such commands as it is launching and stopping.

It's important to notice that OpenStack technologies are independent of the hypervisor. Support is implemented through the appropriate drivers in a Nova project. Primarily, OpenStack development and testing are being made for Kernel-based Virtual Machines (KVMs). Most execution is also implemented on top of the KVM hypervisor.

KVM has been a part of Linux kernel since 2007, and it requires virtualization hardware support on servers with standard architecture (AMD-V or Intel VT-x). At present, KVM is adapted for usage with a number of different platforms, for example, PowerPC. QEMU (short for Quick Emulator) is used for input/output devices for emulation in GNU/Linux.

You can check whether the support is turned on and the processor supports one of the technologies by executing the following command:

```
$ grep -E ' svm | vmx' /proc/cpuinfo
```

You should see svm or vmx among the flags supported by the processor. Also if you execute the command:

```
$ lsmod | grep kvm
kvm_intel           143187  3
kvm                 455843  1 kvm_intel
```

or

```
$ lsmod | grep kvm
kvm_amd           60314  3
kvm               461126  1 kvm_amd
```

you should see two kernel modules loaded in the memory. The kvm is the module independent of the vendor, and the kvm_intel or kvm_amd executes VT-x or AMD-V functionality, respectively. Pay attention to the fact that virtualization hardware support could be disabled in the basic input/output system (BIOS) by default.

The next service, OpenStack Networking (Neutron), is responsible for network connectivity. Users themselves can create virtual networks and routers as well as set up Internet provider (IP) addresses. One of the mechanisms provided by Neutron is called "floating IP." Thanks to this mechanism, virtual machines can get externally fixed IP addresses. Such functionality has a network capability balancer as a service, a firewall as a service, and virtual private network (VPN) as a service can be obtained through the mechanism of connecting modules.

OpenStack Keystone identification service is a centralized catalog of users and services that they have access to. Keystone performs as a united authentication system of the cloud operating system. Keystone checks the validity of users' accounts and the accordance of users to the OpenStack projects and roles. And if it's compliant, it gives the token for access to other services. Keystone runs a services' catalog/directory as well.

OpenStack Image Service (Glance) runs the catalog of virtual machines' images, which users can use as templates to run instances of virtual machines in the cloud. This service also delivers the backup functionality and snapshots creation. Glance supports many different formats, including vhd, vmdk, vdi, iso, qcow2, and ami.

OpenStack Block Storage (Cinder) service manages block storage, which can be used by running instances of virtual machines. This is permanent data storage for virtual machines. Snapshots can be used for data saving and restoring or cloning. In most cases data storage based on GNU/Linux servers is used together with Cinder. However, there are connecting modules for hardware storage.

OpenStack Object Storage (Swift) service is one of the two original projects that appeared in OpenStack besides Nova. Originally it was called Rackspace Cloud Files. This service is an object storage, which allows users to store files. Swift has distributed architecture, allowing horizontal scaling, redundancy, and replication for failover purposes. Swift is oriented mostly to static data, such as virtual machines' copies, backup copies, and archives.

OpenStack Telemetry (Celiometer) service is a centralized information source based on cloud metrics for monitoring data. This component delivers the billing ability for OpenStack.

OpenStack Orchestration (Heat) service has the main task of application life cycle provision in cloud infrastructure. Using the template in AWS CloudFormation format, this service manages all other OpenStack services, allowing the creation of most types of resources (virtual machines, volumes, floating IPs, users, security groups, etc.). Heat can also make application scaling automatic by using data from the Ceilometer service. Templates describe the relation between the resourses, which allows Heat service to make API OpenStack calls in the right order, for example, first to create the server and then to connect volume to it.

Finally, OpenStack Dashboard (Horizon) service allows management of cloud resources through the web console.

History of OpenStack Project

The cloud operational system OpenStack was established in June 2010 as a project that connected NASA's Nova virtual servers development system and US hosting-provider Rackspace's Swift data storage system. The first version, under the code name Austin, was released in October 2010.

The third service for Glance image storage had already appeared in the Bexar version in addition to Nova and Swift. In the Essex version, Horizon management web-console and Keystone identification service were added. There was the Folsom version of network service, which was originally named Quantum but then renamed as that name was already a registered trademark, and then the Cinder cloud block storage service. The Heat orchestration service and Celiometer service were added in the Havana version.

It's important to understand that OpenStack itself is a development project. The web site `Openstack.org` doesn't provide any reference for distribution. Otherwise, different vendors could create their own distributions based on this project code.

At present, OpenStack is being developed under the control of the OpenStack Foundation with about 18,000 individual members and more than 500 corporate members. Almost all IT market leaders support OpenStack. The OpenStack Foundation budget in 2016 was more than US$16 million per year.

As per one Linux Foundation report, OpenStack currently has 2.3 million lines of code. The main programming language is Python. The code itself is distributed under an Apache 2.0 license.

To easily evaluate each vendor contribution to the OpenStack project, visit `http://stackalytics.com`. This service was originally created by Mirantis company to get the statistics and measure the company's engineers' contributions in the project as a whole and its separate parts. Then all the rest of the OpenStack developers began to use it. The top five contributors now are Red Hat, HP, Mirantis, Rackspace, and IBM.

In accordance with a Forrester Research report (`http://www.openstack.org/assets/pdf-downloads/OpenStack-Is-Ready-Are-You.pdf`), at the present time OpenStack is used by many Fortune 100 companies, such as BMW, Disney, and Walmart.

Before going further, perhaps it will be interesting for you to look through the portal `https://www.openstack.org/enterprise/`. You can find some examples of OpenStack usage in production operations at some of these enterprises.

OpenStack Distribution and Vendors

As stated earlier, OpenStack is a cloud infrastructure development project, but not a product. However, many companies that take part in OpenStack development create their products and distributions on the basis of its code, often using their proprietary components. This situation is similar to GNU/Linux distributions' creation. Some examples of OpenStack distributions with links for downloading are shown in Table 1-1.

I have tried to give a very short overview of OpenStack distributions in this chapter. But this overview does not by any means present an overall coverage. Please note that the information in this book is up to date at the time the book was written in 2016. You can find a full list of major distributions at the Marketplace tab of the OpenStack official web site at `https://www.openstack.org/marketplace/distros/`.

RDO (RPM Distribution of OpenStack) is the project on open OpenStack distribution creation sponsored by Red Hat. Unlike for Red Hat commercial distribution, with Red Hat OpenStack Platform (RH OSP), the RDO support cannot be bought. Interrelation between RH OSP and RDO is very similar to the interrelation between Red Hat Enterprise Linux (RHEL) and Fedora. RDO is called up to create a community for Red Hat developments. In the latest versions of RDO, Manager, based on OpenStack Ironic and OpenStack TripleO projects, is offered to be used for installation. RDO can be deployed on top of RHEL and its derivatives (CentOS, Oracle Linux, etc.).

Table 1-1. *Download Links for OpenStack Distributions*

OpenStack Distribution	Web Site Link
Red Hat OpenStack Platform (60-day trial)	`https://www.redhat.com/en/insights/openstack`
RDO by Red Hat	`https://www.rdoproject.org/`
Mirantis OpenStack	`https://www.mirantis.com/products/mirantis-openstack-software/`
Ubuntu OpenStack	`http://www.ubuntu.com/cloud/openstack`
SUSE OpenStack Cloud (60-day trial)	`https://www.suse.com/products/suse-openstack-cloud/`

Another popular GNU/Linux vendor also has its own OpenStack distribution called SUSE OpenStack Cloud. SUSE Linux Enterprise Server 11 or SUSE Linux Enterprise Server 12 is used as an operation system distribution. The Cowbar and Chef projects are used as an installation tool. Chef is one of the leading configuration management tools in the OpenSource world.

The next distribution is Mirantis OpenStack (MOS). Similar to RDO, there are no proprietary components in it. The distinctive feature is the Fuel installation system, which can significantly ease large deployments. The support of OpenStack Community Application Catalog, based on the application's catalog Murano, also needs to be mentioned. As a GNU/Linux distribution, MOS requires either Ubuntu or CentOS. There are scripts for fast deployment on VirtualBox to ease the demo stands deployments or OpenStack research.

Oracle OpenStack for Oracle Linux stands out with quite unexpansive technical support for commercial usage in comparison with its competitors. It's free when you have premium Oracle Linux support. As a specialty Oracle, ZFS support can be noted. Solaris x86 is supported as a virtual machine. Similar to other hardware vendors, for example, IBM and HP, Oracle supports its distribution usage only on its own hardware. OpenStack Kolla project and Docker containers are used for installation.

Ericsson Cloud Execution Environment distribution is created with the requirements of network functions virtualization (NFV) and telecommunication operators specifics in mind. It provides the higher capacity of network subsystem and orientation to applications that require real-time operations. Compared to the distributions of any conventional IT companies, Ericsson Cloud Execution Environment is oriented toward telecommunication operators and provides service-level agreement (SLA) guaranteed by Ericsson. As a functionality example of VLAN Trunking support, virtual switch (Ericsson Virtual Switch) speeded with the help of Intel DPDK library, monitoring, high accessibility of virtual machines, and so on can be considered. As a distinction, it has its own web interface on the Horizon base. The distribution is created on top of the Mirantis OpenStack. Mirantis is a partner of Ericsson.

Hewlett Packard Enterprise (HPE) Helion OpenStack is a Hewlett Packard distribution. The company actively involves its resourses in OpenStack project development.

In any discussion of OpenStack distributions, it's necessary to mention the OPNFV (Open Platform for NFV) project (`https://www.opnfv.org`). OPNFV is a project based on open standard platform building for NFV. OPNFV integrated a number of projects, including OpenStack, OpenDaylight, Ceph Storage, KVM, Open vSwitch, and GNU/Linux. The largest telecommunication companies and vendors are taking part in this project (AT&T, Cisco, EMC, Ericsson, HP, Huawei, IBM, Intel, NEC, Nokia, Vodafone, ZTE, and many more).

■ ■ ■

## CHAPTER 2

How to Build Your Own Virtual Test Environment

This chapter describes how to install a virtual lab in preparation for the Certified OpenStack Administrator exam. You will use the DevStack, PackStack, and Fuel tool options for this installation. Keep in mind that this chapter is not related to exam questions.

Installing Vanilla OpenStack with the DevStack Tool

You have a lot of options for how to create your test environment. I will introduce several of them in this chapter. First, let's have a look at the most generic method of OpenStack installation. In this case, you will install all services from scratch on one PC or virtual machine. You can use one of the common GNU/Linux distributions like Ubuntu, Fedora, or CentOS. Since this method is very generic, you probably need some adaptations for your particular environment. More specific examples will be given later in this chapter.

I recommend using any type of desktop virtual environment like VirtualBox or VMware Workstation. I would recommended 4BG of memory or more for VM, where you will install all of the OpenStack services.

First, you will need the OS installed with access to standard repos. Then you need to get the DevStack tool from GitHub. The main purpose of this tool is to prepare the environment for OpenStack developers, but you can use it for creating this learning environment. The following instructions are for the most recent Ubuntu LTS releases. First, you will install the Git tool and download DevStack:

```
andrey@ubuntu:~$ sudo apt-get -y install git

andrey@ubuntu:~$ sudo git clone https://github.com/openstack-dev/devstack.git /opt/devstack/
Cloning into '/opt/devstack'...
remote: Counting objects: 33775, done.
remote: Compressing objects: 100% (6/6), done.
remote: Total 33775 (delta 2), reused 0 (delta 0), pack-reused 33769
Receiving objects: 100% (33775/33775), 12.25 MiB | 2.11 MiB/s, done.
Resolving deltas: 100% (23470/23470), done.
Checking connectivity... done.
```

© Andrey Markelov 2016
A. Markelov, *Certified OpenStack Administrator Study Guide*, DOI 10.1007/978-1-4842-2125-9_2

Then you create the user with the `create-stack-user.sh` script, change ownership for /opt/devstack/, and switch to the stack user:

```
andrey@ubuntu:~$ cd /opt/devstack/

andrey@ubuntu:/opt/devstack$ sudo tools/create-stack-user.sh
Creating a group called stack
Creating a user called stack
Giving stack user passwordless sudo privileges
andrey@ubuntu:/opt/devstack$ sudo chown -R stack:stack /opt/devstack/
andrey@ubuntu:/opt/devstack$ sudo -i -u stack
stack@ubuntu:~$ cd /opt/devstack/
```

DevStack uses a special file located in the root directory of devstack with instructions that describe how to configure OpenStack services. You can find several examples on the DevStack web site (http://docs.openstack.org/developer/devstack/) or you can use the following minimal example of the local.conf file:

```
[[local|localrc]]

ADMIN_PASSWORD="apress"
SERVICE_PASSWORD="apress"
SERVICE_TOKEN="apress"
MYSQL_PASSWORD="apress"
RABBIT_TOKEN="apress"
RABBIT_PASSWORD="apress"
SWIFT_HASH=sOM3hash1sh3r3

disable_service n-net
enable_service neutron
enable_service q-svc
enable_service q-agt
enable_service q-dhcp
enable_service q-l3
enable_service q-meta
HOST_IP=10.0.2.15

enable_service ceilometer-acompute
enable_service ceilometer-acentral
enable_service ceilometer-anotification
enable_service ceilometer-collector
enable_service ceilometer-alarm-evaluator
enable_service ceilometer-alarm-notifier
enable_service ceilometer-api

enable_service heat h-api h-api-cfn h-api-cw h-eng
enable_service s-proxy s-object s-container s-account
SWIFT_REPLICAS=1

LOGFILE=/opt/stack/logs/stack.sh.log
SCREEN_LOGDIR=/opt/stack/logs
```

Now you need to run the `stack.sh` script from the devstack directory and wait for it to load. Here is an example:

```
stack@ubuntu:/opt/devstack$ ./stack.sh
...
===========================
DevStack Component Timing
===========================
Total runtime          2239

run_process            104
test_with_retry          4
apt-get-update           7
pip_install            490
restart_apache_server   15
wait_for_service        16
git_timed              391
apt-get                195
===========================

This is your host IP address: 10.0.2.15
This is your host IPv6 address: ::1
Horizon is now available at http://10.0.2.15/dashboard
Keystone is serving at http://10.0.2.15:5000/
The default users are: admin and demo
The password: apress
2016-05-21 19:41:48.510 | stack.sh completed in 2239 seconds.
```

Installation can take some time. The process can be different in different environments or with different versions of OS. You will probably have to debug some errors. For a more predictable way of installing, see the next section.

Installing RDO OpenStack Distribution with PackStack

PackStack (`https://wiki.openstack.org/wiki/Packstack`) is another tool that can be used to install OpenStack. The main purpose of PackStack is to prepare OpenStack's test environments with rpm-based distributions. The easiest and most predictable way to use PackStack is to use it with CentOS 7.

Let's start with OS preparation. First, you need to install CentOS 7 with the `Minimal` or `Server with GUI` option. Right after installation, you should update the packages and reboot your server:

```
# yum -y update
# reboot
```

Next, add additional repositories that contain OpenStack and some supplementary packages:

```
# yum -y install epel-release
# yum install -y https://www.rdoproject.org/repos/rdo-release.rpm
```

Also you need to disable Network Manager service because OpenStack does not support it:

```
# systemctl stop NetworkManager.service
# systemctl disable NetworkManager.service
```

I use the old-fashioned "network" service instead:

```
# systemctl start network.service
# systemctl enable network.service
```

Make sure you have a static IP address in /etc/sysconfig/network-scripts/ifcfg-* config files. Here is an example of ifcfg-eth0:

```
TYPE="Ethernet"
BOOTPROTO="STATIC"
DEFROUTE="yes"
IPV6INIT="no"
NAME="eth0"
ONBOOT="yes"
IPADDR0="10.0.2.15"
PREFIX0="24"
GATEWAY="10.0.2.2"
DNS1="10.0.2.2"
NM_CONTROLLED=no
```

If the firewalld daemon is used, you need to change it to iptables. OpenStack can't use firewalld at the moment. Now everything is ready and you can install the PackStack tool:

```
# systemctl stop firewalld; systemctl disable firewalld
$ sudo yum install -y centos-release-openstack-mitaka
$ sudo yum update -y
# yum install -y openstack-packstack
```

Now you can just run the command packstack --allinone, but I recommend another change to generate the answers file for PackStack:

```
# packstack --gen-answer-file ~/answer-file.txt
```

Now you are ready to edit the ~/answer-file.txt. This file contains a lot of different options. Some of them are documented in Table 2-1.

Table 2-1. *PackStack Options*

Option with Example	Definition
`CONFIG_<name of cioponent>_INSTALL=y`	Specify 'y' to install OpenStack component. `<name of component>` can be `CINDER`, `GLANCE`, `NOVA`, `NEUTRON`, etc. For example `CONFIG_SWIFT_INSTALL=y`.
`CONFIG_DEFAULT_PASSWORD=password`	Default password to be used everywhere (overridden by passwords set for individual services or users).
`CONFIG_NTP_SERVERS=192.168.1.1,192.168.1.2`	Comma-separated list of NTP servers.
`CONFIG_CONTROLLER_HOST=10.0.2.15`	Comma-separated list of servers on which to install OpenStack services specific to the controller role.
`CONFIG_COMPUTE_HOSTS=10.0.2.15`	List of servers on which to install the Compute service.
`CONFIG_NETWORK_HOSTS=10.0.2.15`	List of servers on which to install the Network service.
`CONFIG_AMQP_BACKEND=rabbitmq`	Service to be used as the AMQP broker. Usually `rabbitmq`.
`CONFIG_AMQP_HOST=10.0.2.15`	IP address of the server on which to install the AMQP service.
`CONFIG_AMQP_ENABLE_SSL=n`	Specify 'y' to enable SSL for the AMQP service.
`CONFIG_USE_EPEL=y`	Specify 'y' to enable the EPEL repository (Extra Packages for Enterprise Linux). You need to do that if you are using CentOS or Oracle Linux.
`CONFIG_KEYSTONE_ADMIN_PW=password`	Password to use for the Identity service 'admin' user.
`CONFIG_KEYSTONE_DEMO_PW=password`	Password to use for the Identity service 'demo' user.
`CONFIG_GLANCE_BACKEND=file`	Storage backend for the Image service (controls how the Image service stores disk images). Valid options are: `file` or `swift`.
`CONFIG_CINDER_BACKEND=lvm`	Storage backend to use for the Block Storage service. Valid options are: lvm, gluster, nfs, vmdk, netapp.
`CONFIG_CINDER_VOLUMES_CREATE=y`	Specify 'y' to create the Block Storage volumes group. That is, PackStack creates a raw disk image in `/var/lib/cinder`, and mounts it using a loopback device.
`CONFIG_CINDER_VOLUMES_SIZE=20G`	Size of Block Storage volumes group.
`CONFIG_NEUTRON_FWAAS=y`	Specify 'y' to configure OpenStack Networking's Firewall-as-a-Service (FWaaS).
`CONFIG_NEUTRON_VPNAAS=y`	Specify 'y' to configure OpenStack Networking's VPN-as-a-Service (VPNaaS).
`CONFIG_SWIFT_STORAGE_SIZE=2G`	Size of the Object Storage loopback file storage device.
`CONFIG_PROVISION_DEMO=y`	Specify 'y' to provision for demo usage and testing.

It is best to at least change these options:

```
CONFIG_DEFAULT_PASSWORD=password
CONFIG_KEYSTONE_ADMIN_PW=password
CONFIG_KEYSTONE_DEMO_PW=password
CONFIG_USE_EPEL=y
CONFIG_PROVISION_DEMO=y
```

You should for sure use your own password instead of password. Now you are ready to run PackStack:

```
# packstack --answer-file ~/answer-file.txt
```

You must wait until PackStack completes all of its tasks. It can take 15 to 30 minutes. While working, the tool will report about all that is happening at each stage, for example:

```
Welcome to the Packstack setup utility

The installation log file is available at: /var/tmp/packstack/20160325-062215-wbPC1v/
openstack-setup.log

Installing:
Clean Up                                    [ DONE ]
Discovering ip protocol version             [ DONE ]
Setting up ssh keys                         [ DONE ]
...
Applying Puppet manifests                   [ DONE ]
Finalizing                                  [ DONE ]

 **** Installation completed successfully ******

Additional information:
 * Time synchronization installation was skipped. Please note that unsynchronized time on
   server instances might be problem for some OpenStack components.
 * File /root/keystonerc_admin has been created on OpenStack client host 10.0.2.15. To use
   the command line tools you need to source the file.
 * To access the OpenStack Dashboard browse to http://10.0.2.15/dashboard .
   Please, find your login credentials stored in the keystonerc_admin in your home directory.
 * To use Nagios, browse to http://10.0.2.15/nagios username: nagiosadmin, password:
   password
 * The installation log file is available at: /var/tmp/packstack/20160325-062215-wbPC1v/
   openstack-setup.log
 * The generated manifests are available at: /var/tmp/packstack/20160325-062215-wbPC1v/
   manifests
```

■ **Tip** You can rerun PackStack with option -d if you need to update the configuration.

Installing Mirantis OpenStack with Fuel Tool

PackStack should be used only for learning purposes or demo. In the real world for production usage, companies use "enterprise grade" installation tools. This kind of installation tool can simultaneously install OpenStack for hundreds of hosts and can create advanced configuration with high availability of services. The most mature tool is Fuel, which comes with Mirantis OpenStack.

First, you need to download the latest version of Mirantis OpenStack (MOS) in ISO format from https://software.mirantis.com/openstack-download-form/. All documentation is available online at https://docs.mirantis.com/openstack/fuel/. The easiest way to install MOS for learning purposes is described in the QuickStart Guide at the Mirantis web site. You also need the Oracle VirtualBox plus Oracle VM VirtualBox Extension Pack virtualization software and VirtualBox scriprt from Mirantis. You can download this script from the Mirantis web site at www.mirantis.com. You need at least 8GB on your PC with VirtualBox. For Microsoft Windows, you will need to install the Cygwin environment from https://www.cygwin.com/.

The workflow of the installation process is shown in Figure 2-1.

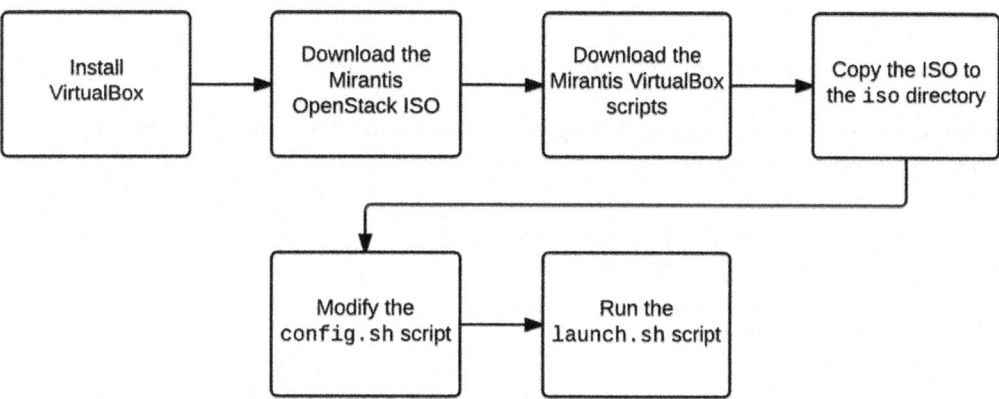

Figure 2-1. *Workflow of installation process (Figure courtesy of Mirantis)*

Unarchive the scripts pack and place the MOS ISO-file into the iso directory. Then run launch.sh script at the Cygwin prompt (see Figure 2-2):

```
cd /cygdrive/c/Users/{name}/Desktop/virtualbox
sh launch.sh
```

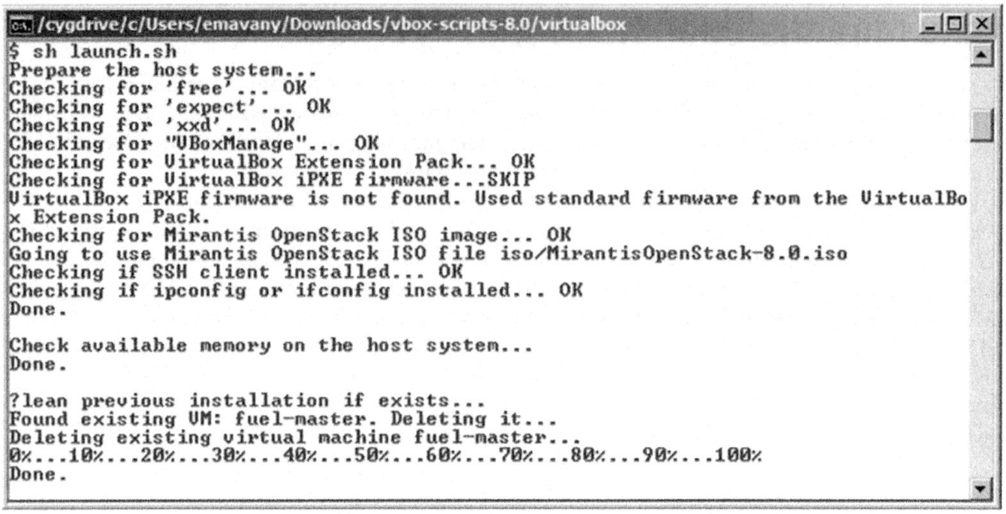

```
/cygdrive/c/Users/emavany/Downloads/vbox-scripts-8.0/virtualbox                    _ □ ×
$ sh launch.sh
Prepare the host system...
Checking for 'free'... OK
Checking for 'expect'... OK
Checking for 'xxd'... OK
Checking for "UBoxManage"... OK
Checking for VirtualBox Extension Pack... OK
Checking for VirtualBox iPXE firmware...SKIP
VirtualBox iPXE firmware is not found. Used standard firmware from the VirtualBo
x Extension Pack.
Checking for Mirantis OpenStack ISO image... OK
Going to use Mirantis OpenStack ISO file iso/MirantisOpenStack-8.0.iso
Checking if SSH client installed... OK
Checking if ipconfig or ifconfig installed... OK
Done.

Check available memory on the host system...
Done.

?lean previous installation if exists...
Found existing VM: fuel-master. Deleting it...
Deleting existing virtual machine fuel-master...
0%...10%...20%...30%...40%...50%...60%...70%...80%...90%...100%
Done.
```

Figure 2-2. *Running launch.sh in Microsoft Windows and Cygwin environment*

The script installs the Fuel Master node on VirtualBox and creates three VMs for the OpenStack environment. When installation of the Fuel node ends, you will see something like Figure 2-3 on the VMs screen.

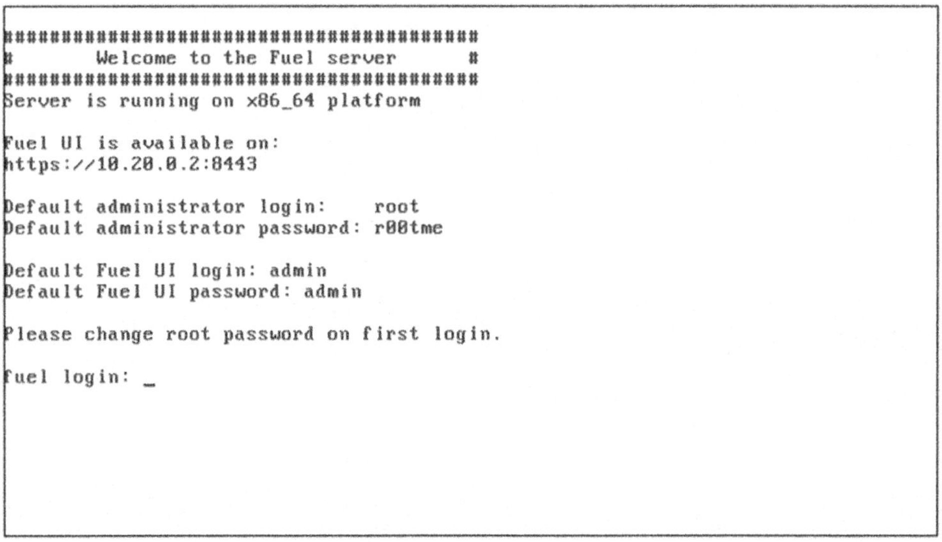

```
############################################
#         Welcome to the Fuel server       #
############################################
Server is running on x86_64 platform

Fuel UI is available on:
https://10.20.0.2:8443

Default administrator login:     root
Default administrator password: r00tme

Default Fuel UI login: admin
Default Fuel UI password: admin

Please change root password on first login.

fuel login: _
```

Figure 2-3. *Fuel node is ready*

As you see, you need to log in on https://10.20.0.2:8443 with the name admin and password admin. Alternatively, it is possible to connect to http://10.20.0.2:8000. Before that, if you need to change some settings for the Fuel host, for example, the DNS server and so on, you can log in to the console prompt and run the command fuelmenu. Go through the text user interface and change the requested settings. Figure 2-4 shows an example of the user interface (UI).

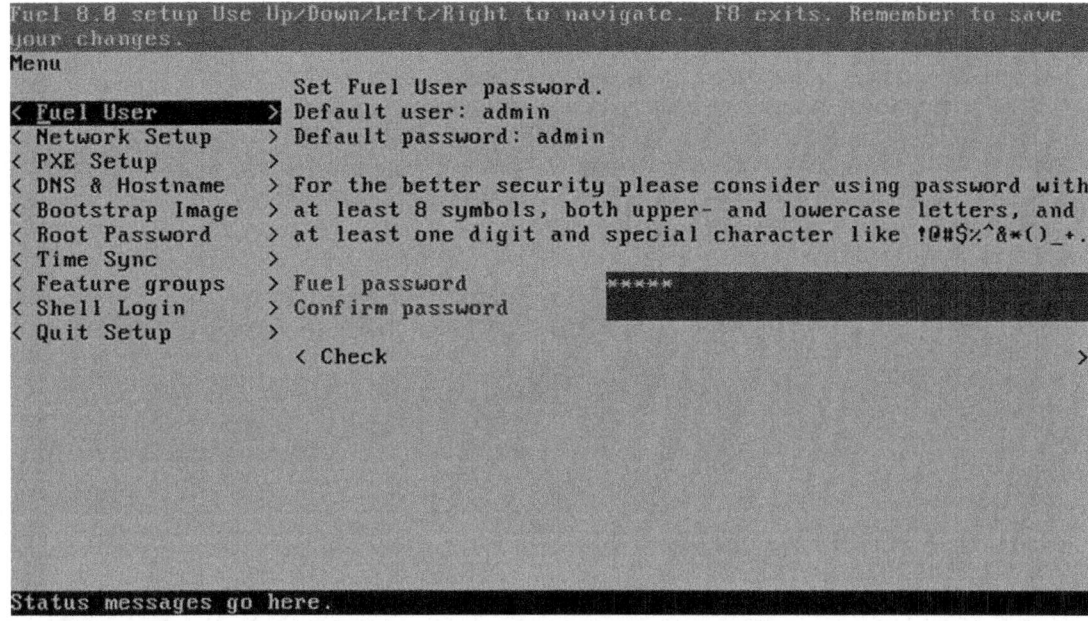

Figure 2-4. *Fuel menu user interface*

After log in, Fuel will ask you a question about a support login. As you do not have paid support from Mirantis, you can skip this step. You need to create a new OpenStack environment from three available virtual machines. Click the "New OpenStack Environment" button (see Figure 2-5). In the first screen, type a name for the OpenStack environment. You need to choose options (OpenStack release, hypervisor, network topology, storage backend) on the next four screens. It is safest to use the default options.

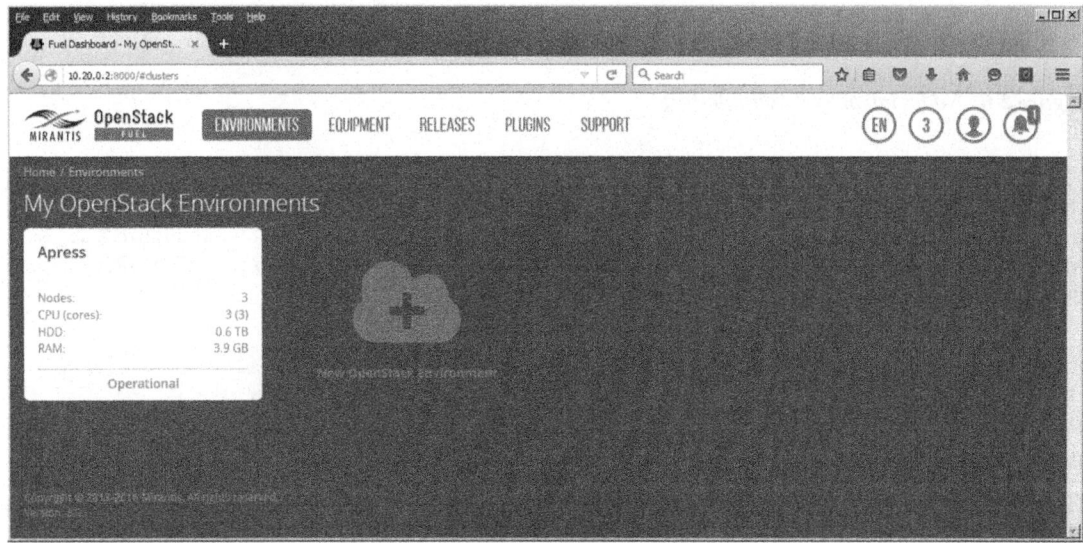

Figure 2-5. *Enviroments main screen of Fuel*

At the top right corner you should see the overall count of nodes and the count of free nodes that can be used in the new environment (3/3). Try to reboot VM if your VM is not shown. VMs should start Ubuntu based on the PXE pre-boot environment that is available from the Fuel host.

Click the button with the name of your OpenStack environment. Click the "Add nodes" button on the Dashboard tab. Go to the Nodes tab and select the roles for each node. To assign roles to the nodes, select the role you want to assign and click the appropriate nodes in the "Unallocated Nodes" list. At the end, click the "Apply Changes" button. You need at least one Controller and one Compute host.

Figure 2-6 shows how the Nodes tab should look now.

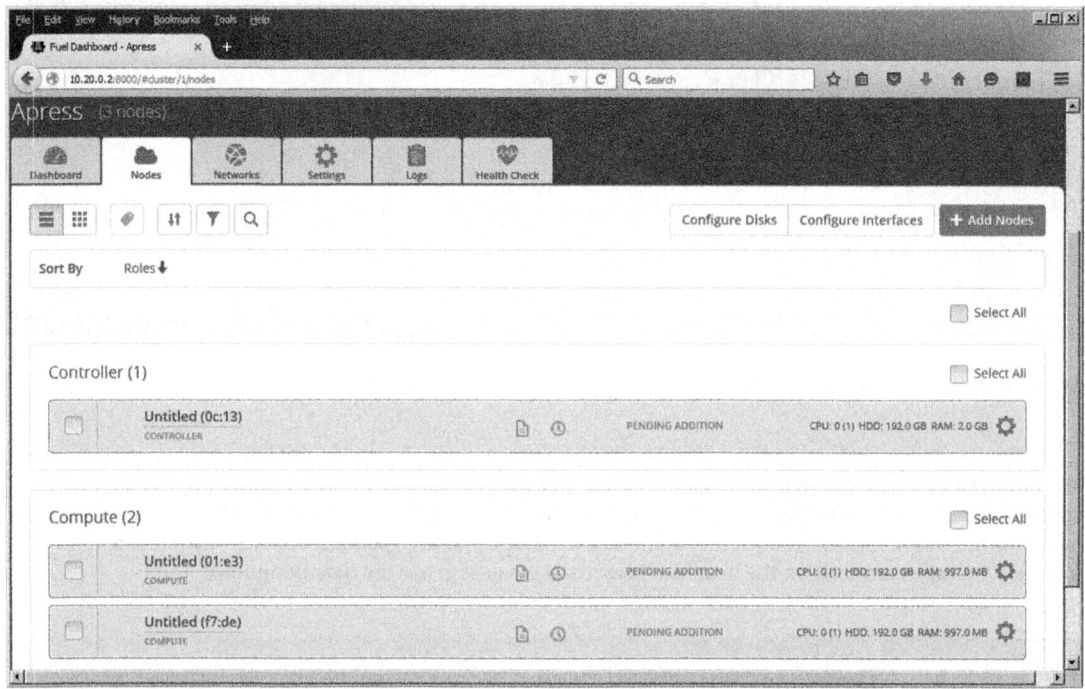

Figure 2-6. *Nodes tab of Fuel user interface*

Now everything is ready for deployment. In the Fuel web UI, select the Dashboard tab and click the "Deploy changes" button. Depending on the configuration of the environment, the deployment may take from 15 minutes to 1 hour. A screenshot of the deploying changes is shown in Figure 2-7. More detailed guidance is available at `https://docs.mirantis.com/openstack/fuel/fuel-8.0/quickstart-guide.html`.

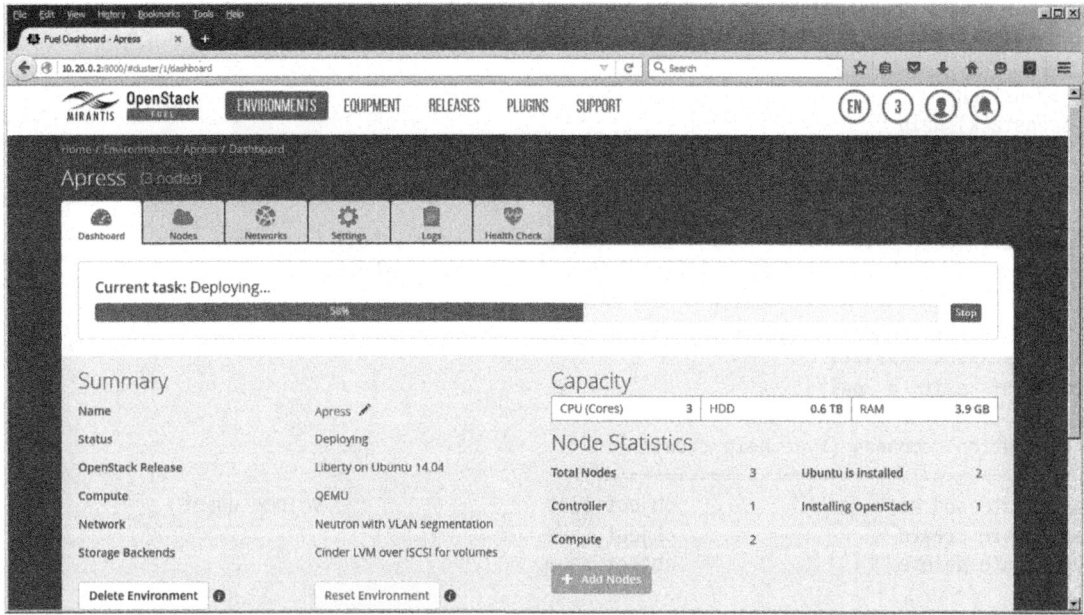

Figure 2-7. *Deploying changes in OpenSource*

Using the OpenStack CLI

OpenStack comes with a number of client utilities. Most services have their own command-line interface (CLI) utility that has the same name as the service itself. Some of these utilities will become obsolete because of the universal openstack CLI. You can use the packet manager to identify installed clients:

```
# rpm -qa | grep python.*client
python-keystoneclient-1.7.2-1.el7.noarch
python-troveclient-1.3.0-1.el7.noarch
python-neutronclient-3.1.0-1.el7.noarch
python-ceilometerclient-1.5.0-1.el7.noarch
python-heatclient-0.8.0-1.el7.noarch
python-glanceclient-1.1.0-1.el7.noarch
python-openstackclient-1.7.2-1.el7.noarch
python-swiftclient-2.6.0-1.el7.noarch
python-saharaclient-0.11.1-1.el7.noarch
python-cinderclient-1.4.0-1.el7.noarch
python2-os-client-config-1.7.4-1.el7.noarch
python-novaclient-2.30.1-1.el7.noarch
```

For a full list, refer to https://wiki.openstack.org/wiki/OpenStackClients. Most clients have an internal help section that can be printed with the help option followed by a subcommand. For example:

```
$ glance help image-create
usage: glance image-create [--architecture <ARCHITECTURE>]
                           [--protected [True|False]] [--name <NAME>]
...
```

Universal python-openstackclient has an interactive mode. This mode is indicated by the (openstack) prompt:

```
$ openstack
(openstack) help

Shell commands (type help <topic>):
====================================
cmdenvironment  edit  hi         l   list  pause  r    save  shell       show
ed                    help  history  li  load  py     run  set   shortcuts

Undocumented commands:
======================
EOF  eof  exit  q  quit

Application commands (type help <topic>):
=========================================
aggregate add host           object list                   volume unset
aggregate create             object save
aggregate delete             object show
...
```

Use the following code to get help regarding the subcommand keypair create:

```
(openstack) help keypair create
usage: keypair create [-h] [-f {html,json,json,shell,table,value,yaml,yaml}]
                      [-c COLUMN] [--max-width <integer>] [--noindent]
                      [--prefix PREFIX] [--public-key <file>]
                      <name>

Create new public key

positional arguments:
  <name>                New public key name
...
```

CHAPTER 3

■ ■ ■

Identity Management

This chapter covers 12% of the Certified OpenStack Administrator exam requirements.

Architecture and Main Components of Keystone

The Keystone or OpenStack Identity service acts as a catalog of all OpenStack services and provides the ability for authenticating and managing user accounts and role information for the cloud environment. If you are familiar with the Microsoft Windows Server environment, you can think of Keystone as the "Active Directory analog" for your OpenStack cloud. Usually Keystone is the first component to be installed when starting an OpenStack cloud. Keystone supports multiple forms of authentication, including login name and password, token-based credentials, and REST API log ins.

First, let's define some terms which Keystone operates with:

- **Service**: OpenStack cloud component listed in Keystone catalog. Examples of the services are Nova, Neutron, Glance, Keystone itself, etc. Service provides one or more endpoints through which users can access service's API.

- **Endpoint**: URL from which the service is available. Service can have three endpoints: internal, public, and administration. They can have different subsets of API calls. Endpoint can look like `https://controller.my-domain.com:35357/v2.0`. At this URL you would find that the service is listening to incoming calls on port number 35357 and the API version is 2.0. Common port numbers for OpenStack services are shown in Table 3-1.

Table 3-1. *Common Port Numbers for OpenStack Services*

Network Port Number	OpenStack Service
5000	Public API endpoint port for Keystone
35357	Admin API endpoint port for Keystone
8776	Cinder Block Storage service
9292	Image service Glance
9191	Glance Registry
8774	Compute service Nova
8080 and 6001-6003	Object Storage services Swift
9696	Networking service Neutron
8777	Telemetry service Ceilometer
8004	Orchestration service Heat

© Andrey Markelov 2016
A. Markelov, *Certified OpenStack Administrator Study Guide*, DOI 10.1007/978-1-4842-2125-9_3

- **Project**: Represents the base unit of ownership in OpenStack. Networks, VMs, users, roles, and so on belong to a particular project. For administrative operations in OpenStack, an environment special administrative project "admin" exists.

- **Domain**: Represents a collection of projects, groups, and users that defines administrative boundaries for managing OpenStack Identity entities.

- **Region**: Separates the OpenStack environment with dedicated API endpoints but with common Keystone service.

- **Token**: Issued by Keystone service then passed to API requests and used by OpenStack to verify that the client is authorized to run the requested operation. The token is issued for a limited time and, if necessary, may be withdrawn prior to the expiration. In order to get the user token, the user must either provide a name and password, or the name and the key to access the API (API key). The token also contains a list of roles that defines the roles available to the user.

- **User**: Individual API consumer. User can be associated with roles, projects, or both.

- **Role**: Specific set of operations associated with a user. A role includes a set of rights and privileges.

From an architectural point of view, Keystone is the simplest service in the cloud. As for many other OpenStack services, OpenStack Identity service uses the MariaDB/MySQL database. As an alternative, it is possible to store information in the LDAP (Lightweight Directory Access Protocol) server or Microsoft Active Directory. Starting from the Miaka release, Keystone uses the Apache web server as the front end, so you no longer need to start `openstack-keystone.service`. Prior to the Mitaka release, Keystone worked under the built-in Eventlet Python service by default.

■ **Tip**   In modern documents, the OpenStack community prefers to use the term "Project." In old documents you can still find the term "tenant." Keep in mind that "project" and "tenant" are synonymous.

Let's have a quick look through the Keystone main configuration file `/etc/keystone/keystone.conf`. Table 3-2 summarizes the main configuration options from config.

Table 3-2. *Main Configuration Options from /etc/keystone/keystone.conf*

Example of Config Options	Description
`[DEFAULT]` `admin_token = ee224e8...`	A "shared secret" that can be used to bootstrap and debug Keystone. This "token" does not represent a user.
`[DEFAULT]` `debug = True`	Set logging level to DEBUG instead of default INFO level in journal.
`[DEFAULT]` `log_dir = /var/log/keystone`	The base directory used for log files.

`[DEFAULT]`
`public_port=5000`
`admin_port=35357`
`admin_bind_host=0.0.0.0`
`public_bind_host=0.0.0.0`
	The port numbers and IP address which the public and admin services listen on. In *_bind_host options, four zeros mean all available ports on the server.

`[database]`
`connection = mysql://keystone_`
`admin:password@10.0.2.15/keystone`
	The SQLAlchemy connection string is used to connect to the database.

`[oslo_messaging_rabbit]`
`rabbit_host = localhost`
`rabbit_port = 5672`
`rabbit_userid = guest`
`rabbit_password = guest`
	The RabbitMQ broker address, port, user name, and password.

`[token]` `expiration = 3600`	Token validity timeframe (in seconds). By default–1 hour.

Managing Keystone Catalog Services and Endpoints

Before initiating something with OpenStack, you need to go through the authorization and authentication processes. You can use the CLI commands options, but it is better and easier to create a file with global variables for GNU/Linux environment and to process this file with the source command. You need to create in any text editor something like the following code:

```
unset OS_SERVICE_TOKEN
export OS_AUTH_URL=http://10.0.2.15:5000/v2.0
export OS_TENANT_NAME=admin
export OS_REGION_NAME=RegionOne
export OS_USERNAME=admin
export OS_PASSWORD=openstack
export OS_IDENTITY_API_VERSION=3
```

You need to use your correct IP address and correct admin password for your environment. Now you can execute the script:

```
$ source keystonerc_admin
```

Let's try to create a service record in Keystone for the OpenStack image service Glance (the Glance service is described in Chapter 4):

```
$ openstack service create --name glance --description "OpenStack Image service" image
+-------------+------------------------------------+
| Field       | Value                              |
+-------------+------------------------------------+
| description | OpenStack Image service            |
| enabled     | True                               |
| id          | 9d33c464f61749cd9f5811cda1ae5444   |
| name        | glance                             |
| type        | image                              |
+-------------+------------------------------------+
```

Only two mandatory options exist in this particular command. First, the name of the service, and second, the type of the service. The name is glance and the type is image. You can check the existing services with their types by using the openstack service list command:

```
$ openstack service list
+----------------------------------+------------+---------------+
| ID                               | Name       | Type          |
+----------------------------------+------------+---------------+
| 1b3b63218f1042a4994b51e8d20078ec | cinderv2   | volumev2      |
| 49b256b46a0f4052acee768b5b0bbe65 | cinder     | volume        |
| 4b815b6d85474c70a449326b6bf4b4ea | ceilometer | metering      |
| 7d5da91499224026a21efdf84300381a | nova_ec2   | ec2           |
| 7e621a56c3aa41f78ed6d5bddaba3a92 | swift      | object-store  |
| 9d33c464f61749cd9f5811cda1ae5444 | glance     | image         |
| b0763e843e0e4e7284e14e76f4dd702c | keystone   | identity      |
| b8367ddba94248cfa16451390684f89c | heat       | orchestration |
| c81578d4864349e1b29a04e2554556bc | nova       | compute       |
| d83dacc916434390b3557c4ff0e893a4 | neutron    | network       |
| e4851946adb14ee481660bd45b76496f | novav3     | computev3     |
| ea9433eec76d49ebb11ed47645b5765b | swift_s3   | s3            |
+----------------------------------+------------+---------------+
```

▨ **Note**   You may find it interesting that there are two versions of the Cinder service. That's because not all other services support the newest second version of Cinder API.

If you made a mistake in service creation, you can easily delete it with the openstack service delete command. After creating the service record in the Keystone catalog, you need to create three endpoints for this service. This can be done with the next command:

```
$ openstack endpoint create \
>    --publicurl http://10.0.2.15:9292 \
>    --internalurl http://10.0.2.15:9292 \
>    --adminurl http://10.0.2.15:9292
>    --region RegionOne image
```

```
+--------------+-----------------------------------+
| Field        | Value                             |
+--------------+-----------------------------------+
| adminurl     | http://10.0.2.15:9292             |
| id           | 5ae58266319446a4837ce0c212c5ad1a  |
| internalurl  | http://10.0.2.15:9292             |
| publicurl    | http://10.0.2.15:9292             |
| region       | RegionOne                         |
| service_id   | 9d33c464f61749cd9f5811cda1ae5444  |
| service_name | glance                            |
| service_type | image                             |
+--------------+-----------------------------------+
```

■ **Note**   Starting with the Mitaka release, the syntax of the command has changed. You need to add three endpoints for service, one by one. Here is an example for the public endpoint: `openstack endpoint create identity public http://controller.test.local:5000/v3 --region RegionOne`.

You can run a check of all of the endpoints:

```
$ openstack endpoint list
+----------------------------------+-----------+--------------+---------------+
| ID                               | Region    | Service Name | Service Type  |
+----------------------------------+-----------+--------------+---------------+
| f312043049e04056a793c16fd4b81bc5 | RegionOne | ceilometer   | metering      |
| 6af17d75bdec498cbc2af32e6625b1b2 | RegionOne | keystone     | identity      |
| 82c5b56f536e446189abbef7c114e9c4 | RegionOne | neutron      | network       |
| 9d6a6b9d9ee744e3a2991dbb39cec995 | RegionOne | cinderv2     | volumev2      |
| ecfb03318bcb4bd588ee7a02833aae31 | RegionOne | nova         | compute       |
| 93591bd7d0394abc8a1e624e5be2f284 | RegionOne | cinder       | volume        |
| 73598ea8c3e8480a965f83f50fbf92bb | RegionOne | nova_ec2     | ec2           |
| bc52befa27da44cfbd709b5c67fc44fe | RegionOne | swift        | object-store  |
| d5d7afeaf892470bac9fc587bb413cb3 | RegionOne | heat         | orchestration |
| 37316205c43746ca96ca6435fd2f4b7a | RegionOne | swift_s3     | s3            |
| 2d8fb2f861a24f5f8964df225a7961cd | RegionOne | novav3       | computev3     |
| 5ae58266319446a4837ce0c212c5ad1a | RegionOne | glance       | image         |
+----------------------------------+-----------+--------------+---------------+
```

And you can show the details about a particular endpoint:

```
$ openstack endpoint show glance
+--------------+-----------------------------------+
| Field        | Value                             |
+--------------+-----------------------------------+
| adminurl     | http://10.0.2.15:9292             |
| enabled      | True                              |
| id           | 5ae58266319446a4837ce0c212c5ad1a  |
| internalurl  | http://10.0.2.15:9292             |
| publicurl    | http://10.0.2.15:9292             |
```

```
| region       | RegionOne                        |
| service_id   | 9d33c464f61749cd9f5811cda1ae5444 |
| service_name | glance                           |
| service_type | image                            |
+--------------+----------------------------------+
```

Horizon can handle approximately 70% of the overall available OpenStack functionality. So you can't create services and endpoints through the web client, although you can check a list of services and their current statuses. Log in as admin and go to Admin ➤ System Information (see Figure 3-1).

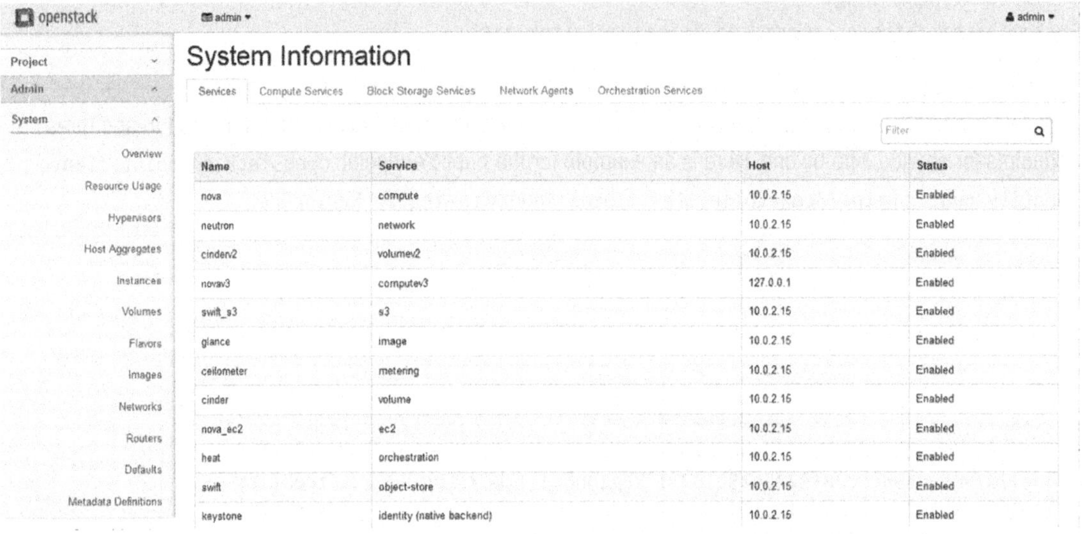

Figure 3-1. *List of services in Horizon*

Managing/Creating Projects, Users, and Roles

You can easily create projects, users, and roles with the help of the openstack command. Let's start from a new project. You need to use admin credentials for this operation:

```
$ source keystonerc_admin
$ openstack project create --description "Test project" apress
+-------------+----------------------------------+
| Field       | Value                            |
+-------------+----------------------------------+
| description | Test project                     |
| enabled     | True                             |
| id          | ee6dbb7d8b5e420da8e8bd1b5e23953b |
| name        | apress                           |
+-------------+----------------------------------+
```

■ **Note**   Starting with the Mitaka release, you need to add the --domain option.

You can get a list of all projects and details about each project as well:

```
$ openstack project list
+-----------------------------------+----------+
| ID                                | Name     |
+-----------------------------------+----------+
| 1542af2b20d349d29710d8c4019ba202  | demo     |
| 233d4bfa02ee46e69194a7594570da45  | services |
| 560a3e76bdc64ea2bee9316038b12793  | admin    |
| ee6dbb7d8b5e420da8e8bd1b5e23953b  | apress   |
+-----------------------------------+----------+
$ openstack project show apress
+-------------+----------------------------------+
| Field       | Value                            |
+-------------+----------------------------------+
| description | Test project                     |
| enabled     | True                             |
| id          | ee6dbb7d8b5e420da8e8bd1b5e23953b  |
| name        | apress                           |
+-------------+----------------------------------+
```

Now you can create a new user—apressadmin—granting _member_ a role in the Apress project:

```
$ openstack user create --password-prompt apressuser
User Password:
Repeat User Password:
+----------+----------------------------------+
| Field    | Value                            |
+----------+----------------------------------+
| email    | None                             |
| enabled  | True                             |
| id       | 639a67455b474a9eae2a9f048ee811b1 |
| name     | apressuser                       |
| username | apressuser                       |
+----------+----------------------------------+
$ openstack role add --project apress --user apressuser _member_
+-------+----------------------------------+
| Field | Value                            |
+-------+----------------------------------+
| id    | 9fe2ff9ee4384b1894a90878d3e92bab |
| name  | _member_                         |
+-------+----------------------------------+
```

■ **Note** The admin role is global, not per project, so granting a user the admin role in any project gives the user administrative rights across the whole environment.

If you want to get a list of all of the roles in OpenStack cloud, you can use the command:

```
$ openstack role list
+----------------------------------+------------------+
| ID                               | Name             |
+----------------------------------+------------------+
| 7f8760410d94476c81fa77589cf7f6e2 | heat_stack_user  |
| 9120dbbe6c324f96978f34ae8e386c36 | heat_stack_owner |
| 9d70fe84f7524503aeb69dfa9a2b987e | admin            |
| 9fe2ff9ee4384b1894a90878d3e92bab | _member_         |
| e39b1852b0674392a4c56a48e37fa7d7 | SwiftOperator    |
+----------------------------------+------------------+
```

The file policy.json exists in each service /etc/service_name/ directory. In such files, policy definitions for roles are described. For example, this is a part of /etc/keystone/policy.json:

```
{
    "admin_required": "role:admin or is_admin:1",
...
    "identity:create_region": "rule:admin_required",
...
    "identity:create_domain": "rule:admin_required",
...
  "identity:list_groups_for_user": "rule:admin_or_owner",
}
```

The first line is the admin role definition and the next three lines are the policy rules, which are represented by the following syntax:

```
"<service>:<action>" : "<subject conditions>"
```

As you can see, to create a region or domain in the identity service, you need an admin role. You will get an HTTP 403 error code if the current policy doesn't allow the command to be performed.

After creating a new user, you may want to create a new keystonerc file for it. You may use the keystonerc_admin file as a template. In this case, you need to change the OS_TENANT_NAME, OS_USERNAME and OS_PASSWORD variables.

If you need to delete a user or project, you can use the same openstack command but with the delete subcommand. For example:

```
$ openstack user delete apressuser
$ openstack project delete apress
```

It is possible to create, delete, and edit users and projects in OpenStack in web interface (Horizon). Go to Identity ➤ Users or Identity ➤ Projects. Examples of editing project and creating user are shown in Figures 3-2 and 3-3, respectively.

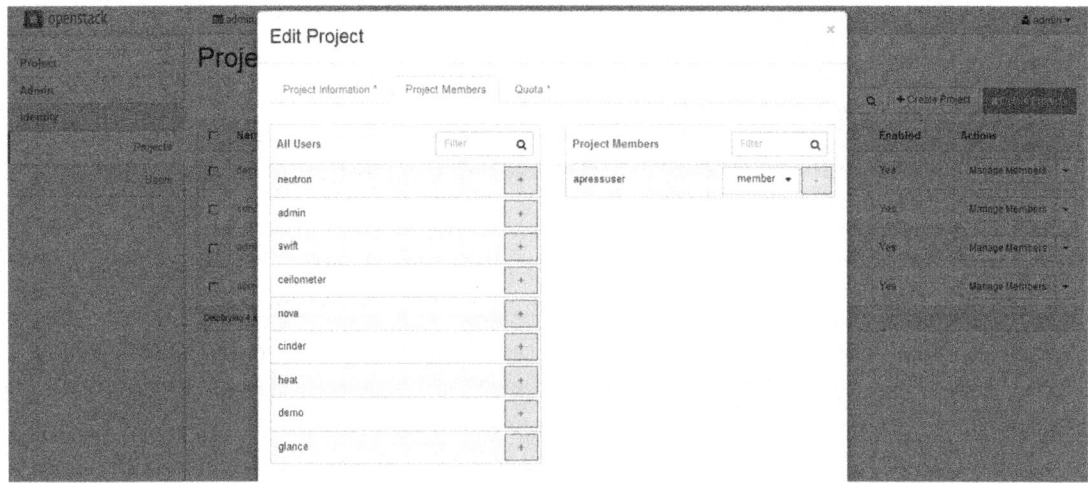

Figure 3-2. *Managing project members in Horizon*

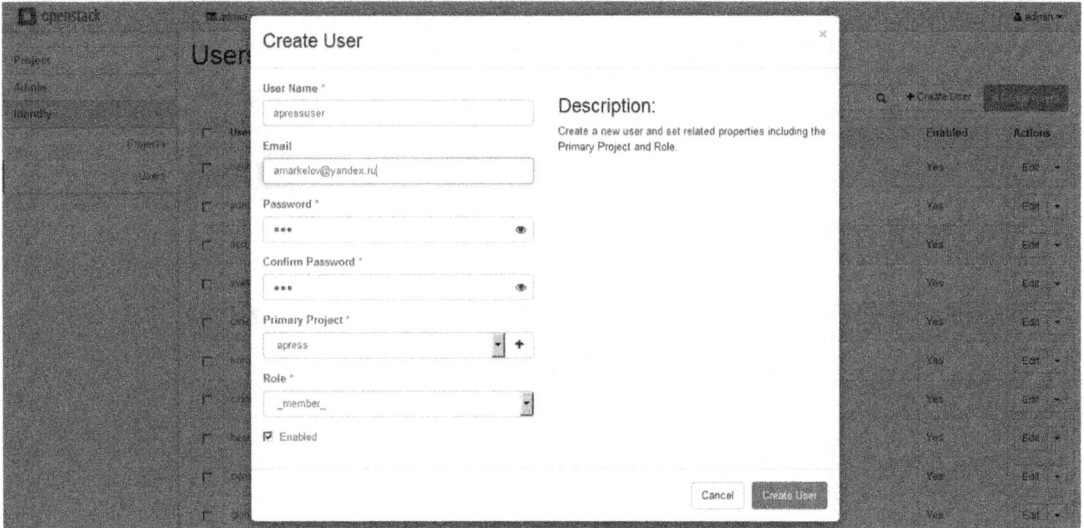

Figure 3-3. *Creating a new user in Horizon*

Managing and Verifying Operation of the Identity Service

For performance, a modern OpenStack installation deploys the Apache HTTP server with mod_wsgi package to handle requests and Memcached fronfend to store tokens. In CentOS, Scientific Linux, Oracle Linux, and other Red Hat Enterprise Linux derivatives, distribution for service management systemd is used. You can check whether Memcached and Apache servers are started and active:

```
# systemctl status memcached.service
● memcached.service - Memcached
   Loaded: loaded (/usr/lib/systemd/system/memcached.service; enabled; vendor preset: disabled)
```

```
    Active: active (running) since Sun 2016-04-10 13:13:45 MSK; 1h 34min ago
...
# systemctl status httpd.service
• httpd.service - The Apache HTTP Server
   Loaded: loaded (/usr/lib/systemd/system/httpd.service; enabled; vendor preset: disabled)
  Drop-In: /usr/lib/systemd/system/httpd.service.d
              └─openstack-dashboard.conf
   Active: active (running) since Sun 2016-04-10 13:14:50 MSK; 1h 33min ago
...
```

■ **Note** Keystone supports the three types of access tokens: PKI tokens (deprecated), UUID, and starting with the Mitaka release, Fernet tokens. The latter are non-persistent, lightweight, and reduce the operational overhead required to run a cloud. In the case of Fernet tokens, you don't need to run the memcached daemon.

The standard GNU/Linux command ps can show you two processes with names containing keystone:

```
# ps aux | grep keystone
root      22377  0.0  0.0 112644    960 pts/0    R+   15:42   0:00 grep --color=auto keystone
keystone 23767  0.0  1.9 595200 78144 ?          Sl   14:14   0:05 keystone-
admin  -DFOREGROUND
keystone 23768  0.0  0.2 397220 10088 ?          Sl   14:14   0:00 keystone-
main   -DFOREGROUND
```

There are two distinct daemon processes created for running through the WSGI module of Apache HTTP server. You can find their configuration files in the /etc/httpd/conf.d/ directory:

```
# ls /etc/httpd/conf.d/*keystone*
/etc/httpd/conf.d/10-keystone_wsgi_admin.conf  /etc/httpd/conf.d/10-keystone_wsgi_main.conf
```

Here is a shorted example of the configuration file for admin's virtual host:

```
<VirtualHost *:35357>
  ServerName centos7.test.local
  DocumentRoot "/var/www/cgi-bin/keystone"

  <Directory "/var/www/cgi-bin/keystone">
    Options Indexes FollowSymLinks MultiViews
    AllowOverride None
    Require all granted
  </Directory>

 ErrorLog /var/log/httpd/keystone-error.log
 CustomLog /var/log/httpd/keystone-access.log combined
  WSGIDaemonProcess keystone_admin display-name=keystone-admin group=keystone processes=1
threads=1 user=keystone
  WSGIProcessGroup keystone_admin
  WSGIScriptAlias / "/var/www/cgi-bin/keystone/admin"
  WSGIPassAuthorization On
</VirtualHost>
```

In case there is a need for troubleshooting, you may also want to check the endpoints by name or by ID:

```
$ openstack endpoint show identity
+--------------+-----------------------------------+
| Field        | Value                             |
+--------------+-----------------------------------+
| adminurl     | http://10.0.2.15:35357/v2.0       |
| enabled      | True                              |
| id           | 6af17d75bdec498cbc2af32e6625b1b2  |
| internalurl  | http://10.0.2.15:5000/v2.0        |
| publicurl    | http://10.0.2.15:5000/v2.0        |
| region       | RegionOne                         |
| service_id   | b0763e843e0e4e7284e14e76f4dd702c  |
| service_name | keystone                          |
| service_type | identity                          |
+--------------+-----------------------------------+
```

As you see, the internal and public URLs are the same, but the admin endpoint uses port 35357, as discussed earlier in this chapter. In case of debugging, you may want to check the log ins using /var/log/httpd/keystone_* and /var/log/leystone/keystone.log.

Review Questions

1. How would you add the user apressuser with a Member role to the apress project?

    A.   openstack role add --project apress --user apressuser _member_

    B.   openstack role add --project apress --user apressuser member

    C.   openstack role add --project apress --user _member_ apressuser

    D.   openstack role add --project apress --user member apressuser

2. Which two system services should be started for a proper Keystone functioning (choose two)?

    A.   keystone-main

    B.   keystone-admin

    C.   memcached

    D.   httpd

3. How would you define a new role in OpenStack cloud (choose all applicable)?

    A.   Enter command openstack role create newrole.

    B.   Restart httpd service.

    C.   Create new "keystonerc" file.

    D.   Add definition to policy.json files.

4. How would you separate two or more cloud instances but manage them with one Keystone instance?

   A. Use Domains feature.

   B. Use Regions feature.

   C. Use availability zones.

   D. Each cloud instance should use own Keystone instance feature.

5. Which HTTP error code would you get if the Keystone token has expired?

   A. ERROR 404.

   B. ERROR 403.

   C. ERROR 401.

   D. All of them.

Answers to Review Questions

1. A

2. C, D

3. A, D

4. A

5. C

CHAPTER 4

Image Management

This chapter covers 10% of the Certified OpenStack Administrator exam requirements.

Architecture and Main Components of Glance

Chapter 3 touched on the Keystone service that acts as a catalog of other OpenStack services. This chapter covers one of the services that always exists in almost all OpenStack installations. The name of this service is Glance, and its purpose is to act as an "Images-as-a-Service" provider. First, let's deconstruct Glance to its particular components. Have a look at Figure 4-1.

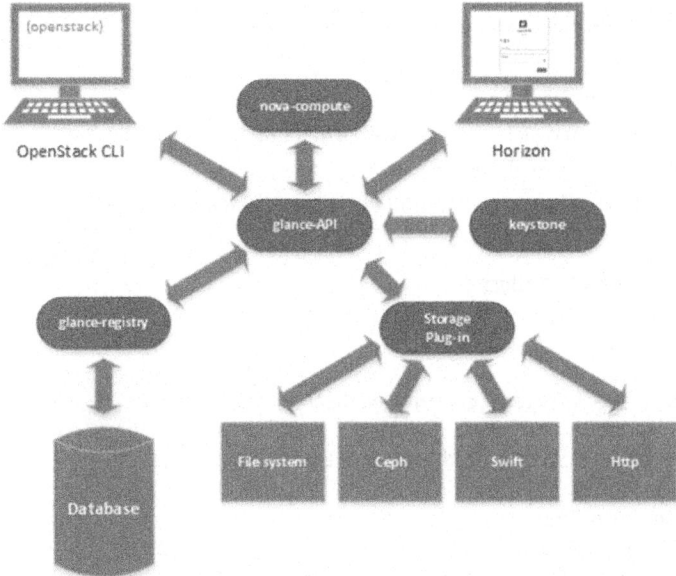

Figure 4-1. *Architecture of Glance (Cinder and Glance integration is not shown to avoid complexity)*

© Andrey Markelov 2016
A. Markelov, *Certified OpenStack Administrator Study Guide*, DOI 10.1007/978-1-4842-2125-9_4

Glance consists of two services that are implemented as GNU/Linux daemons:

- **glance-api**: Accepts Image REST API calls for image discovery, retrieval, and storage.

- **glance-registry**: Stores, processes, and retrieves metadata about images. For example, metadata are size, type, owner, etc. As you can see in Figure 4-1, external services never touches glance-registry directly.

As you can also see in Figure 4-1, Glance itself does not store images by themselves. Glance uses plug-ins for particular storage, which can be your local file system, Swift object storage, Ceph storage, NFS (Network File System), or other back ends. Metadata of images are stored in the Glance database, usually as a MariaDB instance.

Glance supports many disk formats. Table 4-1 describes some of them.

Table 4-1. *Disk Formats Supported by Glance*

Type of Disk	Description
aki	An Amazon kernel image.
ami	An Amazon machine image.
ari	An Amazon ramdisk image.
iso	An archive format for the data contents of an optical disk, such as CD-ROM.
qcow2	Supported by the QEMU emulator that can expand dynamically and supports Copy on Write.
raw	An unstructured disk image format; if you have a file without an extension, it is possibly a raw format.
vdi	Supported by VirtualBox virtual machine monitor and the QEMU emulator.
vhd	The VHD disk format, a common disk format used by virtual machine monitors from VMware, Xen, Microsoft, VirtualBox, and others.
vmdk	Common disk format supported by many common virtual machine monitors.

Let's check these services on the OpenStack controller:

```
# systemctl | grep glance
  openstack-glance-api.service
  loaded active running   OpenStack Image Service (code-named Glance) API server
  openstack-glance-registry.service
  loaded active running   OpenStack Image Service (code-named Glance) Registry server
```

As you can see, both services are up and running.

Usually when the Compute service Nova is trying to spawn a new virtual machine, it sends a GET request to the URL http://path_to_Glance_service/images/paticular_image_ID. If the glance-api finds the requested image, the service will return the URL where the image is located. After that, Nova sends the link to the hypervisor's driver and hypervisor will download the image directly.

Then you need to look through the main configuration files for the glance-api and glance-registry. Both /etc/glance/glance-api.conf and /etc/glance/glance-registry.conf contain similar settings.

▪ **Tip** Default config files come with a huge amount of comments and are a very good source of information. But sometimes you need to have a clear look at what is in the configs. You can use RegEx magic to remove all comments and make the configs shorter. For example, with the command grep -o '^[^#]*' /etc/glance/ glance-registry.conf you can cut the default file from 1200 lines to 29. It can really make your life easier.

As discussed earlier, Glance uses the database for storing metadata. In both config files, you can find something like this:

```
[database]
...
connection=mysql://glance:password@10.0.2.15/glance
```

This is the connection URL for the Glance database. The next important thing you will need is the authentication parameters for Keystone. As with other services, you will need to define the basic authentication credentials:

```
[keystone_authtoken]
auth_uri=http://10.0.2.15:5000/v2.0
identity_uri=http://10.0.2.15:35357
admin_user=glance
admin_password=password
admin_tenant_name=services

[paste_deploy]
flavor=keystone
```

In our set up, Keystone server has the IP address 10.0.2.15 and you can see the public Identity API endpoint and Admins Identity API endpoint definitions. Each has its own port number—5000 and 35357, respectively. Also as you can see, in the config files the user name for Glance, service tenant, and password are in clear text. It is very important to keep the right permissions for all config files because many of them contain the password in clear text.

Depending on the OpenStack version you use you will need to put RabbitMQ settings either in the [oslo_messaging_rabbit] or in[DEFAULT] section of /etc/glance/glance-api.conffile. Here is an example:

```
[oslo_messaging_rabbit]
rabbit_host=10.0.2.15
rabbit_port=5672
rabbit_hosts=10.0.2.15:5672
rabbit_use_ssl=False
rabbit_userid=guest
rabbit_password=guest
sss
```

Deploying a New Image to an OpenStack Instance

You can download various cloud-ready images from the Internet. Most major Linux distributions already have prepared images for OpenStack. Table 4-2 shows several examples.

Table 4-2. *Cloud-Ready Images*

Linux Distro or OS	URL
CirrOS	`http://download.cirros-cloud.net/`
Ubuntu	`http://cloud-images.ubuntu.com/`
Debian	`http://cdimage.debian.org/cdimage/openstack/`
Fedora	`https://getfedora.org/cloud/download/`
CentOS	`http://cloud.centos.org/centos/7/`
Windows Server 2012 R2 Evaluation for OpenStack	`https://cloudbase.it/windows-cloud-images/`

For testing purposes, you can use CirrOS, which is a minimal Linux distro that was designed for testing images on the cloud. First, you need to download the image:

```
$ wget -P /tmp http://download.cirros-cloud.net/0.3.4/cirros-0.3.4-x86_64-disk.img
```

■ **Tip**　In a CirrOS image, the user name of the existing account is cirros. The password is cubswin:).

Then you can deploy the image in the cloud:

```
$ openstack image create --file /tmp/cirros-0.3.4-x86_64-disk.img --disk-format qcow2
--container-format bare --public cirros-0.3.4-x86_64
+------------------+------------------------------------------------------+
| Field            | Value                                                |
+------------------+------------------------------------------------------+
| checksum         | ee1eca47dc88f4879d8a229cc70a07c6                     |
| container_format | bare                                                 |
| created_at       | 2016-03-12T18:24:59Z                                 |
| disk_format      | qcow2                                                |
| file             | /v2/images/e5791edb-30dd-475a-9bc4-5938341db655/file |
| id               | e5791edb-30dd-475a-9bc4-5938341db655                 |
| min_disk         | 0                                                    |
| min_ram          | 0                                                    |
| name             | cirros-0.3.4-x86_64                                  |
| owner            | 560a3e76bdc64ea2bee9316038b12793                     |
| protected        | False                                                |
| schema           | /v2/schemas/image                                    |
| size             | 13287936                                             |
| status           | active                                               |
| updated_at       | 2016-03-12T18:25:00Z                                 |
| virtual_size     | None                                                 |
| visibility       | public                                               |
+------------------+------------------------------------------------------+
```

In this particular command --public means that image can be used across project/tenants for every user in the OpenStack cloud. To get information about the image, you can use the command openstack image show followed by the ID of the image or name. In this case, the ID is e5791edb-30dd-475a-9bc4-5938341db655 and the name is cirros-0.3.4-x86_64.

To get a list of all available images for the current user, use the following:

```
$ openstack image list
+-------------------------------------+----------------------+
| ID                                  | Name                 |
+-------------------------------------+----------------------+
| f42295b8-d600-4a67-86b7-dcda07652db4 | ubuntu-amd64        |
| e5791edb-30dd-475a-9bc4-5938341db655 | cirros-0.3.4-x86_64 |
+-------------------------------------+----------------------+
```

As an admin, you can see all the images in the cloud.

It's good to know information about an image before onboarding it to OpenStack. Use the command qemu-img from the package with the same name:

```
$ qemu-img info /tmp/wily-server-cloudimg-amd64-disk1.img
image: /tmp/wily-server-cloudimg-amd64-disk1.img
file format: qcow2
virtual size: 2.2G (2361393152 bytes)
disk size: 309M
cluster_size: 65536
Format specific information:
    compat: 0.10
```

It is possible to create an image in OpenStack in a web interface (Horizon). Go to Project ➤ Compute ➤ Images. On the top of the right side of interface, click the "Create Image" button (see Figure 4-2). Only the image name, format, and file are mandatory.

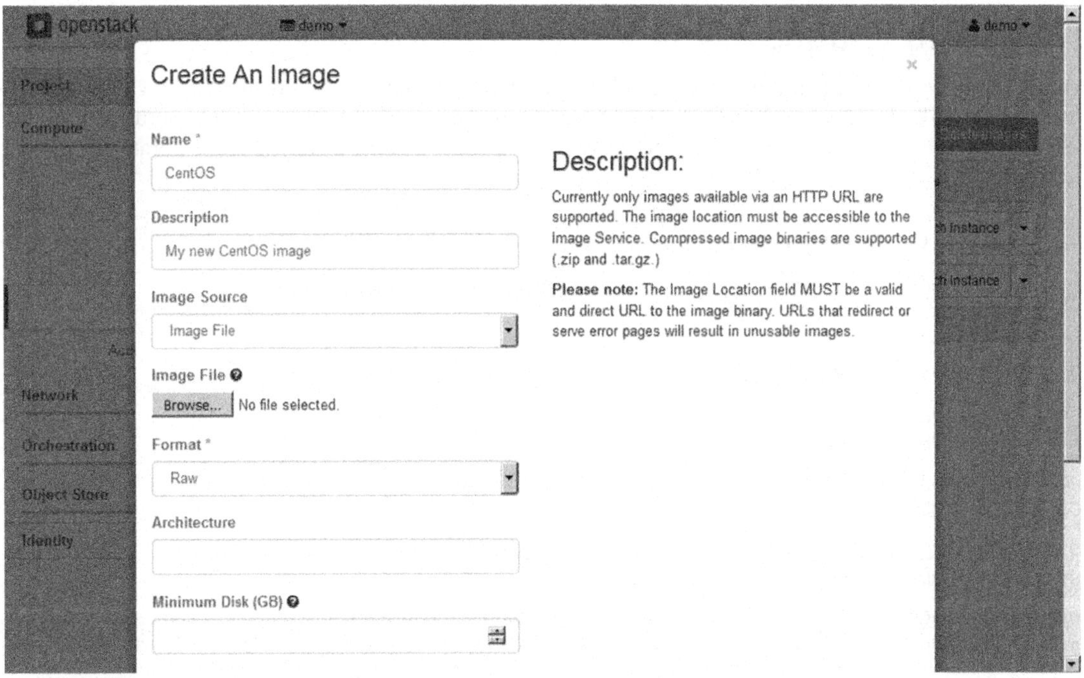

Figure 4-2. *Creating an image in the Horizon web interface*

As a user admin you can also see all images on the Admin ➤ Images page. It is possible to edit or add some part of metadata from this point. Figure 4-3 shows this page.

Figure 4-3. *Admin's view of images in Horizon web interface*

Managing Images

Table 4-3 shows the most common commands for Glance management. In old versions of OpenStack, you can use only the glance command. This command will probably become obsolete in the future. For searching particular options and command descriptions, add –h to the end of your subcommand. For example:

Table 4-3. *CLI Commands for Glance Management*

Command	Purpose of Command
openstack image create or glance image-create	Create/upload an image
openstack image delete or glance image-delete	Delete image(s)
openstack image add project or glance member-create	Associate project with an image
openstack image remove project or glance member-delete	Disassociate project with an image
openstack image list or glance image-list	List available images

(continued)

Table 4-3. (*continued*)

Command	Purpose of Command
openstack image save or glance image-download	Save an image locally on disk
openstack image show or glance image-show	Display image details
openstack image set	Set image properties
glance image-update	Set image metadata

```
$ openstack image add project -h
usage: openstack image add project [-h]
                                   [-f {html,json,json,shell,table,value,yaml,yaml}]
                                   [-c COLUMN] [--max-width <integer>]
                                   [--noindent] [--prefix PREFIX]
                                   [--project-domain <project-domain>]
                                   <image> <project>

Associate project with image

positional arguments:
  <image>              Image to share (name or ID)
  <project>            Project to associate with image (name or ID)

...
```

Table 4-3 shows how some commands work.

Once you have your image set up, you can download it. A simple example looks something like this:

```
$ openstack image save ubuntu-amd64 > local_image.img
$ ls -l local_image.img
-rw-rw-r-- 1 andrey andrey 323682816 Mar 13 18:36 local_image.img
```

You can add your own metadata to an image. For instance, the following command adds two new properties to the existing image:

```
$ glance image-update f42295b8-d600-4a67-86b7-dcda07652db4 --property os_name=linux
--property contact_person="andrey.markelov@ericsson.com"
+------------------+------------------------------------------+
| Property         | Value                                    |
+------------------+------------------------------------------+
| checksum         | 89a76d37ee23111237628d6ea38fd7e9         |
| contact_person   | andrey.markelov@ericsson.com             |
| container_format | bare                                     |
| created_at       | 2016-03-12T18:41:05Z                     |
| disk_format      | qcow2                                    |
| id               | f42295b8-d600-4a67-86b7-dcda07652db4     |
| min_disk         | 0                                        |
| min_ram          | 0                                        |
```

```
| name            | ubuntu-amd64                     |
| os_name         | linux                            |
| owner           | 560a3e76bdc64ea2bee9316038b12793 |
| protected       | False                            |
| size            | 323682816                        |
| status          | active                           |
| tags            | []                               |
| updated_at      | 2016-03-13T15:41:33Z             |
| virtual_size    | None                             |
| visibility      | public                           |
+-----------------+----------------------------------+
```

For deleting a property, use the following command:

```
$ glance image-update f42295b8-d600-4a67-86b7-dcda07652db4 --remove-property contact_person
```

And if you want, you can delete an image itself:

```
$ openstack image delete ubuntu-amd64
$ openstack image list
+--------------------------------------+------------------+
| ID                                   | Name             |
+--------------------------------------+------------------+
| e5791edb-30dd-475a-9bc4-5938341db655 | cirros-0.3.4-x86_64 |
+--------------------------------------+------------------+
```

For almost all commands, you may use either the name of the image or the ID. The utilities glance and openstack have the --debug option, if you want to see what is behind the CLI. It might be useful for troubleshooting or learning more about the API:

```
openstack image list --debug
START with options: ['image', 'list', '--debug']
...
REQ: curl -g -i -X GET http://10.0.2.15:9292/v2/images -H "User-Agent: python-
openstackclient" -H "X-Auth-Token: {SHA1}a7106d46959611d458dbd9a89f01f570bc5fc536"
"GET /v2/images?marker=e5791edb-30dd-475a-9bc4-5938341db655 HTTP/1.1" 200 69
RESP: [200] date: Sun, 13 Mar 2016 16:02:50 GMT connection: keep-alive content-type:
application/json; charset=UTF-8 content-length: 69 x-openstack-request-id: req-bf5875a1-
ba85-46f2-8dea-2918272a80da
RESP BODY: {"images": [], "schema": "/v2/schemas/images", "first": "/v2/images"}


+--------------------------------------+------------------+
| ID                                   | Name             |
+--------------------------------------+------------------+
| e5791edb-30dd-475a-9bc4-5938341db655 | cirros-0.3.4-x86_64 |
+--------------------------------------+------------------+
clean_up ListImage:
END return value: 0
```

Managing Image Back Ends

Glance can support various data store back ends, such as Swift, Ceph, NFS, local file system, and others. Storage vendors like EMC or NetApp produce plug-ins for their own hardware. You can define each particular back end in the [glance_store] section of the configuration file /etc/glance/glance-api.conf. Here is the simplest example of the local file system:

```
[glance_store]
...
default_store = file
filesystem_store_datadir = /var/lib/glance/images/
```

If you look at this directory, you can find files with the names that are equal to the image's ID:

```
# ls -l /var/lib/glance/images/
total 329080
-rw-r----- 1 glance glance  13287936 Mar 12 21:25 e5791edb-30dd-475a-9bc4-5938341db655
-rw-r----- 1 glance glance 323682816 Mar 12 21:41 f42295b8-d600-4a67-86b7-dcda07652db4
ls -l /var/lib/glance/images/
$ openstack image list
+--------------------------------------+--------------------+
| ID                                   | Name               |
+--------------------------------------+--------------------+
| f42295b8-d600-4a67-86b7-dcda07652db4 | ubuntu-amd64       |
| e5791edb-30dd-475a-9bc4-5938341db655 | cirros-0.3.4-x86_64 |
+--------------------------------------+--------------------+
```

Glance can serve multiple back ends at the same time. In this case Glance will choose a particular back end depending on the free space and priority. For example, if you have two mounted disks in /var/lib/glance/images/, you can add something like this:

```
[glance_store]
filesystem_store_datadirs = /var/lib/glance/images/mountA/:10
filesystem_store_datadirs = /var/lib/glance/images/mountB/:20
...
```

To limit the size of images, you need to add the image_size_cap parameter and maximum size in bytes to the glance-api configuration file and restart the glance-api service. Here is an example for adding a 1GB parameter:

```
[default]
image_size_cap = 1073741824
...

# systemctl restart openstack-glance-api
```

If you need to limit the storage amount per user in Glance, use another option:

```
[default]
user_storage_quota = 500MB
...

# systemctl restart openstack-glance-api
```

Verifying Operation of the Image Service

Let's check the presence of Glance service in the Keystone services catalog. You can do that with the old-fashioned command keystone or with the new openstack command. It's better to use the openstack CLI when possible because in the future it will probably be the only command-line client available:

```
$ source keystonerc_admin
$ openstack service show glance
+-------------+-----------------------------------+
| Field       | Value                             |
+-------------+-----------------------------------+
| description | OpenStack Image Service           |
| enabled     | True                              |
| id          | 9d33c464f61749cd9f5811cda1ae5444  |
| name        | glance                            |
| type        | image                             |
+-------------+-----------------------------------+
```

Looks like everything is fine with that. For troubleshooting, you may also need to know where the glance-api endpoint is:

```
$ openstack endpoint show glance
+--------------+-----------------------------------+
| Field        | Value                             |
+--------------+-----------------------------------+
| adminurl     | http://10.0.2.15:9292             |
| enabled      | True                              |
| id           | 5ae58266319446a4837ce0c212c5ad1a  |
| internalurl  | http://10.0.2.15:9292             |
| publicurl    | http://10.0.2.15:9292             |
| region       | RegionOne                         |
| service_id   | 9d33c464f61749cd9f5811cda1ae5444  |
| service_name | glance                            |
| service_type | image                             |
+--------------+-----------------------------------+
```

In this particular environment, the Glance service is listening for incoming connections at the IP address 10.0.2.15 and port number 9292. All communications are happening through http. In real life it can also be done through the https protocol. URLs for admin interface, public interface, and internal interface can also be different. Keep in mind that glance-registry is listening on port 9191, but you will not expose the registry for external services.

You may also want to check Glance's log files. The /var/log/glance/api.log is in charge of glance-api and /var/log/glance/registry.log for glance-registry service. To adjust how the logs are detailed, you can add the option to Glance's configuration files:

```
[DEFAULT]
...
verbose = True
debug = True
```

Review Questions

1. Where are the images stored when using the local file system by default?

    A. /var/cache/glance/

    B. /var/lib/glance/store/

    C. /var/log/glance/

    D. /var/lib/glance/images/

2. Which two main daemons does Glance consist of (choose two)?

    A. glance-endpoint

    B. glance-registry

    C. glance-backend

    D. glance-api

3. What parameter in Glance's configuration files defines the back end for storing files?

    A. default_store

    B. B. default_backend

    C. prefered_store

    D. prefered_backend

4. How can an image in OpenStack cloud be stored with CLI?

    A. openstack image create --file image.img --disk-format qcow2 --container-format bare --public image

    B. openstack image add --file image.img --disk-format qcow2 --container-format bare --public image

    C. openstack image create --file image.img --disk qcow2 --container-format bare --public image

    D. openstack image add --file image.img --disk qcow2 --container-format bare --public image

5. How can the storage volume be limited in Glance per user?

    A. Put image_size_cap option to /etc/glance/glance-api.conf

    B. Put image_size_cap option to /etc/glance/glance-registry.conf

    C. Put user_storage_quota option to /etc/glance/glance-api.conf

    D. Put user_storage_quota option to /etc/glance/glance-registry.conf

Answers to Review Questions

1. D

2. B and D

3. B

4. A

5. C

■ ■ ■

## CHAPTER 5

OpenStack Networking

This chapter covers 16% of the Certified OpenStack Administrator exam requirements.

Architecture and Components of Neutron

OpenStack Networking is one of the most complicated OpenStack services. Let's start by looking at the architecture and general concepts of Neutron. Figure 5-1 shown the objects in the OpenStack Networking.

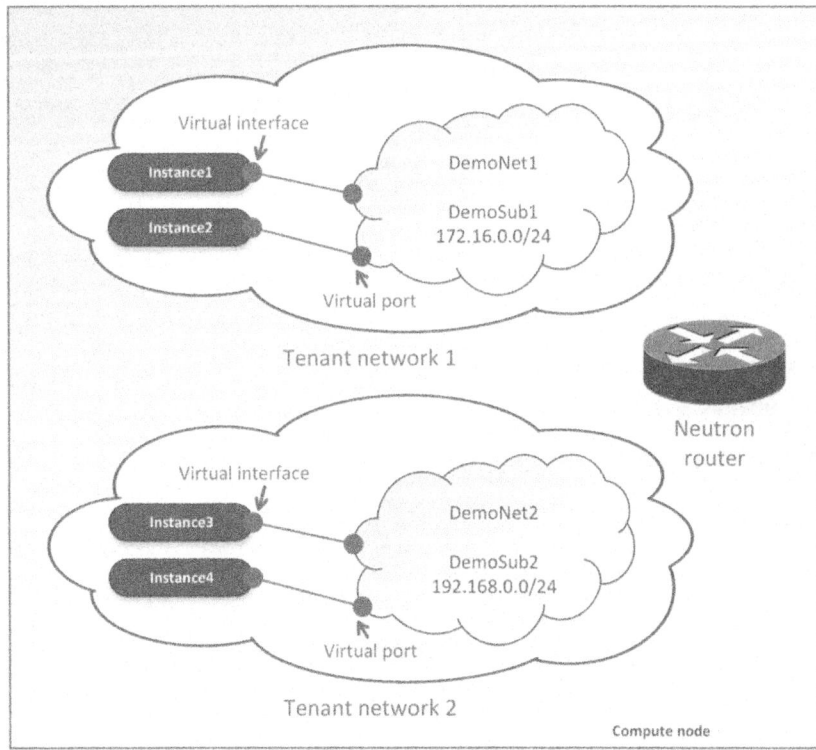

Figure 5-1. *Logical objects in the OpenStack Networking service*

© Andrey Markelov 2016
A. Markelov, *Certified OpenStack Administrator Study Guide*, DOI 10.1007/978-1-4842-2125-9_5

There are several components of most importance in OpenStack Networking:

- **Tenant network**: A virtual network that provides connectivity between entities. The network consists of subnets, and each subnet is a logical subdivision of an IP network. A subnet can be private or public. Virtual machines can get access to an external world through the public subnet. If a virtual machine is connected only to the private subnet, then only other virtual machines from this particular network can access it. Only a user with an admin role can create a public network.

- **Router**: A virtual network device that passes network traffic between different networks. A router can have one gateway and many connected subnets.

- **Security Group**: The set of ingress and egress firewall rules that can be applied to one or many virtual machines. It is possible to change a Security Group at runtime.

- **Floating IP address**: An IP address that can be associated with a virtual machine so that the instance has the same IP from the public network each time it boots.

- **Port:** A virtual network port within OpenStack Networking. It is a connection between the subnet and vNIC or virtual router.

- **vNIC (virtual Network Interface Card) or VIF (Virtual Network Interface)**: An interface that is plugged into a port in a network.

Let's continue this discussion by learning more about Neutron architecture (see Figure 5-2).

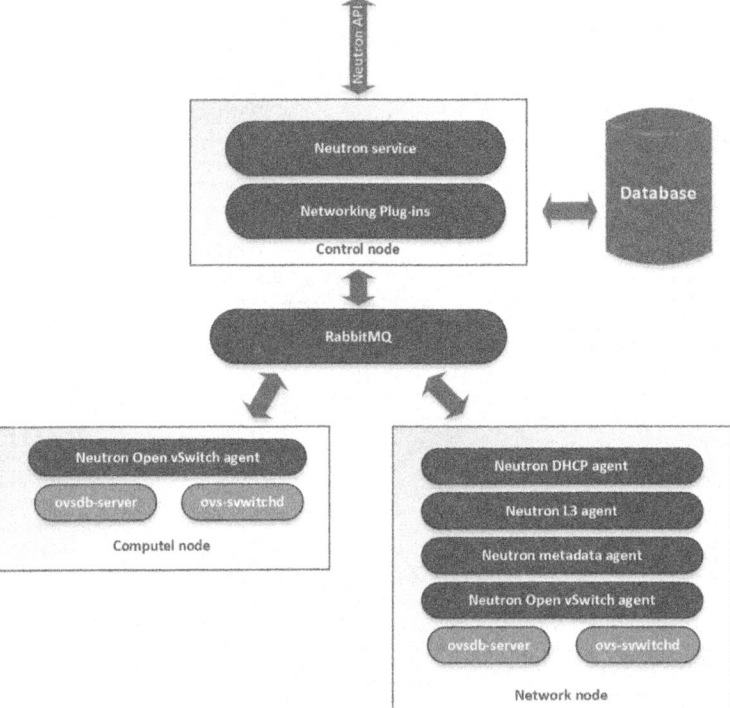

Figure 5-2. *Architecture of OpenStack Networking sevice*

Upstream documentation from docs.openstack.org defines several types of OpenStack nodes. Neutron is usually spread across three of them. API service usually exists at the control node. Open vSwitch and client-side Neutron agents are usually started at the Hypervisor or Compute node. And all server-side components of the OpenStack Networking service work on Networks nodes, which can be gateways to an external network.

Neutron consists of several services that are implemented as standard GNU/Linux daemons:

- **neutron-server**: The main service of Neutron. Accepts and routes API requests through message bus to the OpenStack Networking plug-ins for action.

- **neutron-openvswitch-agent**: Receives commands from neutron-server and sends them to Open vSwitch (OVS) for execution. The neutron-openvswitch-agent uses the local GNU/Linux commands for OVS management.

- **neutron-l3-agent**: Provides routing and Network Address Translation (NAT) using standard GNU/Linux technologies like Linux Routing and Network Namespaces.

- **neutron-dhcp-agent**: Manages dnsmasq services. Dnsmasq is a lightweight Dynamic Host Configuration Protocol (DHCP) and caching DNS server. Also neutron-dhcp-agent starts proxies for the metadata server.

- **neutron-metadata-agent**: Provides the ability for instances to get information such as hostname, SSH keys, etc. Virtual machines can request HTTP protocol information such as an URL http://169.254.169.254 at boot time. Usually this happens with scripts like cloud-init (https://launchpad.net/cloud-init). Agent acts as a proxy to nova-api for retrieving metadata.

Neutron also uses Open vSwitch. Its configuration will be discussed in the next section of this chapter. Table 5-1 lists what type of node (Compute, Network, or Control) services are started and the location of their configs.

Table 5-1. *OpenStack Neutron Services and Their Placement*

Service	Node Type	Configuration Files
neutron-service	Control	/etc/neutron/neutron.conf
neutron-openvswitch-agent	Network and Compute	/etc/neutron/plugins/ml2/openvswitch_agent.ini
neutron-l3-agent	Network	/etc/neutron/l3_agent.ini
neutron-dhcp-agent	Network	/etc/neutron/dhcp_agent.ini
neutron-metadata-agent	Network	/etc/neutron/metadata_agent.ini
Modular Layer 2 agent (it is not run as a daemon)	Network	/etc/neutron/plugins/ml2/ml2_conf.ini and /etc/neutron/plugin.ini (symbolic link to ml2_conf.ini)

Architecture of Open vSwitch

The important part of networking in the OpenStack cloud is OVS. The web site for OVS with documentation and source code is http://openvswitch.org/. Open vSwitch is not a part of OpenStack project. However, OVS is used in most implementations of OpenStack clouds. It has also been integrated into many other virtual management systems including OpenQRM, OpenNebula, and oVirt. Open vSwitch can provide support for protocols such as OpenFlow, GRE, VLAN, VXLAN, NetFlow, sFlow, SPAN, RSPAN, and LACP. It can operate in distributed configurations with a central controller.

Open vSwitch by itself consists of several components:

- **GNU/Linux kernel module** openswitch_mod.ko: The module plays the role of ASIC (application-specific integrated circuit) in hardware switches. This module is an engine of traffic processing.

- **Daemon** ovs-vswitchd: The daemon is in charge of management and logic for data transmitting.

- **Daemon** ovsdb-server: The daemon is used for the internal database. It also provides RPC (remote procedure call) interfaces to one or more Open vSwitch databases (OVSDBs).

Most likely you will not need to manage Open vSwitch at the exam time, but commands can be useful. Let's see some examples of using the management utility ovs-vsctl for interacting with OVS. First, let's check for the version of Open vSwitch:

```
# ovs-vsctl -V
ovs-vsctl (Open vSwitch) 2.4.0
Compiled Oct  7 2015 18:01:06
DB Schema 7.12.1
```

You can create a new bridge and delete it with the help of the commands:

```
# ovs-vsctl add-br br-new
# ovs-vsctl del-br br-new
```

The same with adding or removing a physical interface to or from the bridge:

```
# ovs-vsctl add-port br-ex enp0s3
# ovs-vsctl del-port br-ex enp0s3
```

The most interesting command is ovs-vsctl show. The output of this command is printed from the lab environment with three nodes:

```
# ovs-vsctl show
22a0e0a2-7ac2-493a-9398-65e5683835e9
    Bridge br-int
        fail_mode: secure
        Port br-int
            Interface br-int
                type: internal
        Port "tap7fd27c60-32"
            tag: 1
            Interface "tap7fd27c60-32"
                type: internal
        Port patch-tun
            Interface patch-tun
                type: patch
                options: {peer=patch-int}
        Port int-br-ex
            Interface int-br-ex
                type: patch
                options: {peer=phy-br-ex}
```

```
        Port "qr-8d2a382b-01"
            tag: 1
            Interface "qr-8d2a382b-01"
                type: internal
    Bridge br-ex
        Port "eth1"
            Interface "eth1"
        Port br-ex
            Interface br-ex
                type: internal
        Port "qg-dbd535f0-05"
            Interface "qg-dbd535f0-05"
                type: internal
        Port phy-br-ex
            Interface phy-br-ex
                type: patch
                options: {peer=int-br-ex}
    Bridge br-tun
        fail_mode: secure
        Port "gre-c0a87ad2"
            Interface "gre-c0a87ad2"
                type: gre
                options: {df_default="true", in_key=flow, local_ip="10.0.2.15", out_
key=flow, remote_ip="10.0.2.20"}
        Port br-tun
            Interface br-tun
                type: internal
        Port patch-int
            Interface patch-int
                type: patch
                options: {peer=patch-tun}
        Port "gre-c0a87ad7"
            Interface "gre-c0a87ad7"
                type: gre
                options: {df_default="true", in_key=flow, local_ip="10.0.2.15", out_
key=flow, remote_ip="10.0.2.30"}
    ovs_version: "2.4.0"
```

As you can see, three bridges exist:

- **Integration bridge** (br-int): There is a single integration bridge on each node. This bridge acts as a virtual switch where all virtual network cards from all virtual machines are connected. OVS Neutron agent automatically creates the integration bridge.

- **External bridge** (br-ex): This bridge is for interconnection with external networks. In our example, physical interface eth1 is connected to this bridge.

- **Tunnel bridge** (br-tun): This bridge is a virtual switch like br-int. It connects the GRE and VXLAN tunnel endpoints. As you can see in our particular example, it connects the node with the IP address 10.0.2.15 and two others with IP 10.0.2.20 and 10.0.2.30. In our example, a GRE tunnel was used.

Here is an example of the code from a config file for neutron-openvswitch-agent:

```
# grep -o '^[^#]*' /etc/neutron/plugins/ml2/openvswitch_agent.ini
[DEFAULT]
[agent]
tunnel_types =vxlan,gre
vxlan_udp_port = 4789
l2_population = False
drop_flows_on_start = False
[ovs]
integration_bridge = br-int
tunnel_bridge = br-tun
local_ip = 10.0.2.15
enable_tunneling=True
[securitygroup]
firewall_driver = neutron.agent.linux.iptables_firewall.OVSHybridIptablesFirewallDriver
```

See the Tip in Chapter 4 for an explanation of how RegEx can be used in the grep command.

Manage Network Resources

Now let's go through the process of creating all the necessary network resources for connecting an instance to the external world. For that you can use the neutron command and sometimes nova. Both commands have built-in help. Use nova help <sub-command> or neutron help sub-command for getting help for a particular sub-command. First, let's create a flat external network. You should have admin role before doing that:

```
$ source keystonerc_demo
$ neutron net-create ext-net --router:external True --provider:physical_network external
--provider:network_type flat
Created a new network:
+------------------------------+------------------------------------------+
| Field                        | Value                                    |
+------------------------------+------------------------------------------+
| admin_state_up               | True                                     |
| availability_zone_hints      |                                          |
| availability_zones           |                                          |
| created_at                   | 2016-07-17T16:39:51                      |
| description                  |                                          |
| id                           | 4716a0c7-70c9-44f1-a276-6e159400ba78     |
| ipv4_address_scope           |                                          |
| ipv6_address_scope           |                                          |
| is_default                   | False                                    |
| mtu                          | 1500                                     |
| name                         | ext-net                                  |
| provider:network_type        | flat                                     |
| provider:physical_network    | external                                 |
```

```
| provider:segmentation_id |                                          |
| router:external          | True                                     |
| shared                   | False                                    |
| status                   | ACTIVE                                   |
| subnets                  |                                          |
| tags                     |                                          |
| tenant_id                | ae8d3e3f5cff4a959f1ae1cfe9e80d6d         |
| updated_at               | 2016-07-17T16:39:51                      |
+--------------------------+------------------------------------------+
```

■ **Tip**   If you can't create a network with type `flat`, then add `flat` to the `type_drivers` option in the `/etc/neutron/plugins/ml2/ml2_conf.ini` config file. After changes, you will need to restart Neutron service.

The next step is to create a subnet for this network. It will be an external existing network and you will need to disable DHCP for this network:

```
$ neutron subnet-create ext-net --name ext-subnet --allocation-pool
start=10.0.2.100,end=10.0.2.200 --disable-dhcp --gateway 10.0.2.2 10.0.2.0/24
Created a new subnet:
+------------------+----------------------------------------------+
| Field            | Value                                        |
+------------------+----------------------------------------------+
| allocation_pools | {"start": "10.0.2.100", "end": "10.0.2.200"} |
| cidr             | 10.0.2.0/24                                  |
| created_at       | 2016-07-17T16:43:48                          |
| description      |                                              |
| dns_nameservers  |                                              |
| enable_dhcp      | False                                        |
| gateway_ip       | 10.0.2.2                                     |
| host_routes      |                                              |
| id               | 40d6da8b-b7eb-437e-8e84-ef018b773e4a         |
| ip_version       | 4                                            |
| ipv6_address_mode |                                             |
| ipv6_ra_mode     |                                              |
| name             | ext-subnet                                   |
| network_id       | 4716a0c7-70c9-44f1-a276-6e159400ba78         |
| subnetpool_id    |                                              |
| tenant_id        | ae8d3e3f5cff4a959f1ae1cfe9e80d6d             |
| updated_at       | 2016-07-17T16:43:48                          |
+------------------+----------------------------------------------+
```

If you use Horizon for net and subnet creation, go to Project ➤ Network ➤ Networks and click the "Create Network" button. You will then see an opened window as shown in Figure 5-3. By clicking Next, you will then go to the Subnet tab.

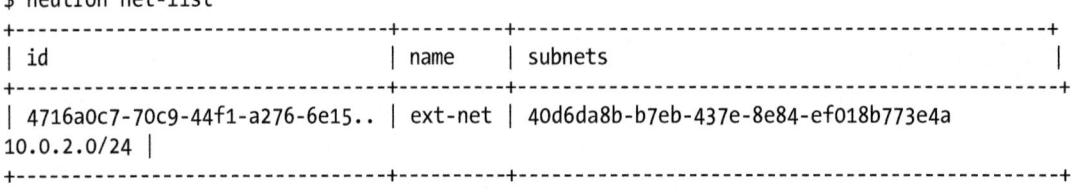

Create Network   ✕

| Network | Subnet | Subnet Details |

Network Name

| ext-net |

Create a new network. In addition, a subnet associated with the network can be created in the following steps of this wizard.

Admin State ❓

| UP   ☑ |

☐ Shared

☑ Create Subnet

Cancel   « Back   Next »

Figure 5-3. *Net creating dialog in Horizon*

Now it is possible to check the work that has already been done. First, let's check the list of all networks:

```
$ neutron net-list
+-------------------------------+----------+-----------------------------------------------+
| id                            | name     | subnets                                       |
+-------------------------------+----------+-----------------------------------------------+
| 4716a0c7-70c9-44f1-a276-6e15..| ext-net  | 40d6da8b-b7eb-437e-8e84-ef018b773e4a          |
10.0.2.0/24 |
+-------------------------------+----------+-----------------------------------------------+
```

Then you may want to check the details of ext-net:

```
$ neutron net-show ext-net
+---------------------------+------------------------------------------+
| Field                     | Value                                    |
+---------------------------+------------------------------------------+
| admin_state_up            | True                                     |
| availability_zone_hints   |                                          |
| availability_zones        | nova                                     |
```

```
| created_at                  | 2016-07-17T16:39:51                  |
| description                 |                                      |
| id                          | 4716a0c7-70c9-44f1-a276-6e159400ba78 |
| ipv4_address_scope          |                                      |
| ipv6_address_scope          |                                      |
| is_default                  | False                                |
| mtu                         | 1500                                 |
| name                        | ext-net                              |
| provider:network_type       | flat                                 |
| provider:physical_network   | external                             |
| provider:segmentation_id    |                                      |
| router:external             | True                                 |
| shared                      | False                                |
| status                      | ACTIVE                               |
| subnets                     | 40d6da8b-b7eb-437e-8e84-ef018b773e4a |
| tags                        |                                      |
| tenant_id                   | ae8d3e3f5cff4a959f1ae1cfe9e80d6d     |
| updated_at                  | 2016-07-17T16:39:51                  |
+-----------------------------+--------------------------------------+
```

The corresponding Networks screen from Horizon is shown in Figure 5-4.

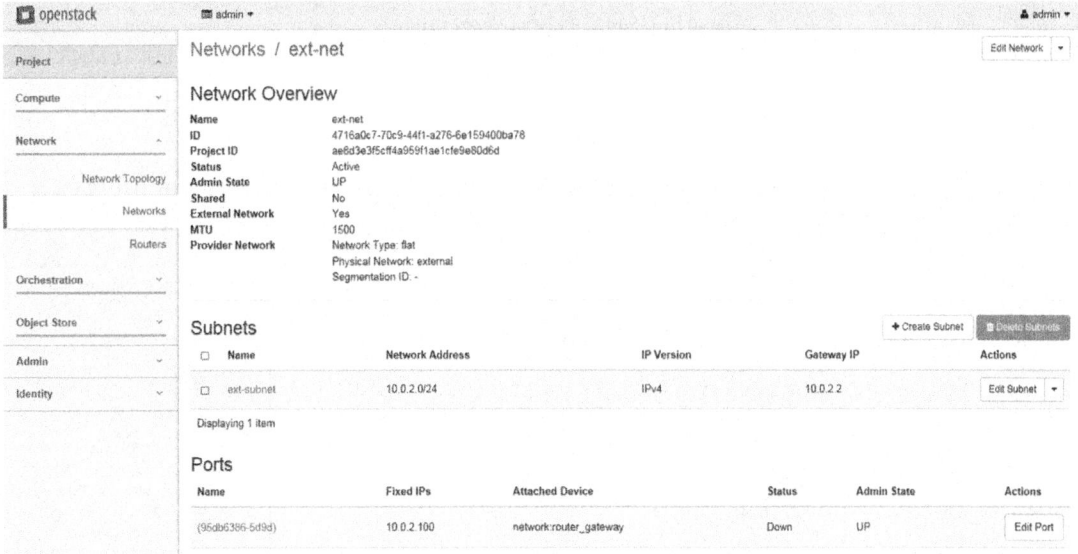

Figure 5-4. *Properties of the chosen network in Horizon*

The rest of the work you can do as a demo user from the demo project. Actually the only action where you need an admin role is when you name the network as external. Now let's create the tenant network:

```
$ source keystonerc_demo
$ neutron net-create demo-net
Created a new network:
+---------------------------+--------------------------------------+
| Field                     | Value                                |
+---------------------------+--------------------------------------+
| admin_state_up            | True                                 |
| availability_zone_hints   |                                      |
| availability_zones        |                                      |
| created_at                | 2016-07-17T16:45:52                  |
| description               |                                      |
| id                        | da07837c-74a5-471b-a79a-810dd3c2a91f |
| ipv4_address_scope        |                                      |
| ipv6_address_scope        |                                      |
| mtu                       | 1450                                 |
| name                      | demo-net                             |
| router:external           | False                                |
| shared                    | False                                |
| status                    | ACTIVE                               |
| subnets                   |                                      |
| tags                      |                                      |
| tenant_id                 | 16f44d2a075a4139a2a5425a42f1b447     |
| updated_at                | 2016-07-17T16:45:53                  |
+---------------------------+--------------------------------------+
```

You will also need a subnet for your network:

```
$ neutron subnet-create demo-net --name demo-subnet --gateway 172.16.0.1 172.16.0.0/24
Created a new subnet:
+-------------------+----------------------------------------------------+
| Field             | Value                                              |
+-------------------+----------------------------------------------------+
| allocation_pools  | {"start": "172.16.0.2", "end": "172.16.0.254"}     |
| cidr              | 172.16.0.0/24                                       |
| created_at        | 2016-07-17T16:46:53                                |
| description       |                                                    |
| dns_nameservers   |                                                    |
| enable_dhcp       | True                                               |
| gateway_ip        | 172.16.0.1                                          |
| host_routes       |                                                    |
| id                | 51a7950a-c132-462e-8b49-72b82ac7a0d2               |
| ip_version        | 4                                                  |
| ipv6_address_mode |                                                    |
| ipv6_ra_mode      |                                                    |
| name              | demo-subnet                                        |
| network_id        | da07837c-74a5-471b-a79a-810dd3c2a91f               |
| subnetpool_id     |                                                    |
| tenant_id         | 16f44d2a075a4139a2a5425a42f1b447                   |
| updated_at        | 2016-07-17T16:46:53                                |
+-------------------+----------------------------------------------------+
```

You will then need to create a virtual router for routing traffic:

```
$ neutron router-create demo-router
Created a new router:
+-------------------------+-----------------------------------------+
| Field                   | Value                                   |
+-------------------------+-----------------------------------------+
| admin_state_up          | True                                    |
| availability_zone_hints |                                         |
| availability_zones      |                                         |
| description             |                                         |
| external_gateway_info   |                                         |
| id                      | c61bbed9-ee0e-4b9f-b385-1e778b915a1b    |
| name                    | demo-router                             |
| routes                  |                                         |
| status                  | ACTIVE                                  |
| tenant_id               | 16f44d2a075a4139a2a5425a42f1b447        |
+-------------------------+-----------------------------------------+
```

Now connect the router with the tenant subnet from one side:

```
$ neutron router-interface-add demo-router demo-subnet
Added interface 875a80bc-adb4-4cff-b029-91af84f6fc86 to router demo-router.
```

And from the other side you will need to set ext-net as a gateway for the router:

```
$ neutron router-gateway-set demo-router ext-net
Set gateway for router demo-router
```

You can now create a virtual router in Horizon by going to Project ➤ Network ➤ Router tab. An example of the router properties is shown in Figure 5-5.

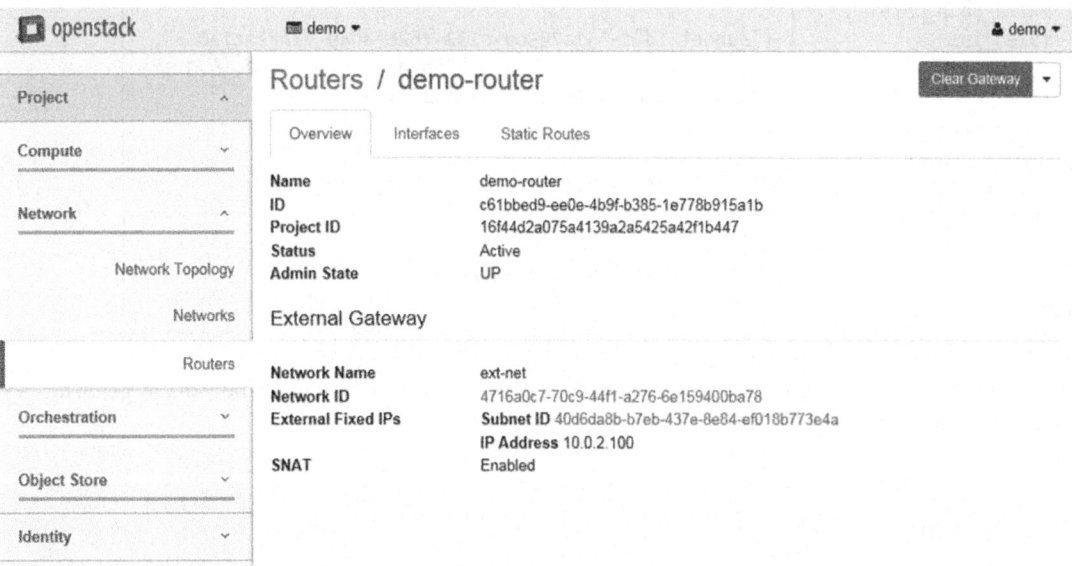

Figure 5-5. *Properties of virtual router in Horizon*

Now you can check all of the ports. Remember, it is the connection between a subnet and vNIC or a virtual router:

```
$ source keystonerc_admin
$ neutron port-list
+---------+------+-------------------+------------------------------------------------------+
| id      | name | mac_address       | fixed_ips                                            |
+---------+------+-------------------+------------------------------------------------------+
| 5c4aa.. |      | fa:16:3e:58:a8:71 | {"subnet_id": "51..", "ip_address": "172.16.0.2"}    |
| 875a8.. |      | fa:16:3e:9f:f4:bb | {"subnet_id": "51..", "ip_address": "172.16.0.1"}    |
| 95db6.. |      | fa:16:3e:64:e2:6d | {"subnet_id": "40..", "ip_address": "10.0.2.100"}    |
+---------+------+-------------------+------------------------------------------------------+
```

Then you can get information about any chosen port:

```
$ neutron port-show  875a80bc-adb4-4cff-b029-91af84f6fc86
+----------------------+------------------------------------------------------------------+
| Field                | Value                                                            |
+----------------------+------------------------------------------------------------------+
| admin_state_up       | True                                                             |
| allowed_address_pairs |                                                                 |
| binding:host_id      | centos7.test.local                                               |
| binding:profile      | {}                                                               |
| binding:vif_details  | {"port_filter": true, "ovs_hybrid_plug": true}                   |
| binding:vif_type     | ovs                                                              |
| binding:vnic_type    | normal                                                           |
| created_at           | 2016-07-17T16:48:31                                              |
| description          |                                                                  |
| device_id            | c61bbed9-ee0e-4b9f-b385-1e778b915a1b                             |
| device_owner         | network:router_interface                                         |
| dns_name             |                                                                  |
| extra_dhcp_opts      |                                                                  |
| fixed_ips            | {"subnet_id": "51a7950a-c132-462e-8b49-72b82ac7a0d2",            |
|                      |                         "ip_address": "172.16.0.1"}             |
| id                   | 875a80bc-adb4-4cff-b029-91af84f6fc86                             |
| mac_address          | fa:16:3e:9f:f4:bb                                                |
| name                 |                                                                  |
| network_id           | da07837c-74a5-471b-a79a-810dd3c2a91f                             |
| security_groups      |                                                                  |
| status               | ACTIVE                                                           |
| tenant_id            | 16f44d2a075a4139a2a5425a42f1b447                                 |
| updated_at           | 2016-07-17T16:48:35                                              |
+----------------------+------------------------------------------------------------------+
```

At this stage, you can start the instance and get an overall picture of configured network by going to Project ➤ Network ➤ Network Topology. It is shown in Figure 5-6.

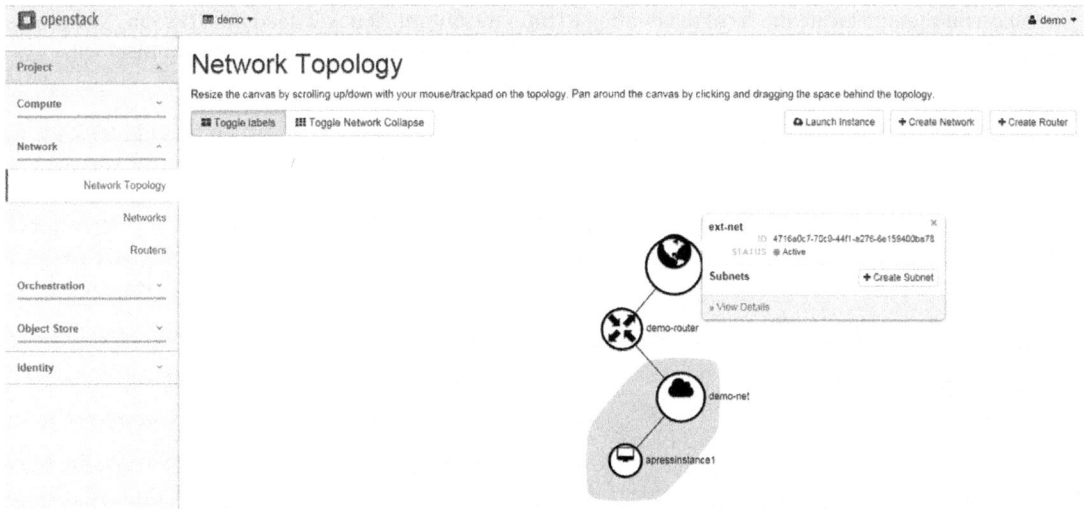

Figure 5-6. *Network Topology tab in Horizon*

At this point you have only one missing part. Your instances within the one tenant network can connect to each other. But none of the instances can reach out to an external network. You need to add a floating IP from ext-net to the virtual machine.

First, let's create the floating IP. The default quota for the number of floating IPs is 10, and this can be adjusted by anyone who has admin capacity:

```
$ neutron floatingip-create ext-net
Created a new floatingip:
+---------------------+--------------------------------------+
| Field               | Value                                |
+---------------------+--------------------------------------+
| description         |                                      |
| dns_domain          |                                      |
| dns_name            |                                      |
| fixed_ip_address    |                                      |
| floating_ip_address | 10.0.2.101                           |
| floating_network_id | 4716a0c7-70c9-44f1-a276-6e159400ba78 |
| id                  | 2c60a8b3-591d-475e-bb81-2d7c9bd4f18d |
| port_id             |                                      |
| router_id           |                                      |
| status              | DOWN                                 |
| tenant_id           | 16f44d2a075a4139a2a5425a42f1b447     |
+---------------------+--------------------------------------+
```

Take a moment to locate the ID of the floating IP from the output. You will need this ID soon. Next, you should determine which port you will associate the IP with. You can get an internal IP of your instance:

```
$ nova list
+------------------------------------------+------------------+--------+-------------+----------+
| ID                                       | Name             | Status | Power State | Networks |
+------------------------------------------+------------------+--------+-------------+----------+
| 4b80e2f5-c331-49f3-b653-33aa4ae77233     | apressinstance1  | ACTIVE | Running     | demo-net=|
|                                          |                  |        |             | 172.16.0.3 |
+------------------------------------------+------------------+--------+-------------+----------+
```

After locating the IP, you can then determine the port ID from the list:

```
$ neutron port-list
+-------------------------------------+- .. ---------------+
| id                                  | ..      fixed_ips  |
+-------------------------------------+- .. ---------------+
| 5c4aa20c-6f85-4f1c-a807-f39db46e7ce5 | .. "172.16.0.2"} |
| 875a80bc-adb4-4cff-b029-91af84f6fc86 | .. "172.16.0.1"} |
| e30e079a-985a-4ff2-ab3a-ba79f1841b3b | .. "172.16.0.3"} |
+-------------------------------------+- .. ---------------+
```

Now you can associate the floating IP with the port. In the example, the ID of the IP is 2c60a8b3-591d-475e-bb81-2d7c9bd4f18d and the ID of the port is e30e079a-985a-4ff2-ab3a-ba79f1841b3b:

```
$ neutron floatingip-associate 2c60a8b3-591d-475e-bb81-2d7c9bd4f18d e30e079a-985a-4ff2-ab3a-
ba79f1841b3b
Associated floating IP 2c60a8b3-591d-475e-bb81-2d7c9bd4f18d
```

If you check the nova list again, you will find the second external IP and the virtual machine properties:

```
$ nova list
+------------------------------------------+------------------+--------+-------------+----------+
| ID                                       | Name             | Status | Power State | Networks |
+------------------------------------------+------------------+--------+-------------+----------+
| 4b80e2f5-c331-49f3-b653-33aa4ae77233     | apressinstance1  | ACTIVE | Running     | demo-net=|
|                                          |                  |        |             | 172.16.0.3,|
|                                          |                  |        |             | 10.0.2.101 |
+------------------------------------------+------------------+--------+-------------+----------+
```

You can find information related to the floating IPs in Horizon by going to Project ➤ Compute ➤ Access & Security ➤ Floating IPs. An example of information provided at this tab is shown in Figure 5-7.

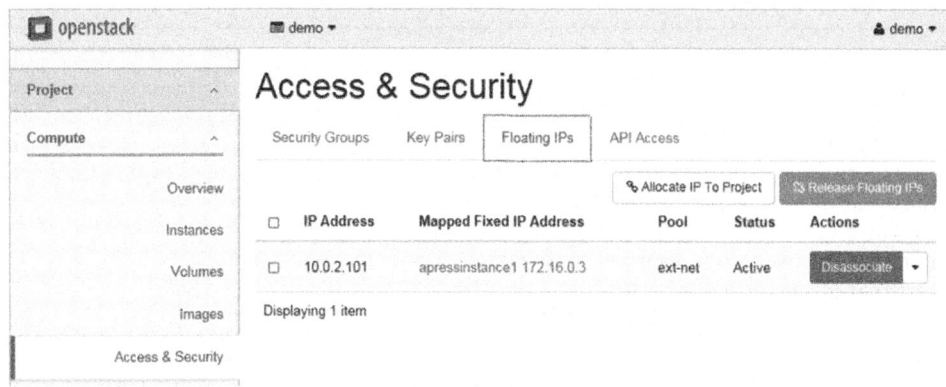

Figure 5-7. *Floating IPs tab in Horizon*

Manage Project Security Group Rules

Security Groups are firewall rules that can filter ingress and egress traffic for virtual machines. They are implemented with iptables rules in the reference configuration. To create the Security Group use the command:

```
$ nova secgroup-create apress-sgroup "Apress secgroup"
+--------------------------------------+---------------+-----------------+
| Id                                   | Name          | Description     |
+--------------------------------------+---------------+-----------------+
| 2ad4b67a-f943-451b-bcd2-14853704bcee | apress-sgroup | Apress secgroup |
+--------------------------------------+---------------+-----------------+
```

Then you can add a rule:

```
$ nova secgroup-add-rule apress-sgroup tcp 22 22 0.0.0.0/0
+-------------+-----------+----------+-----------+--------------+
| IP Protocol | From Port | To Port  | IP Range  | Source Group |
+-------------+-----------+----------+-----------+--------------+
| tcp         | 22        | 22       | 0.0.0.0/0 |              |
+-------------+-----------+----------+-----------+--------------+
```

And you can also apply Security Groups to instances at boot time:

```
$ nova boot --flavor m1.tiny --image cirros-raw --security-groups apress-sgroup
apressinstance1
+---------------------------------+----------------------------------------------------+
| Property                        | Value                                              |
+---------------------------------+----------------------------------------------------+
| OS-DCF:diskConfig               | MANUAL                                             |
| OS-EXT-AZ:availability_zone     |                                                    |
| OS-EXT-STS:power_state          | 0                                                  |
| OS-EXT-STS:task_state           | scheduling                                         |
| OS-EXT-STS:vm_state             | building                                           |
| OS-SRV-USG:launched_at          | -                                                  |
| OS-SRV-USG:terminated_at        | -                                                  |
| accessIPv4                      |                                                    |
| accessIPv6                      |                                                    |
| adminPass                       | EDZh9ctFcfHz                                       |
| config_drive                    |                                                    |
| created                         | 2016-07-17T17:17:31Z                               |
| flavor                          | m1.tiny (1)                                        |
| hostId                          |                                                    |
| id                              | 4b80e2f5-c331-49f3-b653-33aa4ae77233               |
| image                           | cirros-raw (039daa2e-6b3e-4e31-b1da-ab3e6feb8b30)  |
| key_name                        | -                                                  |
| metadata                        | {}                                                 |
| name                            | apressinstance1                                    |
| os-extended-volumes:volumes_attached | []                                            |
| progress                        | 0                                                  |
| security_groups                 | apress-sgroup                                      |
| status                          | BUILD                                              |
| tenant_id                       | 16f44d2a075a4139a2a5425a42f1b447                   |
| updated                         | 2016-07-17T17:17:34Z                               |
| user_id                         | 8e28b302669042e58e7ceb642d4f9708                   |
+---------------------------------+----------------------------------------------------+
```

Also it is possible to add or remove a Security Group on the fly:

```
$ nova add-secgroup apressinstance11 apress-sgroup
$ nova remove-secgroup apressinstance1 default
```

To list the rules, you would use the command:

```
nova secgroup-list-rules apress-sgroup
+-------------+-----------+---------+-----------+--------------+
| IP Protocol | From Port | To Port | IP Range  | Source Group |
+-------------+-----------+---------+-----------+--------------+
| tcp         | 22        | 22      | 0.0.0.0/0 |              |
+-------------+-----------+---------+-----------+--------------+
```

You can find information related to Security Groups in Horizon by going to Project ➤ Compute ➤ Access & Security ➤ Security Groups tab. An example of the information provided on this tab is shown in Figure 5-8.

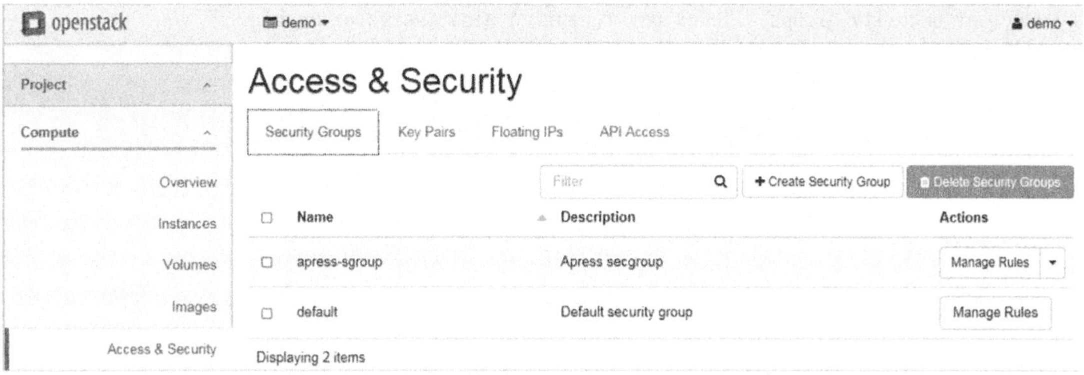

Figure 5-8. *Security Groups tab in Horizon*

Manage Quotas

A quota limits the number of available resources. The default number of resources allowed per tenant is defined in the main configuration file /etc/neutron/neutron.conf in the [quota] section. Here is an example:

```
[quota]
# Number of networks allowed per tenant. A negative value means unlimited.
# (integer value)
quota_network = 10

# Number of subnets allowed per tenant, A negative value means unlimited.
# (integer value)
quota_subnet = 10

# Number of ports allowed per tenant. A negative value means unlimited.
# (integer value)
quota_port = 50

# Default driver to use for quota checks (string value)
quota_driver = neutron.db.quota.driver.DbQuotaDriver

# Keep in track in the database of current resourcequota usage. Plugins which
# do not leverage the neutron database should set this flag to False (boolean
# value)
track_quota_usage = true

# Number of routers allowed per tenant. A negative value means unlimited.
# (integer value)
quota_router = 10

# Number of floating IPs allowed per tenant. A negative value means unlimited.
# (integer value)
quota_floatingip = 50
```

```
# Number of security groups allowed per tenant. A negative value means
# unlimited. (integer value)
quota_security_group = 10

# Number of security rules allowed per tenant. A negative value means
# unlimited. (integer value)
quota_security_group_rule = 100
```

Regular users can get their quotas with the neutron quota-show command:

```
$ neutron quota-show
+----------------------+-------+
| Field                | Value |
+----------------------+-------+
| floatingip           | 50    |
| network              | 10    |
| port                 | 50    |
| rbac_policy          | 10    |
| router               | 10    |
| security_group       | 10    |
| security_group_rule  | 100   |
| subnet               | 10    |
| subnetpool           | -1    |
+----------------------+-------+
```

Admins can do the same, but only for any project with the --tenant_id option. If an admin needs to change the quotas for a particular project, the following command would be used:

```
$ neutron quota-update --tenant_id 16f44d2a075a4139a2a5425a42f1b447 --floatingip 7
+----------------------+-------+
| Field                | Value |
+----------------------+-------+
| floatingip           | 7     |
| network              | 10    |
| port                 | 50    |
| rbac_policy          | 10    |
| router               | 10    |
| security_group       | 10    |
| security_group_rule  | 100   |
| subnet               | 10    |
| subnetpool           | -1    |
+----------------------+-------+
```

The neutron quota-list command lists tenants for which the per-tenant quota is enabled. The command does not list tenants with default quotas:

```
$ neutron quota-list
+------------+---------+------+--------+-----------+----------------+--------+-----------+
| floatingip | network | port | router | sec_group | sec_group_rule | subnet | tenant_id |
+------------+---------+------+--------+-----------+----------------+--------+-----------+
|          7 |      10 |   50 |     10 |        10 |            100 |     10 | 16f44d2.. |
+------------+---------+------+--------+-----------+----------------+--------+-----------+
```

Admins can manage quotas on a per-project basis in Horizon by going to Identity ➤ Projects ➤ Modify Quotas through the drop-down menu to the right of the project's name. Part of the networks quotas edit page is shown in Figure 5-9. A user can check the overall limits, including Neutron quotas, in Horizon by going to Project ➤ Compute ➤ Overview tab.

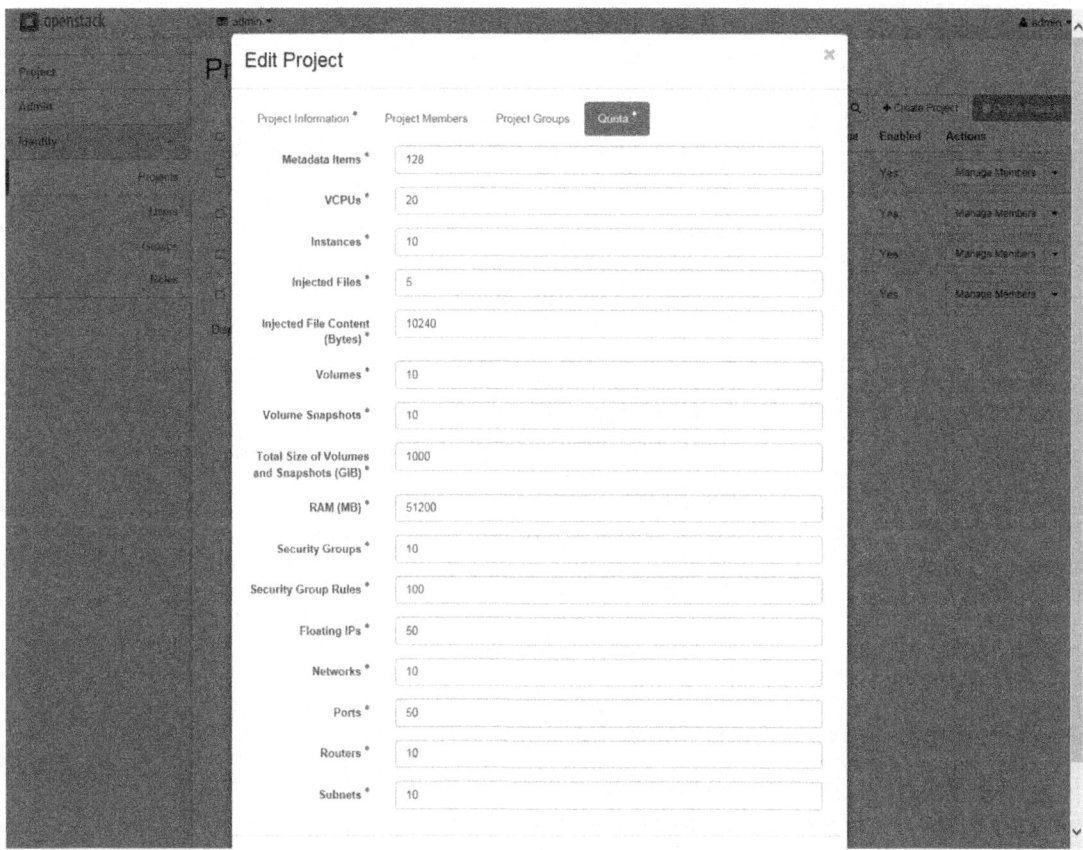

Figure 5-9. *Checking quotas in Horizon*

Verify Operation of Network Service

As mentioned earlier, Neutron consists of several components. Its configuration files were shown at the beginning of this chapter. Neutron API service is bound to port 9696. The log file for the Neutron server is available at /var/log/neutron/server.log.

You can check the supported extension for Neutron with the command:

```
$ neutron ext-list
+---------------------------+-------------------------------------------------+
| alias                     | name                                            |
+---------------------------+-------------------------------------------------+
| default-subnetpools       | Default Subnetpools                             |
| network-ip-availability   | Network IP Availability                         |
| network_availability_zone | Network Availability Zone                       |
| auto-allocated-topology   | Auto Allocated Topology Services                |
| ext-gw-mode               | Neutron L3 Configurable external gateway mode   |
| binding                   | Port Binding                                    |
| metering                  | Neutron Metering                                |
| agent                     | agent                                           |
| subnet_allocation         | Subnet Allocation                               |
| l3_agent_scheduler        | L3 Agent Scheduler                              |
| tag                       | Tag support                                     |
| external-net              | Neutron external network                        |
| net-mtu                   | Network MTU                                      |
| availability_zone         | Availability Zone                               |
| quotas                    | Quota management support                        |
| l3-ha                     | HA Router extension                             |
| provider                  | Provider Network                                |
| multi-provider            | Multi Provider Network                          |
| address-scope             | Address scope                                   |
| extraroute                | Neutron Extra Route                             |
| timestamp_core            | Time Stamp Fields addition for core resources   |
| extra_dhcp_opt            | Neutron Extra DHCP opts                         |
| dns-integration           | DNS Integration                                 |
| security-group            | security-group                                  |
| dhcp_agent_scheduler      | DHCP Agent Scheduler                            |
| router_availability_zone  | Router Availability Zone                        |
| rbac-policies             | RBAC Policies                                   |
| standard-attr-description | standard-attr-description                       |
| router                    | Neutron L3 Router                               |
| allowed-address-pairs     | Allowed Address Pairs                           |
| dvr                       | Distributed Virtual Router                      |
+---------------------------+-------------------------------------------------+
```

And you can check the state of the running agents with the command:

```
$ neutron agent-list
+------+-------------------+---------+-------------------+-------+----------------+-------+
| id   | agent_type        | host    | availability_zone | alive | admin_state_up | binary|
+------+-------------------+---------+-------------------+-------+----------------+-------+
| 38.. | Open vSwitch agent | centos7 |                   | :-)   | True           |       |
neutron-openvswitch-agent |
| 66.. | L3 agent          | centos7 | nova              | :-)   | True           |       |
neutron-l3-agent          |
| 7c.. | Metering agent    | centos7 |                   | :-)   | True           |       |
neutron-metering-agent    |
| 82.. | DHCP agent        | centos7 | nova              | :-)   | True           |       |
neutron-dhcp-agent        |
| 9b.. | Metadata agent    | centos7 |                   | :-)   | True           |       |
neutron-metadata-agent    |
+------+-------------------+---------+-------------------+-------+----------------+-------+
```

Review Questions

1. What service provides routing and Network Address Translation?

    A. neutron-server

    B. neutron-openvswitch-agent

    C. neutron-l3-agent

    D. neutron-metadata-agent

2. How can you check the status of running Neutron agents?

    A. neutron agents-list-state

    B. neutron agent-list

    C. neutron list-agent

    D. neutron agents-list

3. Name the Neutron API service config.

    A. /etc/neutron/neutron.conf

    B. /etc/neutron.conf

    C. /etc/neutron/plugin.ini

    D. /etc/neutron/api-server.conf

4. How can you correctly add a new rule to an existing Security Group?

    A. nova secgroup-add-rule apress-sgroup tcp 22 22 0.0.0.0/0

    B. nova secgroup-add-rule apress-sgroup tcp 22 0.0.0.0/0

    C. nova secgroup-add-new-rule apress-sgroup tcp 22 22 0.0.0.0/0

    D. nova secgroup-add-new-rule apress-sgroup tcp 22 0.0.0.0/0

5.   Where is the Neutron API log file situated?

   A.   /var/log/neutron/neutron.log

   B.   /var/log/neutron/server.log

   C.   /var/log/neutron/api.log

   D.   /var/log/neutron/api-server.log

Answers to Review Questions

1.   B

2.   C

3.   A

4.   A

5.   B

CHAPTER 6

OpenStack Compute

This chapter covers 15% of the Certified OpenStack Administrator exam requirements.

Architecture and Components of Nova

OpenStack Compute (Nova) service is the heart of the OpenStack cloud. Its main goal is to manage basic virtual machines functions like creating, starting, stopping, and so on. Let's look at the architecture and general parts of Nova. As with other services, Nova uses a message broker and database. As usual, by default the database is MariaDB and the message broker is RabbitMQ. The main services that support Nova are:

- **nova-api**: This service receives REST API calls from other services and clients and responds to them.

- **nova-scheduler**: This is Nova's scheduling service. It takes requests for starting instances from the queue and selects a compute node for running a virtual machine on it. The selection of Hypervisor is based on its weight and filters. Filters can include an amount of memory, a requested availability zone, a set of group hosts, among others. The rules apply each time the instance is started or when migrating to another Hypervisor.

- **nova-conductor**: This is the proxy service between the database and the nova-compute services. It helps with horizontal scalability.

- **nova-compute**: This is the main part of an IaaS system. This daemon usually runs only on compute nodes. Its role is to rule Hypervisor through the Hypervisor's specific API. It is designed to manage pools of computer resources and can work with widely available virtualization technologies.

- **nova-nonvncproxy and nova-consoleauth**: These are two services for providing access to the instances console through remote access VNC protocol. The former acts as the VNC-proxy and the latter is responsible for authorization.

Figures 6-1 and 6-2 illustrate the process of starting an instance.

© Andrey Markelov 2016
A. Markelov, *Certified OpenStack Administrator Study Guide*, DOI 10.1007/978-1-4842-2125-9_6

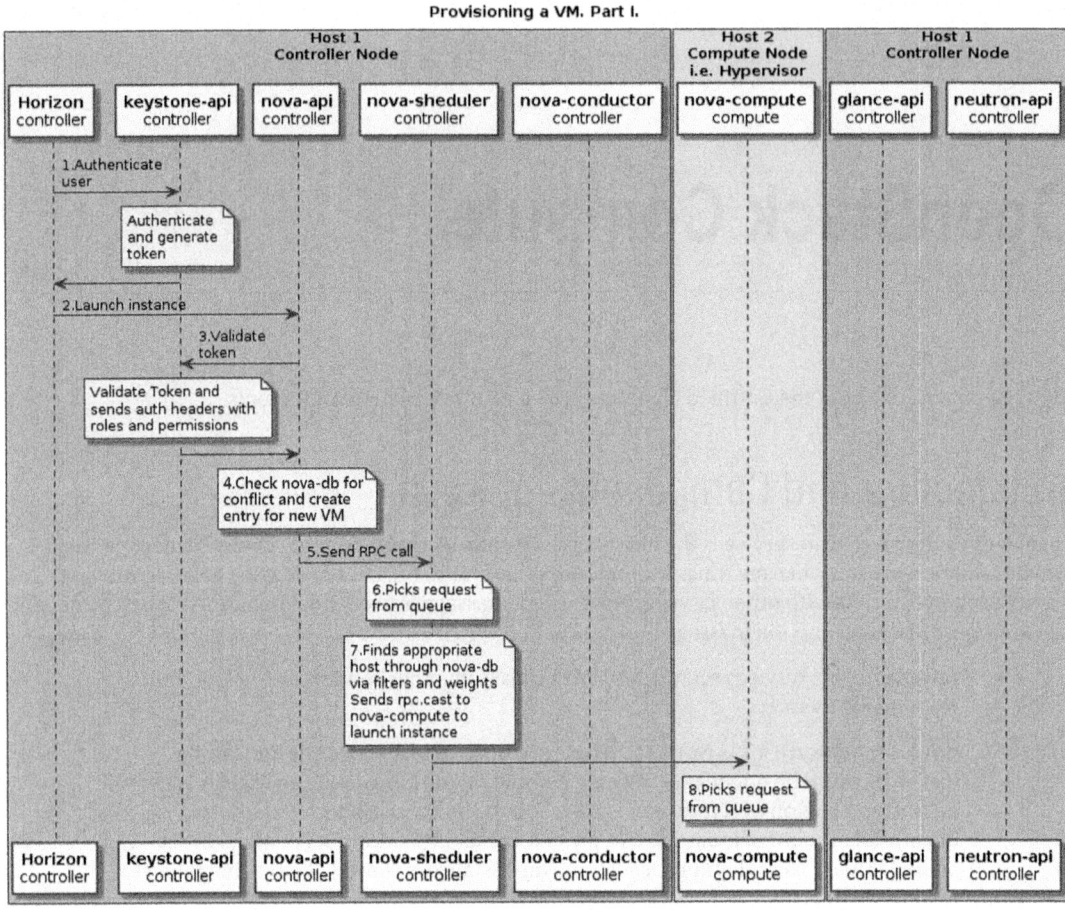

Figure 6-1. *Instance provision workflow—Part I*

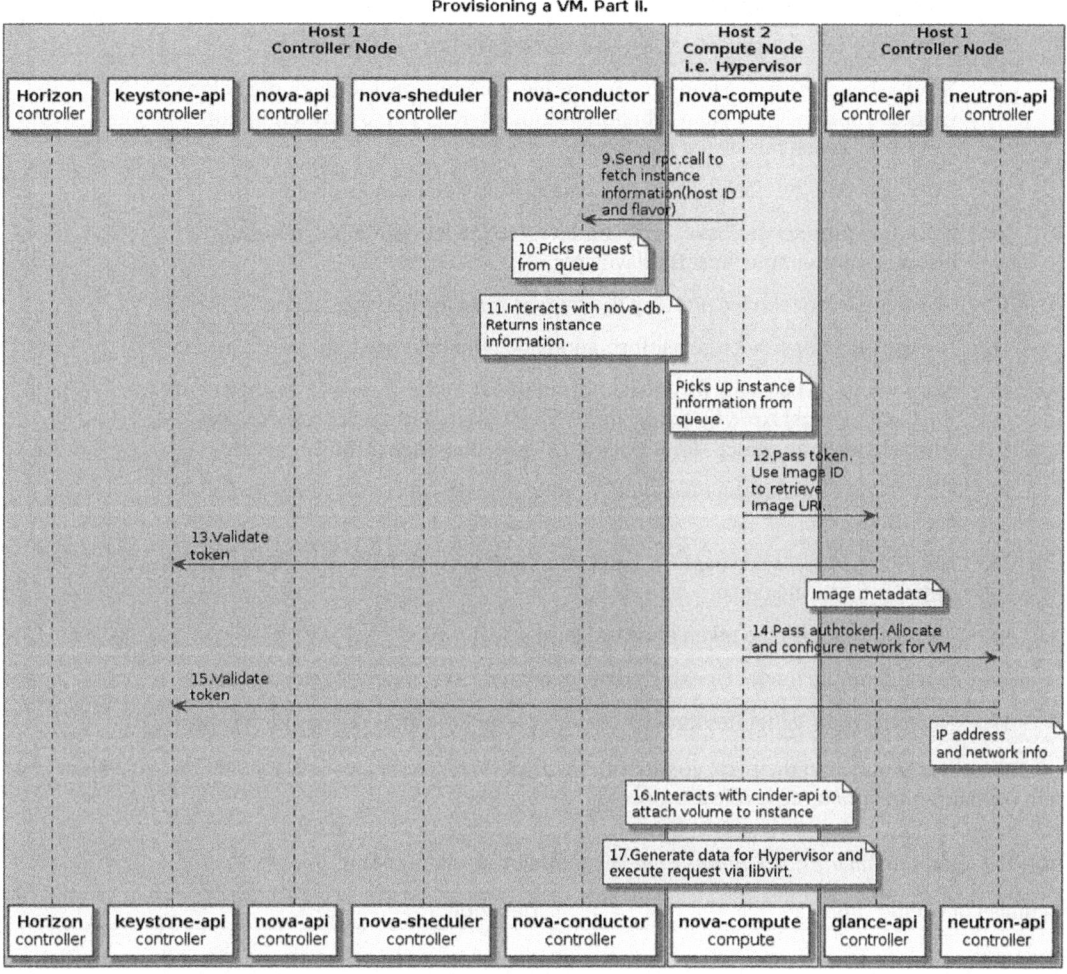

Figure 6-2. Instance provision workflow—Part II

In this example two hosts are used: compute host, which acts as the Hypervisor when nova-compute service is running, and controller node, with all its management services. The workflow of the starting instance is:

1. The client (in this particular example the client is Horizon web client, but it can be nova CLI command) asks keystone-api for authentication and generates the access token.

2. If authentication succeeds, the client sends a request for a running instance to nova-api. It is similar to the nova boot command.

3. Nova service validates the token and receives headers with roles and permissions from keystone-api.

4. Nova checks the database for conflicts with existing names of objects and creates a new entry for this instance in its database.

5. Nova-api sends the RPC for a scheduling instance to nova-scheduler service.

6. Nova-scheduler service picks up the request from the message queue.

7. Nova-scheduler service finds an appropriate compute host through the database via filters and weights. Then scheduler sends the RPC call to nova-compute service to launch the virtual machine.

8. Nova-compute service picks up the request from the message queue.

9. Nova-compute service asks nova-conductor to fetch information about the instance, for example: host ID, flavor, etc.

10. Nova-conductor service picks up the request from the message queue.

11. Nova-conductor service gets information about an instance from the database.

12. Nova-compute takes the instance information from the queue. At this moment the compute host knows what image will be used to start the instance. Nova-compute asks the glance-api service for a particular image URL.

13. Glance-api validates the token and returns the metadata of the image including the URL.

14. Nova-compute service passes a token to neutron-api and asks it to configure the network for the instance.

15. Neutron validates the token and configures the network.

16. Nova-compute interacts with cinder-api to attach the volume to the instance.

17. Nova-compute generates data for Hypervisor and executes the request via libvirt.

Now let's have a look at the main configuration file of Nova: /etc/nova/nova.conf. Table 6-1 shows the main configuration options available from config.

Table 6-1. *Main Configuration Options from* /etc/cinder/cinder.conf

Examples of Config Options	Description
[DEFAULT] my_ip = 10.0.2.15	Management interface IP address of the controller node
[DEFAULT] use_neutron = True firewall_driver = nova.virt.firewall. NoopFirewallDriver	Enables support for the networking service
[DEFAULT] auth_strategy = keystone [keystone_authtoken] auth_uri = http:// 10.0.2.15:5000 auth_url = http:// 10.0.2.15:35357 auth_type = password project_domain_name = default user_domain_name = default project_name = service username = nova password = openstack	Authentication parameters: auth_uri-public Identity API endpoint and auth_url-admin Identity API endpoint Other parameters set a default project name, domain name, project name for services, and account information for Cinder user

(continued)

Table 6-1. (*continued*)

Examples of Config Options	Description
[api_database] connection=mysql+pymysql://nova_ api:password@10.0.2.15/nova_api [database] connection=mysql+pymysql:// nova:password@10.0.2.15/nova	Connection strings are used to connect to Nova's databases
[DEFAULT] rpc_backend = rabbit [oslo_messaging_rabbit] rabbit_host = localhost rabbit_port = 5672 rabbit_userid = guest rabbit_password = guest	RabbitMQ broker address, port, user name, and password
[vnc] vncserver_listen = $my_ip vncserver_proxyclient_address = $my_ip	Management interface IP address of the VNC proxy
[glance] api_servers=10.0.2.15:9292	Location of the Image Service API

Managing Flavors

Instance flavor is a template of a virtual machine that describes the main parameters. It is also known as an instance type. Immediately after installation of OpenStack cloud, you will have several predefined flavors. You can also add new flavors and delete existing ones. To list the flavors use the following command:

```
$ openstack flavor list
+----+-----------+-------+------+-----------+-------+-----------+
| ID | Name      |   RAM | Disk | Ephemeral | VCPUs | Is Public |
+----+-----------+-------+------+-----------+-------+-----------+
|  1 | m1.tiny   |   512 |    1 |         0 |     1 | True      |
|  2 | m1.small  |  2048 |   20 |         0 |     1 | True      |
|  3 | m1.medium |  4096 |   40 |         0 |     2 | True      |
|  4 | m1.large  |  8192 |   80 |         0 |     4 | True      |
|  5 | m1.xlarge | 16384 |  160 |         0 |     8 | True      |
+----+-----------+-------+------+-----------+-------+-----------+
```

You can also use the Nova `flavor-list` command with the same result. To list the details of the flavor use:

```
$ openstack flavor show m1.tiny
+----------------------------+---------+
| Field                      | Value   |
+----------------------------+---------+
| OS-FLV-DISABLED:disabled   | False   |
| OS-FLV-EXT-DATA:ephemeral  | 0       |
| disk                       | 1       |
| id                         | 1       |
| name                       | m1.tiny |
| os-flavor-access:is_public | True    |
| properties                 |         |
| ram                        | 512     |
| rxtx_factor                | 1.0     |
| swap                       |         |
| vcpus                      | 1       |
+----------------------------+---------+
```

By default only admin can list all the flavors and create new ones. Here is an example of creation of a new publicly available flavor:

```
$ source keystonerc_admin
$ nova flavor-create --is-public true m10.tiny auto 400 3 1
+-------+----------+-----------+------+-----------+------+-------+-------------+-----------+
| ID    | Name     | Memory_MB | Disk | Ephemeral | Swap | VCPUs | RXTX_Factor | Is_Public |
+-------+----------+-----------+------+-----------+------+-------+-------------+-----------+
| 33e.. | m10.tiny | 400       | 3    | 0         |      | 1     | 1.0         | True      |
+-------+----------+-----------+------+-----------+------+-------+-------------+-----------+
```

In this example a new flavor was created with the name `m10.tiny` that has a 3GB disk, 400Mb RAM, and 1 vCPU. You can delete the flavor with the command:

```
$ nova flavor-delete m10.tiny
```

For managing flavors in Horizon go to System ➤ Flavors.

Managing and Accessing an Instance Using a Keypair

Before launching instances, you should know how to work with OpenSSH keypairs. Getting access to virtual machines with OpenSSH key-based authentication is essential for using GNU/Linux in the cloud computing environment.

SSH (Secure Shell) allows you to authenticate users by using the private-public keypair. You should generate two linked cryptographic keys: public and private. The public key can be given to anyone. Your private key should be kept in a secure place—it is only yours. An instance with running the OpenSSH server that has your public key can issue a challenge that can only be answered by the system holding your private key. As a result, it can be authenticated through the presence of your key. This allows you to access a virtual machine in a way that does not require passwords.

OpenStack can store public keys and put them inside the instance at the moment it is started. It is your responsibility to keep the private key secured. If you lose the key, you can't recover it. In that case you should remove the public key from your cloud and generate a new keypair. If somebody stole a private key, they can get access to your instances.

■ **Tip** In a GNU/Linux system, public keys are stored in the `~/.ssh/authorized_keys` file.

Let's start by creating a keypair. The corresponding command is:

```
$ nova keypair-add apresskey1 > ~/apresskey1
```

With this command you create a keypair. The private key is stored in the file `~/apresskey1` at your workstation:

```
$ cat ~/apresskey1
-----BEGIN RSA PRIVATE KEY-----
FliElAoNnAoKvQaELyeHnPaLwb8KlpnIC65PunAsRz5FsoBZ8VbnYhD76DON/BDVT
...
gdYjBM1CqqmUw54HkMJp8DLcYmBP+CRTwia9iSyY42Zw7eAi/QTIbQ574d8=
-----END RSA PRIVATE KEY-----
```

A public key is stored in your OpenStack cloud and ready to use. You can check the list of public keys accessible to you with the command:

```
$ nova keypair-list
+------------+-------------------------------------------------+
| Name       | Fingerprint                                     |
+------------+-------------------------------------------------+
| apresskey1 | f4:64:d2:51:91:04:13:f7:4a:76:e7:36:a6:17:05:77 |
+------------+-------------------------------------------------+
```

Before an SSH client can use a private key, you should make sure that the file has the correct GNU/Linux permissions:

```
$ chmod 600 apresskey1
$ ls -l apresskey1
-rw------- 1 andrey andrey 1684 Aug 24 18:05 apresskey1
```

If you want to create and delete keypairs in Horizon, go to Project ➤ Compute ➤ Access & Security ➤ Key Pairs.

When your instance is running and has a floating IP, you can connect to it with a similar command:

```
$ ssh -i ~/apresskey1 cirros@10.100.1.103
```

Option -i points to your private key. You will learn in the next section how to run an instance and how to insert a public key to it.

Launching, Shutting Down, and Terminating the Instance

In general, you need at least three parameters to start an instance: the name of an instance, the flavor, and the source of an instance. The instance source can be an image, snapshot, or block storage volume. At boot time you can also specify optional parameters like keypair, security group, user data files, and volume for persistent storage. Here is the general command line for instance launching:

```
$ nova boot --flavor FLAVOR_ID --image IMAGE_ID --key-name KEY_NAME \
  --user-data USER_DATA_FILE --security-groups SEC_GROUP_NAME --meta KEY=VALUE \
  INSTANCE_NAME
```

To be more specific, you can try this example:

```
$ nova boot --flavor m1.tiny --image cirros-raw --security-groups apress-sgroup --key-name
apresskey1 apressinstance1
```

Property	Value
OS-DCF:diskConfig	MANUAL
OS-EXT-AZ:availability_zone	
OS-EXT-STS:power_state	0
OS-EXT-STS:task_state	scheduling
OS-EXT-STS:vm_state	building
OS-SRV-USG:launched_at	-
OS-SRV-USG:terminated_at	-
accessIPv4	
accessIPv6	
adminPass	et4XhfLmwL7e
config_drive	
created	2016-08-24T16:41:16Z
flavor	m1.tiny (1)
hostId	
id	a526612a-75ce-4856-930e-6bc4e7a54d77
image	cirros-raw (039daa2e-6b3e-4e31-b1da-ab3e6feb8b30)
key_name	apresskey1
metadata	{}
name	apressinstance1
os-extended-volumes:volumes_attached	[]
progress	0
security_groups	apress-sgroup
status	BUILD
tenant_id	16f44d2a075a4139a2a5425a42f1b447
updated	2016-08-24T16:41:16Z
user_id	8e28b302669042e58e7ceb642d4f9708

In this example you tried to run the instance with the name apressinstance1 by the flavor m1.tiny from an image named cirros-raw. You also specified the security group named apress-sgroup and the keypair apresskey1. To check the current state of the instances available to you, use the command:

```
$ nova list
```

```
+--------------+------------------+--------+------------+-------------+----------------------+
| ID           | Name             | Status | Task State | Power State | Networks             |
+--------------+------------------+--------+------------+-------------+----------------------+
| a526612a-... | apressinstance1  | ACTIVE | -          | Running     | demo-net=172.16.0.5  |
+--------------+------------------+--------+------------+-------------+----------------------+
```

You may want to connect to the instance console in your browser by the noVNC client, which is the VNC client using HTML5 with encryption support. To get the URL, use the command:

```
$ nova get-vnc-console apressinstance1 novnc
+-------+--------------------------------------------------------------------------------+
| Type  | Url                                                                            |
+-------+--------------------------------------------------------------------------------+
| novnc | http://10.0.2.15:6080/vnc_auto.html?token=9e2a16e9-904e-4764-b0fa-cebf396f55c6  |
+-------+--------------------------------------------------------------------------------+
```

If you put the URL in the address bar of your browser, you can connect to the machine. The example is shown in Figure 6-3.

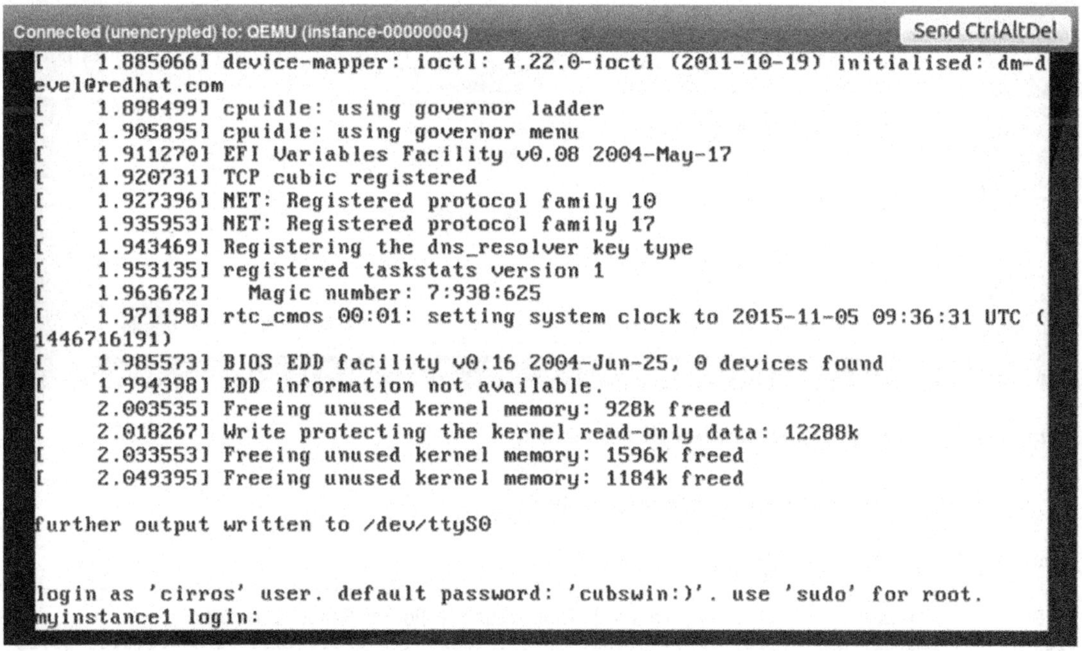

Figure 6-3. *Example of console of running instance in browser*

If you prefer to work with instances in GUI, you can use the Horizon web interface. For that go to Project ➤ Compute ➤ Instances. The example of the launch dialog is shown in Figure 6-4.

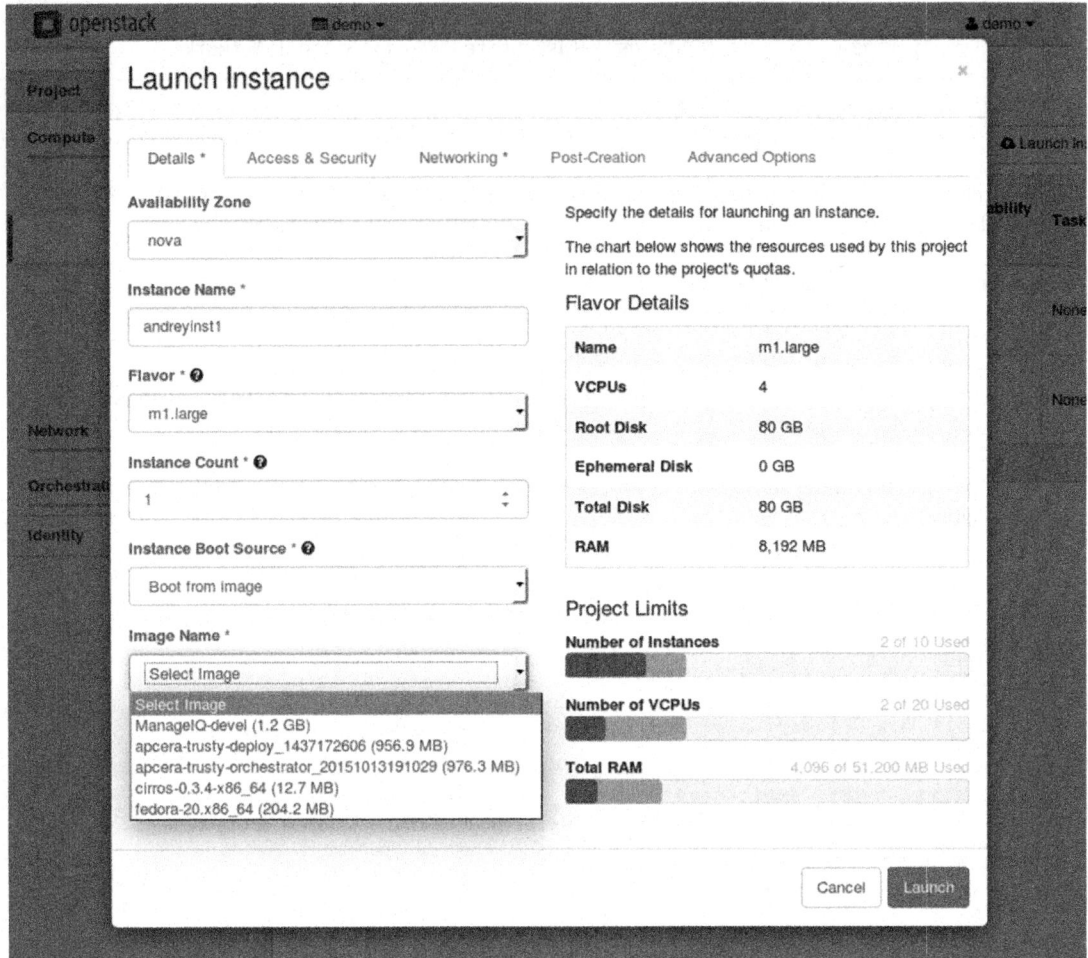

Figure 6-4. *Example of a launch instance dialog window*

In case of an error, you may see something like this:

```
$ nova list
+-------------+----------------+--------+------------+-------------+--------------------+
| ID          | Name           | Status | Task State | Power State | Networks           |
+-------------+----------------+--------+------------+-------------+--------------------+
| a526612a-.. | apressinstance1 | ACTIVE | -          | Running     | demo-net=172.16.0.5 |
| 7ee3f1e8-.. | apressinstance2 | ERROR  | -          | NOSTATE     |                    |
+-------------+----------------+--------+------------+-------------+--------------------+
```

To get the detailed information about the instance, you can run the command:

```
$ nova show apressinstance2
+-------------------------------------+------------------------------------------------+
| Property                            | Value                                          |
+-------------------------------------+------------------------------------------------+
| OS-DCF:diskConfig                   | MANUAL                                         |
| OS-EXT-AZ:availability_zone         |                                                |
| OS-EXT-STS:power_state              | 0                                              |
| OS-EXT-STS:task_state               | -                                              |
| OS-EXT-STS:vm_state                 | error                                          |
| OS-SRV-USG:launched_at              | -                                              |
| OS-SRV-USG:terminated_at            | -                                              |
| accessIPv4                          |                                                |
| accessIPv6                          |                                                |
| config_drive                        |                                                |
| created                             | 2016-08-24T17:39:45Z                           |
| fault                               | {"message": "No valid host was found.          |
|                                     | There are not enough hosts available.",        |
|                                     | "code": 500, "created": "2016-08-24T17:39:46Z"}|
| flavor                              | m1.xlarge (5)                                  |
| hostId                              |                                                |
| id                                  | 7ee3f1e8-278f-4212-9318-c35eb35fbd37           |
| image                               | cirros-raw (039daa2e-6b3e-4e31-b1da-ab3e6feb..)|
| key_name                            | apresskey1                                     |
| metadata                            | {}                                             |
| name                                | apressinstance2                                |
| os-extended-volumes:volumes_attached| []                                             |
| status                              | ERROR                                          |
| tenant_id                           | 16f44d2a075a4139a2a5425a42f1b447               |
| updated                             | 2016-08-24T17:39:46Z                           |
| user_id                             | 8e28b302669042e58e7ceb642d4f9708               |
+-------------------------------------+------------------------------------------------+
```

The command for starting this instance was:

```
$ nova boot --flavor m1.xlarge --image cirros-raw --security-groups apress-sgroup --key-name
apresskey1 apressinstance2
```

From the output above, it is easy to see that there is no room to put such a big instance within flavor m1.xlarge. Flavor m1.xlarge requires 16GB of RAM.

The next command will completely delete this instance:

```
$ nova delete apressinstance2
Request to delete server apressinstance2 has been accepted.
```

If you need to reboot your virtual machine, then use the command:

```
$ nova reboot apressinstance1
Request to reboot server <Server: apressinstance1> has been accepted.
```

For a hard reset of the server you can add the --hard option. You may stop and start an instance if needed:

```
$ nova stop apressinstance1
Request to stop server apressinstance1 has been accepted.
$ nova list
+-------------+----------------+----------+------------+-------------+----------------------+
| ID          | Name           | Status   | Task State | Power State | Networks             |
+-------------+----------------+----------+------------+-------------+----------------------+
| 27a86b68-.. | apressinstance1| SHUTOFF  | -          | Shutdown    | demo-net=172.16.0.6  |
+-------------+----------------+----------+------------+-------------+----------------------+
$ nova start apressinstance1
Request to start server apressinstance1 has been accepted.
$ nova list
+-------------+----------------+----------+------------+-------------+----------------------+
| ID          | Name           | Status   | Task State | Power State | Networks             |
+-------------+----------------+----------+------------+-------------+----------------------+
| 27a86b68-.. | apressinstance1| ACTIVE   | -          | Running     | demo-net=172.16.0.6  |
+-------------+----------------+----------+------------+-------------+----------------------+
```

Managing Instance Snapshots

OpenStack can create snapshots of instances, even if a virtual machine is running. In this case it is the user's obligation to keep the data consistent. It is important to know that snapshot is not an instance recovery point. Snapshot is the same as a regular Glance image. You can start a new virtual machine from the snapshot of another virtual machine.

Let's check whether there is at least one image in Glance and one instance:

```
$ nova image-list
+--------------------------------------+------------------+--------+--------+
| ID                                   | Name             | Status | Server |
+--------------------------------------+------------------+--------+--------+
| 039daa2e-6b3e-4e31-b1da-ab3e6feb8b30 | cirros-raw       | ACTIVE |        |
+--------------------------------------+------------------+--------+--------+
$ nova list
+-------------+----------------+----------+------------+-------------+----------------------+
| ID          | Name           | Status   | Task State | Power State | Networks             |
+-------------+----------------+----------+------------+-------------+----------------------+
| 27a86b68-.. | apressinstance1| ACTIVE   | -          | Running     | demo-net=172.16.0.6  |
+-------------+----------------+----------+------------+-------------+----------------------+
```

Now you can create a snapshot from a running instance:

```
$ nova image-create apressinstance1 apressinstance1_snap
```

And after that you can list the available images:

```
$ nova image-list
+-------------+----------------------+---------+------------------------------------------+
| ID          | Name                 | Status  | Server                                   |
+-------------+----------------------+---------+------------------------------------------+
| 5b385bc6-.. | apressinstance1_snap | ACTIVE  | 27a86b68-80ce-4e4b-925a-9d0f558bd49a     |
| 039daa2e-.. | cirros-raw           | ACTIVE  |                                          |
+-------------+----------------------+---------+------------------------------------------+
```

As you can see, snapshot was added to the list. You are free to create a new instance from this snapshot:

```
$ nova boot --flavor m1.tiny --image apressinstance1_snap apressinstance_from_sn
+--------------------------------------+--------------------------------------------+
| Property                             | Value                                      |
+--------------------------------------+--------------------------------------------+
| OS-DCF:diskConfig                    | MANUAL                                     |
| OS-EXT-AZ:availability_zone          |                                            |
| OS-EXT-STS:power_state               | 0                                          |
| OS-EXT-STS:task_state                | scheduling                                 |
| OS-EXT-STS:vm_state                  | building                                   |
| OS-SRV-USG:launched_at               | -                                          |
| OS-SRV-USG:terminated_at             | -                                          |
| accessIPv4                           |                                            |
| accessIPv6                           |                                            |
| adminPass                            | Ciuh4iXBBzcX                               |
| config_drive                         |                                            |
| created                              | 2016-08-26T14:19:54Z                       |
| flavor                               | m1.tiny (1)                                |
| hostId                               |                                            |
| id                                   | 46c28143-ab85-425e-a5a7-46014a43ec32       |
| image                                | apressinstance1_snap (5b385bc6-8d1..)      |
| key_name                             | -                                          |
| metadata                             | {}                                         |
| name                                 | apressinstance_from_sn                     |
| os-extended-volumes:volumes_attached | []                                         |
| progress                             | 0                                          |
| security_groups                      | default                                    |
| status                               | BUILD                                      |
| tenant_id                            | 16f44d2a075a4139a2a5425a42f1b447           |
| updated                              | 2016-08-26T14:19:54Z                       |
| user_id                              | 8e28b302669042e58e7ceb642d4f9708           |
+--------------------------------------+--------------------------------------------+
```

Managing Quotas

A quota limits the number of available resources. The default number of resources allowed per tenant is defined in the main configuration file: /etc/nova/nova.conf. Here is an example:

```
# Number of instances allowed per project (integer value)
quota_instances=10

# Number of instance cores allowed per project (integer value)
quota_cores=20

# Megabytes of instance RAM allowed per project (integer value)
quota_ram=51200

# Number of floating IPs allowed per project (integer value)
quota_floating_ips=10

# Number of fixed IPs allowed per project (this should be at least the number
# of instances allowed) (integer value)
quota_fixed_ips=-1

# Number of metadata items allowed per instance (integer value)
quota_metadata_items=128

# Number of injected files allowed (integer value)
quota_injected_files=5

# Number of bytes allowed per injected file (integer value)
quota_injected_file_content_bytes=10240

# Length of injected file path (integer value)
quota_injected_file_path_length=255

# Number of security groups per project (integer value)
quota_security_groups=10

# Number of security rules per security group (integer value)
quota_security_group_rules=20

# Number of key pairs per user (integer value)
quota_key_pairs=100
```

Regular users can get their quotas by using the nova quota-show command:

```
$ nova quota-show
+-----------------------------+--------+
| Quota                       | Limit  |
+-----------------------------+--------+
| instances                   | 10     |
| cores                       | 20     |
| ram                         | 51200  |
| floating_ips                | 10     |
| fixed_ips                   | -1     |
| metadata_items              | 128    |
| injected_files              | 5      |
| injected_file_content_bytes | 10240  |
| injected_file_path_bytes    | 255    |
| key_pairs                   | 100    |
| security_groups             | 10     |
| security_group_rules        | 20     |
| server_groups               | 10     |
| server_group_members        | 10     |
+-----------------------------+--------+
```

With the command nova quota-defaults, users can see the default quotas for comparison with their own quotas. Users can see a part of the current quotas in a graphical view on the Overview page of the project. An example is shown in Figure 6-5.

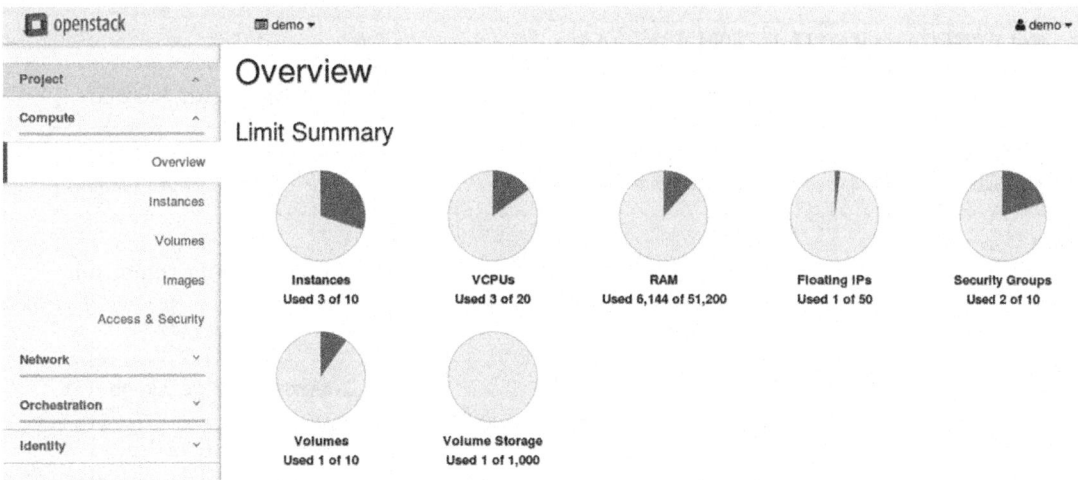

Figure 6-5. *User's overview of the current quota status*

Admins can do the same but for any project with the `--tenant_id` option. If an admin needs to change the quotas for a particular project, this command would be used:

```
$ source keystonerc_admin
$ nova quota-update 16f44d2a075a4139a2a5425a42f1b447 --instances 4
$ source keystonerc_demo
$ nova quota-show | grep instances
| instances                    | 4     |
```

Admins can manage quotas on a per-project basis in Horizon by going to Identity ➤ Projects ➤ Modify Quotas and accessing the drop-down menu to the right of the project's name.

Getting Nova Stats

First let's grab the list of all Hypervisors:

```
$ nova hypervisor-list
+----+---------------------+-------+---------+
| ID | Hypervisor hostname | State | Status  |
+----+---------------------+-------+---------+
| 1  | centos7.test.local  | up    | enabled |
+----+---------------------+-------+---------+
```

In this example only one compute node is presented and it is up and running. You can check which instances are running at this particular host:

```
$ nova hypervisor-servers centos7.test.local
+-------------------------+--------------------+---------------+---------------------+
| ID                      | Name               | Hypervisor ID | Hypervisor Hostname |
+-------------------------+--------------------+---------------+---------------------+
| 27a86b68-80ce-4e4b-925a-.. | instance-0000000b | 1          | centos7.test.local  |
| ca0b7a1e-8aca-41e4-ac2d-.. | instance-0000000c | 1          | centos7.test.local  |
+-------------------------+--------------------+---------------+---------------------+
```

To get a summary of resource usage of all of the instances running on the host, use the command:

```
$ nova host-describe centos7.test.local
+--------------------+----------------------------------+-----+-----------+---------+
| HOST               | PROJECT                          | cpu | memory_mb | disk_gb |
+--------------------+----------------------------------+-----+-----------+---------+
| centos7.test.local | (total)                          | 1   | 3952      | 49      |
| centos7.test.local | (used_now)                       | 3   | 2048      | 3       |
| centos7.test.local | (used_max)                       | 3   | 1536      | 3       |
| centos7.test.local | 16f44d2a075a4139a2a5425a42f1b447 | 3   | 1536      | 3       |
+--------------------+----------------------------------+-----+-----------+---------+
```

To search for all running virtual machines, you can use the Nova database:

```
# nova-manage vm list | grep active
apressinstance2 centos7.test.local m1.tiny    active    2016-08-24
18:55:30+00:00  039daa2e-6b3e-4e31-b1da-ab3e6feb8b30                16f44d2a075a4139a2a
5425a42f1b447 8e28b302669042e58e7ceb642d4f9708 None      0
apressinstance1 centos7.test.local m1.tiny    active    2016-08-24
18:14:01+00:00  039daa2e-6b3e-4e31-b1da-ab3e6feb8b30                16f44d2a075a4139a2a
5425a42f1b447 8e28b302669042e58e7ceb642d4f9708 None      0
```

And as admin you can see an overall picture of all Hypervisors in Horizon. An example is shown in Figure 6-6.

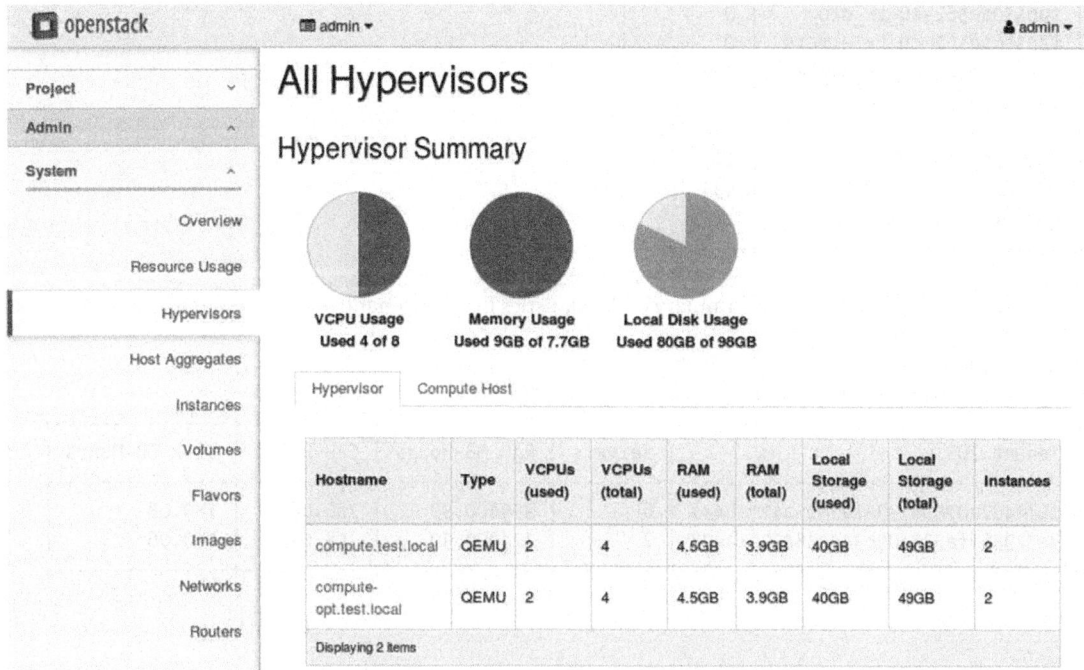

Figure 6-6. *Example of the Hypervisors' summary picture*

If needed you can easily get diagnostic information about any instance:

```
$ nova diagnostics 27a86b68-80ce-4e4b-925a-9d0f558bd49a
+--------------------------+----------+
| Property                 | Value    |
+--------------------------+----------+
| memory                   | 524288   |
| memory-actual            | 524288   |
| memory-rss               | 46568    |
| tap550ae562-c0_rx        | 8710     |
| tap550ae562-c0_rx_drop   | 0        |
| tap550ae562-c0_rx_errors | 0        |
| tap550ae562-c0_rx_packets| 80       |
| tap550ae562-c0_tx        | 10614    |
| tap550ae562-c0_tx_drop   | 0        |
| tap550ae562-c0_tx_errors | 0        |
| tap550ae562-c0_tx_packets| 106      |
| vda_errors               | -1       |
| vda_read                 | 20419584 |
| vda_read_req             | 1151     |
| vda_write                | 434176   |
| vda_write_req            | 125      |
+--------------------------+----------+
```

And at the end, you can get a summary of the statistics for each tenant:

```
$ nova usage-list
Usage from 2016-07-30 to 2016-08-28:
+----------------------------------+---------+--------------+-----------+---------------+
| Tenant ID                        | Servers | RAM MB-Hours | CPU Hours | Disk GB-Hours |
+----------------------------------+---------+--------------+-----------+---------------+
| 16f44d2a075a4139a2a5425a42f1b447 | 6       | 399400.59    | 780.08    | 780.08        |
| 3e52946ffa538409b34cc3849201aa78 | 2       | 124000.30    | 58.02     | 120.06        |
+----------------------------------+---------+--------------+-----------+---------------+
```

Verifying Operation and Managing Nova Compute Servers

You can check whether all Nova servers are started and active by using the systemctl command:

```
# systemctl status *nova* -n 0
● openstack-nova-compute.service - OpenStack Nova Compute Server
   Loaded: loaded (/usr/lib/systemd/system/openstack-nova-compute.service; enabled; vendor
preset: disabled)
   Active: active (running) since Sat 2016-08-27 15:20:00 MSK; 2h 40min ago
 Main PID: 1728 (nova-compute)
   CGroup: /system.slice/openstack-nova-compute.service
           └─1728 /usr/bin/python2 /usr/bin/nova-compute
```

- openstack-nova-conductor.service - OpenStack Nova Conductor Server
    Loaded: loaded (/usr/lib/systemd/system/openstack-nova-conductor.service; enabled; vendor
preset: disabled)
    Active: active (running) since Sat 2016-08-27 15:19:54 MSK; 2h 40min ago
 Main PID: 982 (nova-conductor)
    CGroup: /system.slice/openstack-nova-conductor.service
            └─982 /usr/bin/python2 /usr/bin/nova-conductor

- openstack-nova-novncproxy.service - OpenStack Nova NoVNC Proxy Server
    Loaded: loaded (/usr/lib/systemd/system/openstack-nova-novncproxy.service; enabled;
vendor preset: disabled)
    Active: active (running) since Sat 2016-08-27 15:19:08 MSK; 2h 40min ago
 Main PID: 1014 (nova-novncproxy)
    CGroup: /system.slice/openstack-nova-novncproxy.service
            └─1014 /usr/bin/python2 /usr/bin/nova-novncproxy --web /usr/share/novnc/

- openstack-nova-consoleauth.service - OpenStack Nova VNC console auth Server
    Loaded: loaded (/usr/lib/systemd/system/openstack-nova-consoleauth.service; enabled;
vendor preset: disabled)
    Active: active (running) since Sat 2016-08-27 15:19:54 MSK; 2h 40min ago
 Main PID: 989 (nova-consoleaut)
    CGroup: /system.slice/openstack-nova-consoleauth.service
            └─989 /usr/bin/python2 /usr/bin/nova-consoleauth

- openstack-nova-api.service - OpenStack Nova API Server
    Loaded: loaded (/usr/lib/systemd/system/openstack-nova-api.service; enabled; vendor
preset: disabled)
    Active: active (running) since Sat 2016-08-27 15:20:00 MSK; 2h 40min ago
 Main PID: 1010 (nova-api)
    CGroup: /system.slice/openstack-nova-api.service
            ├─1010 /usr/bin/python2 /usr/bin/nova-api
            ├─1879 /usr/bin/python2 /usr/bin/nova-api
            ├─1896 /usr/bin/python2 /usr/bin/nova-api

- openstack-nova-scheduler.service - OpenStack Nova Scheduler Server
    Loaded: loaded (/usr/lib/systemd/system/openstack-nova-scheduler.service; enabled; vendor
preset: disabled)
    Active: active (running) since Sat 2016-08-27 15:20:19 MSK; 2h 39min ago
 Main PID: 1017 (nova-scheduler)
    CGroup: /system.slice/openstack-nova-scheduler.service
            └─1017 /usr/bin/python2 /usr/bin/nova-scheduler

As you can see in this example, all services are running on the same host. In the production environment, all are running on the control nodes except nova-compute and nova-compute, which are running on the compute nodes. You can also use nova host-list for listing the hosts and the Nova-related services that run on them:

```
$ nova host-list
+--------------------+-------------+----------+
| host_name          | service     | zone     |
+--------------------+-------------+----------+
| centos7.test.local | consoleauth | internal |
| centos7.test.local | scheduler   | internal |
| centos7.test.local | conductor   | internal |
| centos7.test.local | compute     | nova     |
+--------------------+-------------+----------+
```

Let's check for the presence of Nova service in the Keystone services catalog:

```
$ source keystonerc_admin
$ openstack service show nova
+-------------+----------------------------------+
| Field       | Value                            |
+-------------+----------------------------------+
| description | Openstack Compute Service        |
| enabled     | True                             |
| id          | fae23070b15b428f9cb8b59e5cb2323f |
| name        | nova                             |
| type        | compute                          |
+-------------+----------------------------------+
```

For troubleshooting, you may also need to know where the glance-api endpoint is:

```
$ openstack endpoint show nova
+--------------+---------------------------------------+
| Field        | Value                                 |
+--------------+---------------------------------------+
| adminurl     | http://10.0.2.15:8774/v2/%(tenant_id)s |
| enabled      | True                                  |
| id           | a1472fcf100140c3a0d1cbf42c35502b      |
| internalurl  | http://10.0.2.15:8774/v2/%(tenant_id)s |
| publicurl    | http://10.0.2.15:8774/v2/%(tenant_id)s |
| region       | RegionOne                             |
| service_id   | fae23070b15b428f9cb8b59e5cb2323f      |
| service_name | nova                                  |
| service_type | compute                               |
+--------------+---------------------------------------+
```

The Nova service is listening for incoming connections at the IP address 10.0.2.15 and port number 8774.

You may also want to check Nova's log files. With the help of the `lsof` command, you can enumerate the log files and services that are using it:

```
# lsof /var/log/nova/*
COMMAND     PID USER   FD   TYPE DEVICE SIZE/OFF      NODE NAME
nova-cond   982 nova    3w   REG   253,0   100016 136665685 /var/log/nova/nova-conductor.log
nova-cons   989 nova    3w   REG   253,0   414239 136665681 /var/log/nova/nova-consoleauth.log
nova-cert   990 nova    3w   REG   253,0   192460 136665677 /var/log/nova/nova-cert.log
nova-api   1010 nova    3w   REG   253,0  6150041 136538093 /var/log/nova/nova-api.log
nova-novn  1014 nova    3w   REG   253,0    28222 136665680 /var/log/nova/nova-novncproxy.log
nova-sche  1017 nova    3w   REG   253,0   696714 136665683 /var/log/nova/nova-scheduler.log
nova-comp  1728 nova    3w   REG   253,0  7423359 136665687 /var/log/nova/nova-compute.log
nova-api   1879 nova    3w   REG   253,0  6150041 136538093 /var/log/nova/nova-api.log
nova-api   1896 nova    3w   REG   253,0  6150041 136538093 /var/log/nova/nova-api.log
```

Review Questions

1. Which service acts as a proxy service between the database and nova-compute services?

   A. nova-conductor

   B. nova-nonvncproxy

   C. nova-api

   D. nova-scheduler

2. How can you add a new flavor with name m5.tiny that has 5GB disk, 2 vCPU, and 500Mb RAM?

   A. nova flavor-create --is-public true m5.tiny auto 500 2 5

   B. nova flavor-create --is-public true m5.tiny auto 5 2 500

   C. nova flavor-create --is-public true m5.tiny auto 500 5 2

   D. nova flavor-create --is-public true m5.tiny auto 5 500 2

3. Which GNU/Linux permissions should be applied to the private SSH key?

   A. 640

   B. 660

   C. 600

   D. 620

4. How can the regular user get Nova quotes for the project?

   A. nova quota-list

   B. nova quota-show

   C. nova show-quota

   D. nova list-quota

5. How can you get summary statistics for all tenants?

   A. nova show-stat

   B. nova usage-list all

   C. nova statistics

   D. nova usage-list

Answers to Review Questions

1. A
2. C
3. C
4. B
5. D

CHAPTER 7

OpenStack Dashboard

This chapter covers 3% of the Certified OpenStack Administrator exam requirements.

Architecture of Horizon

I am assuming that you started using OpenStack Dashboard (Horizon) from the first chapter of this book. And for first-time OpenStack users, it is probably the easiest interface rather than using CLI. However, you need to know that Horizon gives access to only about 70-80% of its overall functions. In certain situations you will be forced to use CLI. Figure 7-1 shows the log-in page for the OpenStack Dashboard. But just what is OpenStack Dashboard?

Figure 7-1. *Log-in screen of OpenStack Dashboard*

OpenStack Dashboard is a Python project aimed at providing a complete dashboard along with an extensible framework for building new dashboards. Horizon aims to support all core OpenStack projects. The minimum required set of running OpenStack services comprises Keystone, Nova, Neutron, and Glance.

© Andrey Markelov 2016
A. Markelov, *Certified OpenStack Administrator Study Guide*, DOI 10.1007/978-1-4842-2125-9_7

If the Keystone endpoint for a service is configured, Horizon detects it and enables support for optional services, such as Cinder, Swift, and Heat. Horizon can also work with services that are out of the scope of Certified OpenStack Administrator exam and this book, such as Ceilometer, Sahara, and Trove.

OpenStack Dashboard runs under a web server, which is commonly Apache or NGINX. For large-scale deployments, it is recommended that you configure a caching layer in front of Horizon, for example, the memcached daemon.

You will need to use a web browser with JavaScript and HTML5 support while working with Horizon. Horizon is primarily tested and supported on the latest versions of Firefox, Chrome, and Internet Explorer.

▓ **Tip** You can enable SSL support for the Dashboard with the `packstack` installation tool if you used it. You need to provide the `CONFIG_HORIZON_SSL=y` option in the answer file for that.

Verify Operation of the Dashboard

When you start to work with Horizon, you should put your server IP or name in the web-browser address bar and connect to port 80 or 443, in case you have SSL-enabled deployment, of your Horizon server. It can be a separate server or one of the control nodes. You may actually be familiar with most of the menu structure. Figure 7-2 shows the structure of the Dashboard menu.

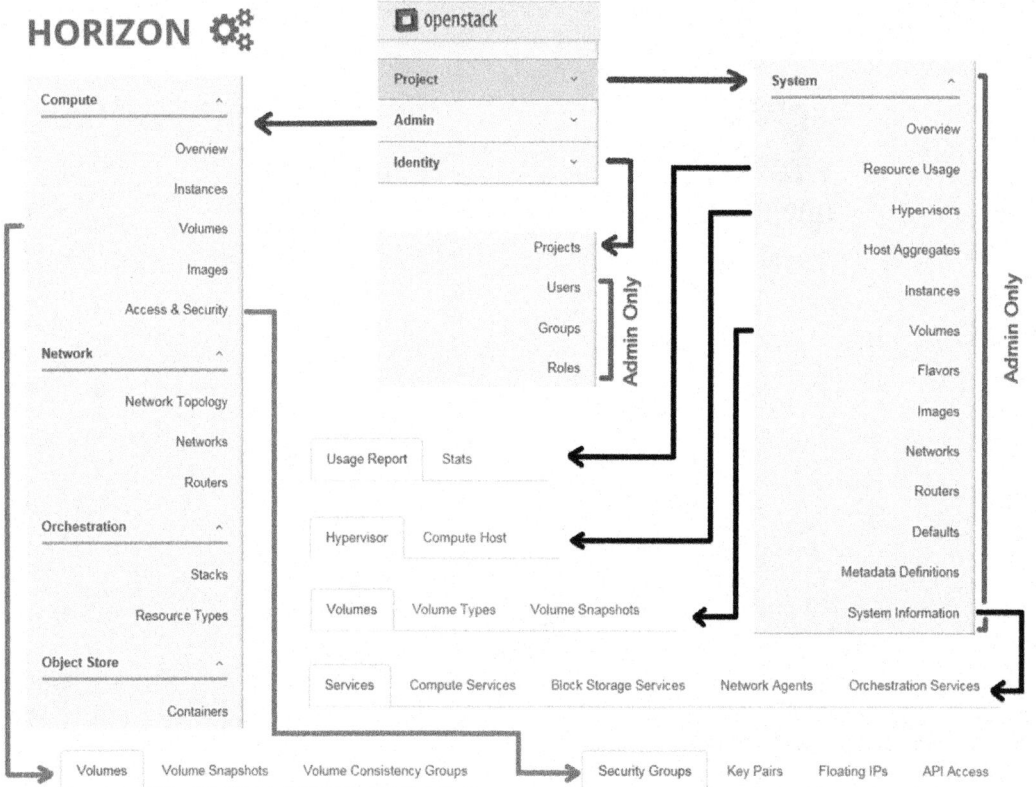

Figure 7-2. Scheme of OpenStack Dashboard menu

The main configuration file of OpenStack Dashboard is `/etc/openstack-dashboard/local_settings`. There are lots of different options in this configuration file, however, the most important is:

```
OPENSTACK_HOST = "10.0.2.15"
```

This is the IP address of the Keystone server. The other interesting option is a session timeout defined in seconds:

```
SESSION_TIMEOUT=3600
```

■ **Tip** Some vendors may supply their own themes with dashboard installation. If you have a standard look of your Horizon installation, you can delete additional packages with branded themes. For Ubuntu, use `apt-get remove --auto-remove openstack-dashboard-ubuntu-theme`. For Red Hat OpenStack Platform, use `rpm -e openstack-dashboard-theme --nodeps`.

Review Question

1. What is the main configuration file of the OpenStack Dashboard?

   A. /var/www/html/openstack-dashboard/local_settings

   B. /etc/openstack-dashboard/local_settings

   C. /etc/horizon/horizon.conf

   D. /etc/horizon/local_settings

Answer to Review Question

1. B

CHAPTER 8

■ ■ ■

OpenStack Object Storage

This chapter covers 10% of the Certified OpenStack Administrator exam requirements.

Overview of Swift Object Storage

OpenStack Swift is a highly available, distributed, eventually consistent object Software Defined Storage (SDS) system. In contrast to file storage, object storage works with an object that contains data and metadata itself. Generally, object storage provides access through an API. Objects are available via URLs and HTTP/HTTPS protocols. Object storage can distribute requests across a number of storage hosts. All objects are accessible in one single namespace, and object storage systems are usually highly scalable.

For passing the Certified OpenStack Administrator exam, you need to know the basic operations with objects. Logically, Swift consists of three levels: accounts, containers, and objects.

Account in Swift corresponds to the Project/Tenant in other OpenStack services. Swift users are primarily people who have a username and password. Swift users correspond to accounts in other OpenStack services. Objects are stored in containers that belong to the accounts. You can imagine an account as a file system, with the container as a directory and the object as a file. Figure 8-1 illustrates this.

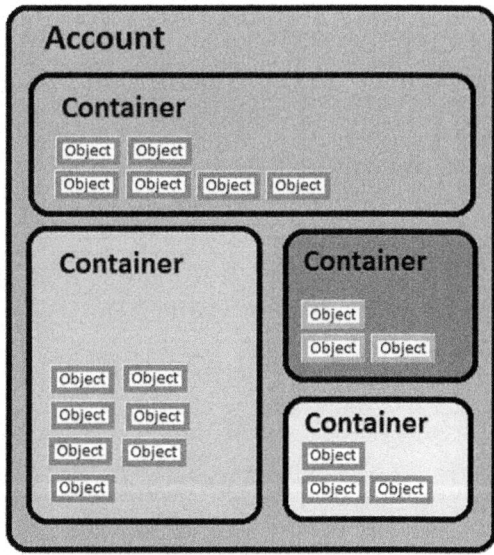

Figure 8-1. *Logical objects in Swift*

© Andrey Markelov 2016
A. Markelov, *Certified OpenStack Administrator Study Guide*, DOI 10.1007/978-1-4842-2125-9_8

You can identify each object by its path:

```
/account_name/container_name/object_name
```

By default, the data stored in Swift will be replicated three times. The main services of Swift are object, account, and container services.

You can start working with containers from the command line with the `swift stat` command. This command will show the summary for the containers and objects:

```
$ swift stat
         Account: AUTH_ae8d3e3f5cff4a959f1ae1cfe9e80d6d
      Containers: 0
         Objects: 0
           Bytes: 0
X-Put-Timestamp: 1472659483.68240
    X-Timestamp: 1472659483.68240
     X-Trans-Id: tx2c1ec5c92e084c19b9843-0057c7001b
   Content-Type: text/plain; charset=utf-8
```

As you see, there are no objects or containers yet. Let's try to upload a file to an object store. As a part of the upload command, you will need to define a container. A container will be created automatically if you point to a nonexisting container:

```
$ swift upload apress_cont1 /etc/hosts
etc/hosts
$ swift stat | grep Containers
                    Containers: 1
Containers in policy "policy-0": 1
```

With the `swift list` command, you can list the containers and the objects within the containers:

```
$ swift list
apress_cont1
$ swift list apress_cont1
etc/hosts
```

To check the status of the object, you can also use the `swift stat` command:

```
$ swift stat apress_cont1 etc/hosts
        Account: AUTH_ae8d3e3f5cff4a959f1ae1cfe9e80d6d
      Container: apress_cont1
         Object: etc/hosts
   Content Type: application/octet-stream
 Content Length: 158
  Last Modified: Wed, 31 Aug 2016 16:05:36 GMT
           ETag: 54fb6627dbaa37721048e4549db3224d
     Meta Mtime: 1370615492.000000
  Accept-Ranges: bytes
    X-Timestamp: 1472659535.94284
     X-Trans-Id: txdc3f00cd63d74a54895c7-0057cb10bf
```

For downloading the content of a container, use the swift download command as shown:

```
$ swift download apress_cont1
etc/hosts [auth 0.120s, headers 0.236s, total 0.236s, 0.001 MB/s]
$ cat etc/hosts
127.0.0.1    localhost localhost.localdomain localhost4 localhost4.localdomain4
::1          localhost localhost.localdomain localhost6 localhost6.localdomain6
```

You may also specify a particular object in the container:

```
$ swift download apress_cont1 etc/hosts
etc/hosts [auth 0.328s, headers 0.535s, total 0.537s, 3.212 MB/s]
```

Figure 8-2 shows the Horizon web interface.

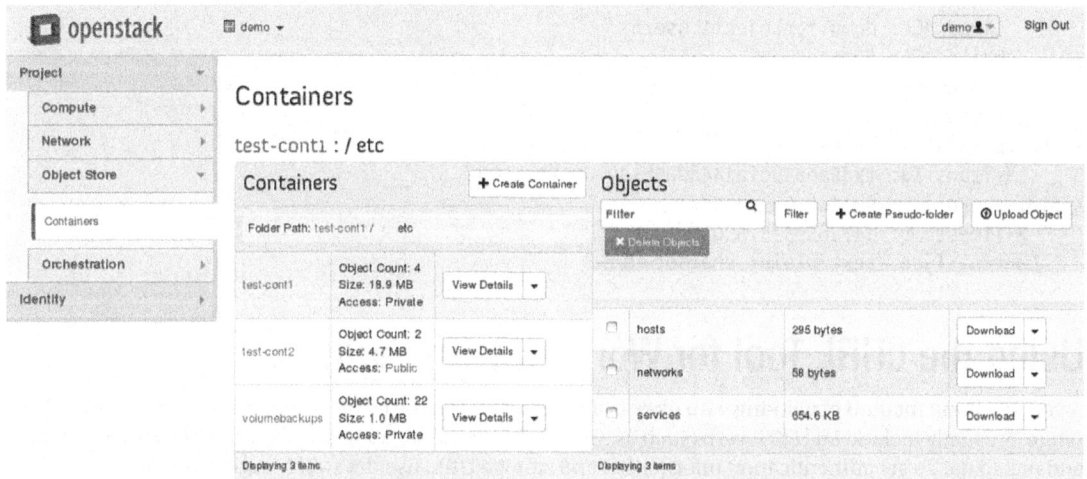

Figure 8-2. *Swift user interface in the Horizon web client*

Managing Permissions on a Container in Object Storage

Users can set up access control lists (ACLs) at the container level and define the read and write access. To successfully write to a container, in addition to write access, a user must also have read access on the container.

Here is an example of how to set up a read ACL for users from a demo project, here specifically for user8 from project1:

```
$ swift post apress_cont1 -r "demo:demo, project1:user8"
$ swift stat apress_cont1
        Account: AUTH_ae8d3e3f5cff4a959f1ae1cfe9e80d6d
      Container: apress_cont1
        Objects: 1
          Bytes: 158
       Read ACL: demo:*,project1:user8
      Write ACL:
```

```
          Sync To:
         Sync Key:
    Accept-Ranges: bytes
       X-Trans-Id: tx69e4a7910fe94075851c1-0057cb0dd4
X-Storage-Policy: Policy-0
      X-Timestamp: 1472659535.59030
     Content-Type: text/plain; charset=utf-8
```

Working with write ACL is similar:

```
$ swift post apress_cont1 -w "demo:demo"
$ swift stat apress_cont1
          Account: AUTH_ae8d3e3f5cff4a959f1ae1cfe9e80d6d
        Container: apress_cont1
          Objects: 1
            Bytes: 158
         Read ACL: demo:*,project1:user8
        Write ACL: demo:demo
          Sync To:
         Sync Key:
    Accept-Ranges: bytes
       X-Trans-Id: txd5ade59cfa1448da9b1a9-0057cb1009
X-Storage-Policy: Policy-0
      X-Timestamp: 1472659535.59030
     Content-Type: text/plain; charset=utf-8
```

Using the cURL Tool for Working with Swift

A very common method of working with object storage is by using the cURL command-line tool. cURL requests usually include an HTTP verb (such as, GET, PUT), authentication information, storage URL, data, and metadata. To get authentication information and storage URL, use the swift auth command:

```
$ swift auth
export OS_STORAGE_URL=http://10.0.2.15:8080/v1/AUTH_ae8d3e3f5cff4a959f1ae1cfe9e80d6d
export OS_AUTH_TOKEN=51c5c5fb2ad44e2390cffbff736e4224
```

You can create a new container with the PUT verb:

```
$ curl -X PUT -H 'X-Auth-Token: 51c5c5fb2ad44e2390cffbff736e4224'  http://10.0.2.15:8080/v1/
AUTH_ae8d3e3f5cff4a959f1ae1cfe9e80d6d/apress_cont2
```

And here is an example that is similar to using the swift list command:

```
$ curl -X GET -H 'X-Auth-Token: 51c5c5fb2ad44e2390cffbff736e4224'  http://10.0.2.15:8080/v1/
AUTH_ae8d3e3f5cff4a959f1ae1cfe9e80d6d/
apress_cont1
apress_cont2
```

Next, you can put the file /etc/networks into the apress_cont2 container:

```
$ curl -X PUT -H 'X-Auth-Token: 51c5c5fb2ad44e2390cffbff736e4224' http://10.0.2.15:8080/v1/
AUTH_ae8d3e3f5cff4a959f1ae1cfe9e80d6d/apress_cont2/ -T /etc/networks
```

For checking the content of the apress_cont2 container, use the command:

```
$ curl -X GET -H 'X-Auth-Token: 51c5c5fb2ad44e2390cffbff736e4224' http://10.0.2.15:8080/v1/
AUTH_ae8d3e3f5cff4a959f1ae1cfe9e80d6d/apress_cont2/
networks
```

And at the end, you can get the contents of the object:

```
$ curl -X GET -H 'X-Auth-Token: 51c5c5fb2ad44e2390cffbff736e4224' http://10.0.2.15:8080/v1/
AUTH_ae8d3e3f5cff4a959f1ae1cfe9e80d6d/apress_cont2/networks
default 0.0.0.0
loopback 127.0.0.0
link-local 169.254.0.0
```

Managing Expiring Objects

Swift Object storage has the ability to schedule deletion of an object. To do that you need to add the X-Delete-At or X-Delete-After header during an object PUT or POST command. The date and time of deletion should be in Unix Epoch timestamp format. You can use the date command to learn the current date and time in Unix Epoch timestamp format or for conversion:

```
$ date +%s
1472994354
$ date -d @1472994354
Sun Sep  4 15:05:54 CEST 2016
```

Also you can use the web site www.epochconverter.com/ for conversion. Here is an example of how to automatically delete object etc/sysctl.conf in the container apress_cont1 on Wed, 30 Nov 2016 00:00:00 GMT (1473510189):

```
$ swift auth
export OS_STORAGE_URL=http://10.0.2.15:8080/v1/AUTH_ae8d3e3f5cff4a959f1ae1cfe9e80d6d
export OS_AUTH_TOKEN=cca554f2330c4e859c8c4903729b7166
$ curl -X POST -H 'X-Auth-Token: dade6fa4180343c895406765d59b1d42' -H 'X-Delete-On:
1473510189' http://10.0.2.15:8080/v1/AUTH_ae8d3e3f5cff4a959f1ae1cfe9e80d6d/apress_cont1/
etc/sysctl.conf
<html><h1>Accepted</h1><p>The request is accepted for processing.</p></html>
```

Monitoring Swift Cluster

For Swift cluster monitoring of the account, container, and object servers, special recon server middleware and the swift-recon tool are used. If you installed the OpenStack lab environment with the packstack tool, you need to do additional configuration of the middleware server. You should change the existing pipeline option in the [pipeline:main] section and add the new [filter:recon] section in three configuration files.

Here is an example of changes made in /etc/swift/object-server.conf:

```
[pipeline:main]
pipeline = recon object-server

[filter:recon]
use = egg:swift#recon
recon_cache_path = /var/cache/swift
```

Here is an example of changes made in /etc/swift/container-server.conf:

```
[pipeline:main]
pipeline = recon container-server

[filter:recon]
use = egg:swift#recon
recon_cache_path = /var/cache/swift
```

This is an example of changes made in /etc/swift/account-server.conf:

```
[pipeline:main]
pipeline = recon account-server

[filter:recon]
use = egg:swift#recon
recon_cache_path = /var/cache/swift
```

After that you need to check whether the cache directory exists and has the right permissions:

```
# ls -ld /var/cache/swift/
drwx------ 2 swift swift 67 Sep  4 14:32 /var/cache/swift/
```

For tracking asynchronous pending on your object servers, you need to add a job in cron to run the swift-recon-cron script:

```
# crontab -e
*/5 * * * * swift /usr/bin/swift-recon-cron /etc/swift/object-server.conf
```

Now you can try to obtain the cluster load average stats:

```
# swift-recon -l
===========================================================================
--> Starting reconnaissance on 1 hosts
===========================================================================
[2016-09-04 11:46:03] Checking load averages
[5m_load_avg] low: 1, high: 1, avg: 1.5, total: 1, Failed: 0.0%, no_result: 0, reported: 1
[15m_load_avg] low: 1, high: 1, avg: 1.1, total: 1, Failed: 0.0%, no_result: 0, reported: 1
[1m_load_avg] low: 1, high: 1, avg: 1.3, total: 1, Failed: 0.0%, no_result: 0, reported: 1
===========================================================================
```

To obtain disk usage stats, use the -d option:

```
# swift-recon -d
===============================================================================
--> Starting reconnaissance on 1 hosts
===============================================================================
[2016-09-04 11:46:09] Checking disk usage now
Distribution Graph:
  10%     1 ********************************************************************
Disk usage: space used: 201555968 of 1945976832
Disk usage: space free: 1744420864 of 1945976832
Disk usage: lowest: 10.36%, highest: 10.36%, avg: 10.357572849%
===============================================================================
```

And the last example will allow you to obtain replication stats:

```
# swift-recon -r
===============================================================================
--> Starting reconnaissance on 1 hosts
===============================================================================
[2016-09-04 11:45:57] Checking on replication
[replication_failure] low:2, high:2, avg:2.0, total: 2, Failed: 0.0%, no_result: 0,
reported: 1
[replication_success] low:0, high:0, avg:0.0, total: 0, Failed: 0.0%, no_result: 0,
reported: 1
[replication_time] low: 0, high: 0, avg: 0.0, total: 0, Failed: 0.0%, no_result: 0,
reported: 1
[replication_attempted] low: 1514, high: 1514, avg: 1514.0, total: 1514, Failed: 0.0%,
no_result: 0, reported: 1
Oldest completion was 2016-09-04 11:45:51 (5 seconds ago) by 10.0.2.15:6000.
Most recent completion was 2016-09-04 11:45:51 (5 seconds ago) by 10.0.2.15:6000.
===============================================================================
```

For a complete options list, see the swift-recon(1) main page.

Review Questions

1. How can you upload all of the files from the ~user directory to the container tempcontainer?

    A.   swift upload tempcontainer ~user/all

    B.   swift upload tempcontainer ~user/*

    C.   swift upload ~user/* tempcontainer

    D.   swift upload ~user/* tempcontainer all

2. How can you check the status of the object test in container cont?

    A.   swift stat test cont

    B.   swift cont test stat

    C.   swift stat cont test

    D.   swift test cont stat

3.   How can you get disk usage stats in Swift?

    A.   recon -l

    B.   swift-recon -d

    C.   swift-recon -l

    D.   recon -d

4.   How can you get a list of all objects in `test` container?

    A.   swift list test

    B.   swift test list

    C.   swift list

    D.   swift list container test

5.   How can you get the object with `curl` command?

    A.   curl -X GET -H 'X-Auth-Token: token' http://server/AUTH_User/container/object

    B.   curl -X GET -H 'X-Auth-Token: token' http://server/v1/AUTH_User/ -c container -o object

    C.   curl -X GET -H 'X-Auth-Token: token' http://server/v1/AUTH_User/container/object

    D.   curl -X GET -H 'X-Auth-Token: token' `http://server/AUTH_User/ container object`

Answers to Review Questions

1.   B

2.   C

3.   B

4.   A

5.   C

CHAPTER 9

■ ■ ■

Block Storage

This chapter covers 10% of the Certified OpenStack Administrator exam requirements.

Architecture and Components of Cinder

Instances use an ephemeral volume by default. This kind of volume does not save the changes made on it and reverts to its original state when the current user relinquishes control. One of the methods for storing data permanently in OpenStack cloud is the use of a block storage service named Cinder. This service is similar to the Amazon EBS service by its functions.

Figure 9-1 shows the main components of Cinder.

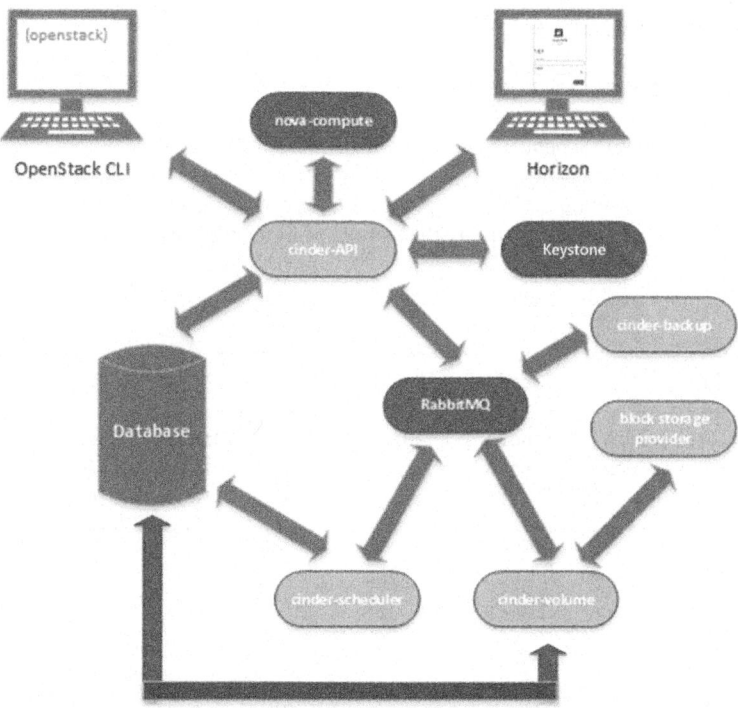

Figure 9-1. *Architecture of Cinder*

© Andrey Markelov 2016
A. Markelov, *Certified OpenStack Administrator Study Guide*, DOI 10.1007/978-1-4842-2125-9_9

OpenStack block storage service consists of four services implemented as GNU/Linux daemons:

- **cinder-api**: API service provides an HTTP endpoint for API requests. At the time of this writing, two versions of API are supported and required for the cloud. So Cinder provides six endpoints. The cinder-api verifies the identity requirements for an incoming request and after that routes them to the cinder-volume for action through the message broker.

- **cinder-scheduler**: Scheduler service reads requests from the message queue and selects the optimal storage provider node to create or manage the volume.

- **cinder-volume**: The service works with a storage back end through the drivers. The cinder-volume gets requests from the scheduler and responds to read and write requests sent to the block storage service to maintain state. You can use several back ends at the same time. For each back end you need one or more dedicated cinder-volume service.

- **cinder-backup**: The backup service works with the backup back end through the driver architecture.

As you can see in Figure 9-1, Cinder uses block storage providers for particular storage. You can find a list of supported drivers at `https://wiki.openstack.org/wiki/CinderSupportMatrix`. There are a lot of storage providers for Cinder, such as LVM/iSCSI, Ceph, Swift, EMC VNX, ScaleIO, IBM Storwize, and others.

Let's look at these services in the OpenStack node:

```
# systemctl | grep cinder
  openstack-cinder-api.service
loaded active running   OpenStack Cinder API Server
  openstack-cinder-backup.service
loaded active running   OpenStack Cinder Backup Server
  openstack-cinder-scheduler.service
loaded active running   OpenStack Cinder Scheduler Server
  openstack-cinder-volume.service
```

You can use the `cinder service-list` command to query the status of Cinder services:

```
$ source keystonerc_admin
$ cinder service-list
```

Binary	Host	Zone	Status	State	Updated_at
cinder-backup	centos7.test.local	nova	enabled	up	2016-04-24T16:34:08
cinder-scheduler	centos7.test.local	nova	enabled	up	2016-04-24T16:34:06
cinder-volume	centos7.test.local@lvm	nova	enabled	up	2016-04-24T16:34:07

After testing the environment, you can see that all services are running on one host. In the production environment, it is more common to have cinder-volume service running on separate storage nodes. By default in test environments Cinder uses the Linux Logical Volume Manager (LVM) back end and the iSCSI target provided by Targetcli (http://linux-iscsi.org/wiki/Targetcli):

```
# systemctl | grep lvmetad.service
  lvm2-lvmetad.service
loaded active running   LVM2 metadata daemon
# systemctl | grep target.service
  target.service
loaded active exited    Restore LIO kernel target configuration
```

Now let's look through the Keystone main configuration file /etc/cinder/cinder.conf. Table 9-1 shows the main configuration options available from the config file.

Table 9-1. *Main Configuration Options from /etc/cinder/cinder.conf*

Example of Config Options	Description
[DEFAULT] glance_host = 10.0.2.15	Default Glance host name or IP.
[DEFAULT] backup_driver = cinder.backup.drivers.swift	Driver to use for backups.
[DEFAULT] auth_strategy = keystone [keystone_authtoken] auth_uri = http:// 10.0.2.15:5000 auth_url = http:// 10.0.2.15:35357 auth_type = password project_domain_name = default user_domain_name = default project_name = service username = cinder password = openstack	Authentication parameters: auth_uri, which is the public Identity API endpoint, and auth_url, which is the admin Identity API endpoint. Other parameters set a default project name, domain name, project name for services, and account information for the Cinder user.
[DEFAULT] backup_swift_url = http://10.0.2.15:8080/v1/AUTH_ backup_swift_container = volumes_backup backup_swift_object_size = 52428800 backup_swift_retry_attempts = 3 backup_swift_retry_backoff = 2	The URL of the Swift endpoint and other Swift parameters such as: name of Swift container to use, maximum object size, the number of retries to make for Swift operations, and the back-off time in seconds between Swift retries.
[DEFAULT] enabled_backends = lvm	A list of back-end names to use.
[database] connection = mysql:// cinder:password@10.0.2.15/cinder	The SQLAlchemy connection string is used to connect to the database.

(*continued*)

Table 9-1. (*continued*)

Example of Config Options	Description
[DEFAULT} rpc_backend = rabbit [oslo_messaging_rabbit] rabbit_host = localhost rabbit_port = 5672 rabbit_userid = guest rabbit_password = guest	The RabbitMQ broker address, port, user name, and password.
[lvm] iscsi_helper=lioadm	iSCSI target user-land tool to use. The old one tgtadm is default. Use lioadm for modern LIO iSCSI support.
[lvm] volume_group=cinder-volumes iscsi_ip_address=10.0.2.15 volume_driver=cinder.volume.drivers.lvm. LVMVolumeDriver volumes_dir=/var/lib/cinder/volumes iscsi_protocol=iscsi volume_backend_name=lvm	LVM back-end options: name of LVM volume group, iSCSI target IP address, volume driver, volume configuration file storage directory, and the back-end name for a given driver implementation.

Manage Volume and Mount It to a Nova Instance

Let's start our example from volume creation. There are two CLI commands that can be used: openstack or cinder. Also you can use the Horizon web client. Here is an example using the cinder command:

```
$ source keystonerc_demo
$ cinder create --display-name apresstest1 1
+-------------------------------------+--------------------------------------+
|               Property              |                Value                 |
+-------------------------------------+--------------------------------------+
|             attachments             |                  []                  |
|          availability_zone          |                 nova                 |
|               bootable              |                false                 |
|          consistencygroup_id        |                 None                 |
|              created_at             |       2016-04-21T05:22:11.000000     |
|             description             |                 None                 |
|              encrypted              |                False                 |
|                  id                 | 08c41630-4da9-42c5-99bb-f9aa389ce2dc |
|               metadata              |                  {}                  |
|              multiattach            |                False                 |
|                 name                |             apresstest1              |
|      os-vol-tenant-attr:tenant_id   |   1542af2b20d349d29710d8c4019ba202   |
|    os-volume-replication:driver_data|                 None                 |
| os-volume-replication:extended_status|                None                 |
|          replication_status         |               disabled               |
|                 size                |                  1                   |
```

```
|            snapshot_id         |                    None                  |
|            source_volid        |                    None                  |
|              status            |                  creating                |
|             user_id            |    ec92590f7ff84887ab9c0329f5ce850c      |
|           volume_type          |                    None                  |
+-------------------------------+------------------------------------------+
```

The next example shows use of the universal openstack command:

```
$ openstack volume create --size 1 apresstest2
+---------------------+--------------------------------------+
| Field               | Value                                |
+---------------------+--------------------------------------+
| attachments         | []                                   |
| availability_zone   | nova                                 |
| bootable            | false                                |
| created_at          | 2016-04-21T05:23:43.504895           |
| display_description  | None                                 |
| display_name        | apresstest2                          |
| encrypted           | False                                |
| id                  | e42d8fe1-7475-46b6-a769-20a2ce462d3c |
| multiattach         | false                                |
| properties          |                                      |
| size                | 1                                    |
| snapshot_id         | None                                 |
| source_volid        | None                                 |
| status              | creating                             |
| type                | None                                 |
+---------------------+--------------------------------------+
```

Now you can check to make sure that both volumes were created and are now available:

```
$ openstack volume list
+--------------------------------------+--------------+-----------+------+-------------+
| ID                                   | Display Name | Status    | Size | Attached to |
+--------------------------------------+--------------+-----------+------+-------------+
| e42d8fe1-7475-46b6-a769-20a2ce462d3c | apresstest2  | available |    1 |             |
| 08c41630-4da9-42c5-99bb-f9aa389ce2dc | apresstest1  | available |    1 |             |
+--------------------------------------+--------------+-----------+------+-------------+
$ cinder list
+--------------------+---------+-----------+----+--------+--------+-----------+-----------+
| ID                 |Status   |Name       |Size|Volume  |Bootable|Multiattach|Attached to|
|                    |         |           |    |Type    |        |           |           |
+--------------------+---------+-----------+----+--------+--------+-----------+-----------+
| 08c41630-4da9-42c5-|available|apresstest1| 1  |-       |false   |False      |           |
| 99bb-f9aa389ce2dc  |         |           |    |        |        |           |           |
| e42d8fe1-7475-46b6-|available|apresstest2| 1  |-       |false   |False      |           |
| a769-20a2ce462d3c  |         |           |    |        |        |           |           |
+--------------------+---------+-----------+----+--------+--------+-----------+-----------+
```

As mentioned earlier, Cinder uses Linux Logical Volume Manager in test environments by default. You can easily check this fact by using the `lvs` command. As you see below, there are two LVM volumes in the cinder-volumes group with the names that contain the OpenStack's volumes' IDs:

```
# lvs
  LV                                      VG             Attr       LSize
  home                                    centos         -wi-ao---- 55.64g
  root                                    centos         -wi-ao---- 50.00g
  swap                                    centos         -wi-ao----  3.88g
  volume-08c41630-4da9-42c5-99bb-f9aa389ce2dc cinder-volumes -wi-a-----  1.00g
  volume-e42d8fe1-7475-46b6-a769-20a2ce462d3c cinder-volumes -wi-a-----  1.00g
```

■ **Note**   The command `lvs` is used to report information about logical volumes. Using the Logical Volume Manager (LVM) is a common way to create the abstraction level of block devices for modern GNU/Linux distributions. LVM is able to create, delete, resize, mirror, or snapshot logical volumes. Logical volumes are created from volume groups and volume groups are usually created from physical devices. If you are not familiar with LVM you can start from a manual page for LVM (`man lvm` in linux prompt).

You can also manage existing and create new volumes from within the Horizon web interface. Go to Compute ➤ Volumes if you are working as a user or System ➤ Volumes if you want to see all of the volumes as an administrator. In each case, different subsets of options are available. Examples of the different web interface screenshots are shown in Figures 9-2 and 9-3.

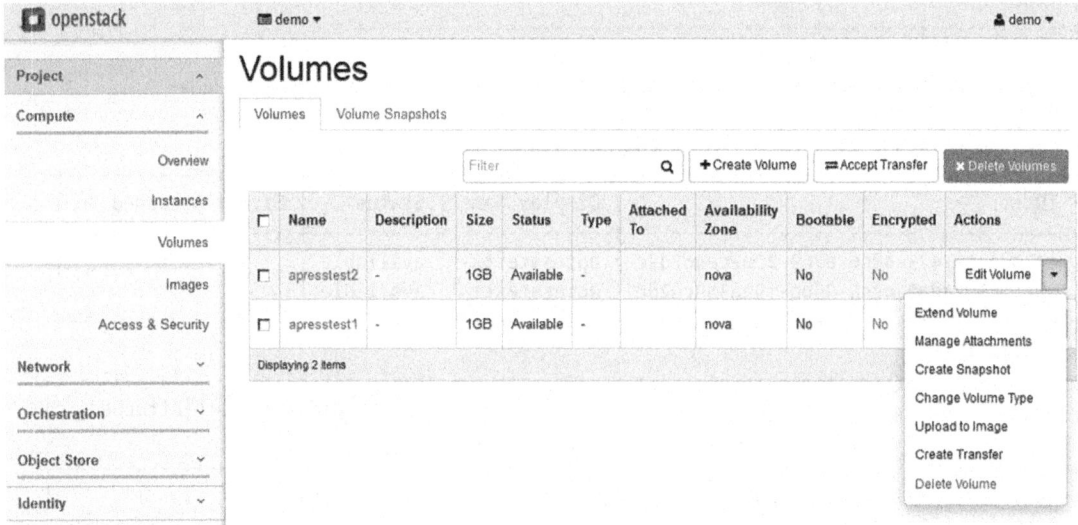

Figure 9-2. *Volumes in regular users Horizon web interface view*

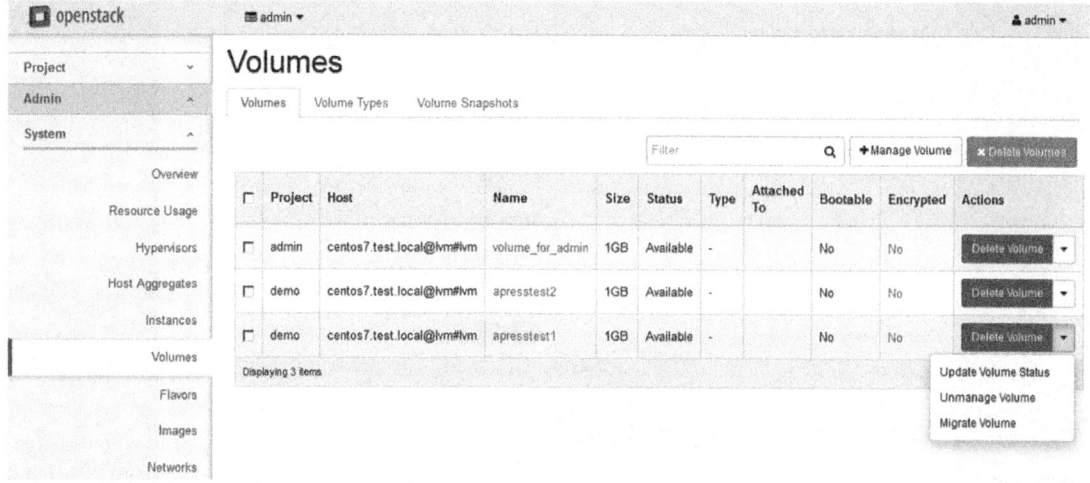

Figure 9-3. *Volumes for admin users in the Horizon web interface view*

Deleting a volume is as easy as creating one. To delete a volume, for example, using the `cinder` CLI command, use the following code:

```
$ cinder delete apresstest2
Request to delete volume apresstest2 has been accepted.
```

In Figure 9-4 you can see the volume creation dialog used in the Horizon user interface. In the drop-down menu you can see additional options for creating the image. You can create a volume from another volume or from the image instead by creating a volume from scratch. For these actions the `--image` and `--source` options of the `openstack` CLI command are used. Here is an example of creating a volume from Glance's image:

```
$ openstack volume create --size 1 --image cirros-0.3.4-x86_64 apresstest3
+---------------------+--------------------------------------+
| Field               | Value                                |
+---------------------+--------------------------------------+
| attachments         | []                                   |
| availability_zone   | nova                                 |
| bootable            | false                                |
| created_at          | 2016-04-24T12:22:47.445562           |
| display_description | None                                 |
| display_name        | apresstest3                          |
| encrypted           | False                                |
| id                  | e5ac6599-d1a9-4d27-a338-6989e2abc0fc |
| image_id            | e5791edb-30dd-475a-9bc4-5938341db655 |
| multiattach         | false                                |
| properties          |                                      |
| size                | 1                                    |
| snapshot_id         | None                                 |
| source_volid        | None                                 |
| status              | creating                             |
| type                | None                                 |
+---------------------+--------------------------------------+
```

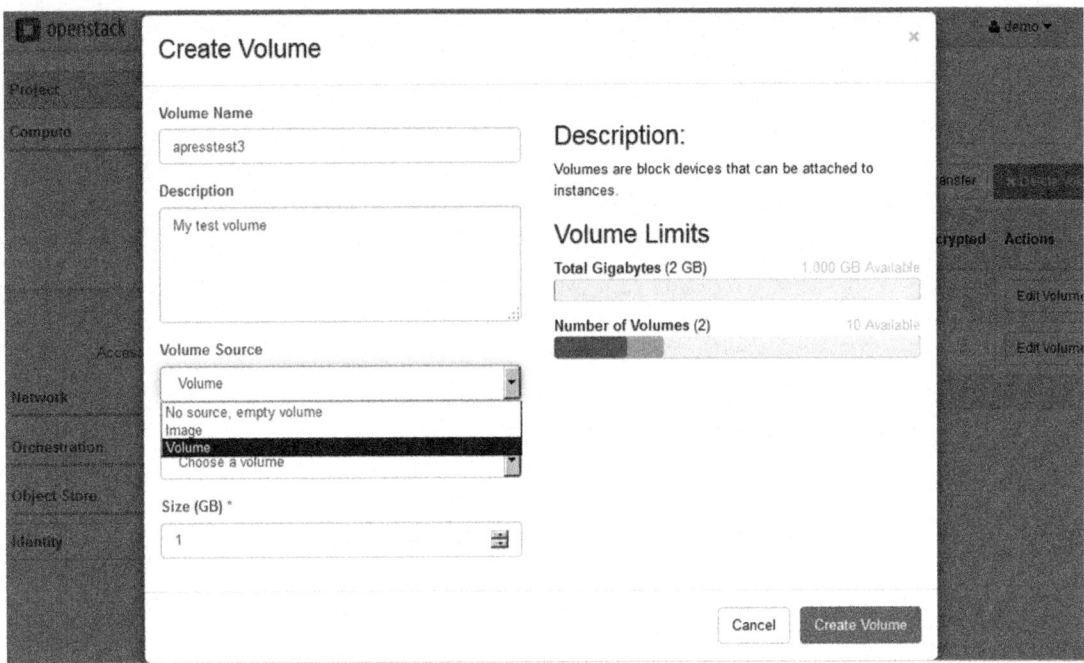

Figure 9-4. *Creation of a volume from the Horizon web interface view*

You can use the openstack volume show command with the image name or ID if you need to look at the particular volume properties.

Volumes are useless by themselves. So let's try to start a new instance of VM and to access a volume from within this VM:

```
$ nova boot --flavor m1.tiny --image cirros-0.3.4-x86_64 apresstestinstance1
...
$ nova list
+--------------+---------------------+--------+------------+-------------+-----------------+
| ID           | Name                | Status | Task State | Power State | Networks        |
+--------------+---------------------+--------+------------+-------------+-----------------+
| a2deaa34-... | apresstestinstance1 | ACTIVE | -          | Running     | private=10.0.0.3|
+--------------+---------------------+--------+------------+-------------+-----------------+
```

Now you can attach the volume apresstest1 to the instance apresstestinstance1:

```
$ openstack server add volume apresstestinstance1 apresstest1
$ openstack volume list
+--------------+--------------+--------+------+-----------------------------------------+
| ID           | Display Name | Status | Size | Attached to                             |
+--------------+--------------+--------+------+-----------------------------------------+
| 78680241-... | apresstest1  | in-use |    1 | Attached to apresstestinstance1 on /dev/vdb |
+--------------+--------------+--------+------+-----------------------------------------+
```

As an alternative, you can use the nova volume-attach command in conjunction with the volume ID:

```
nova volume-attach apresstestinstance1 78680241-7928-41d5-b9bc-f2f82dad7bba /dev/vdb
+----------+--------------------------------------+
| Property | Value                                |
+----------+--------------------------------------+
| device   | /dev/vdb                             |
| id       | 78680241-7928-41d5-b9bc-f2f82dad7bba |
| serverId | a2deaa34-2ca0-406f-9ef7-cf2a92cb6751 |
| volumeId | 78680241-7928-41d5-b9bc-f2f82dad7bba |
+----------+--------------------------------------+
```

For detaching a volume you can use one of these commands:

```
$ openstack server remove volume apresstestinstance1 apresstest1
$ nova volume-detach apresstestinstance1 78680241-7928-41d5-b9bc-f2f82dad7bba
```

Create Volume Group for Block Storage

One of the Certified OpenStack Administrator exam objectives is to create the LVM volume group for block storage. It is very easy but you need to be aware of the hard disks partitions and the LVM hierarchy.

Let's assume that you do not have free space in your current storage. First, you will need to add a new block device (virtual hard drive in this case) to the controller VM. Usually you will need to reboot the VM after that.

Then you need to find a new device name. A device name refers to the entire disk. Device names can be /dev/sda, /dev/sdb, and so on when you are using the virtualization-aware disk driver. For example, if you use the native KVM-based virtualization in GNU/Linux, this code would show the devise name:

```
# fdisk -l | grep [vs]d
Disk /dev/sda: 118.2 GB, 118182313984 bytes, 230824832 sectors
/dev/sda1    *         2048      1026047       512000    83  Linux
/dev/sda2          1026048    230823935    114898944    8e  Linux LVM
Disk /dev/sdb: 103.8 GB, 103834320896 bytes, 202801408 sectors
```

You can see the new disk /dev/sdb has no partitions on it. Let's create one partition for the whole disk:

```
# fdisk /dev/sdb
Welcome to fdisk (util-linux 2.23.2).

Changes will remain in memory only, until you decide to write them.
Be careful before using the write command.

Device does not contain a recognized partition table
Building a new DOS disklabel with disk identifier 0xc2ccdc51.

Command (m for help): n
Partition type:
   p   primary (0 primary, 0 extended, 4 free)
   e   extended
```

```
Select (default p): p
Partition number (1-4, default 1):
First sector (2048-202801407, default 2048):
Using default value 2048
Last sector, +sectors or +size{K,M,G} (2048-202801407, default 202801407):
Using default value 202801407
Partition 1 of type Linux and of size 96.7 GiB is set
```

Before saving changes to the partition table, you also need to change the partition type number from 83 (Linux) to 8e (Linux LVM):

```
Command (m for help): t
Selected partition 1
Hex code (type L to list all codes): 8e
Changed type of partition 'Linux' to 'Linux LVM'

Command (m for help): w
The partition table has been altered!

Calling ioctl() to re-read partition table.
Syncing disks.
# partprobe
```

Now you can create the new volume group for the LVM back end:

```
# vgcreate cinder-volumes-2 /dev/sdb1
  Physical volume "/dev/sdb1" successfully created
  Volume group "cinder-volumes-2" successfully created
```

Manage Quotas

It is possible to add quotas for Cinder volumes. Default quotas for new projects are in the Cinder configuration file. Some of them are shown in Table 9-2.

Table 9-2. *Quota Configuration Options from /etc/cinder/cinder.conf*

Example of Config Options	Description
quota_volumes = 10	Number of volumes allowed per project.
quota_snapshots = 10	Number of volume snapshots allowed per project.
quota_gigabytes = 1000	Total amount of storage, in gigabytes, allowed for volumes and snapshots per project.
quota_backups = 10	Number of volume backups allowed per project.
quota_backup_gigabytes = 1000	Total amount of storage, in gigabytes, allowed for backups per project.

You can show or modify Cinder quotes by using the `cinder` CLI command or through the Horizon web interface. In Horizon, all quotas for projects that exist can be found by going to Identity ➤ Projects. Then you would need to choose "Modify Quotas" from the drop-down menu to the right of the project name. You need to know the project ID if you work from the command line:

```
$ openstack project list
+----------------------------------+---------+
| ID                               | Name    |
+----------------------------------+---------+
| 007cad0f17df4b6f9ece6e5f630cec83 | admin   |
| 7cd5f81dc5d849bbb76295e317128373 | service |
| 90829e88e94a4a39b9860ac61183e98d | demo    |
+----------------------------------+---------+
```

Then you can show the quotas for project demo:

```
$ cinder quota-show 90829e88e94a4a39b9860ac61183e98d
+-----------------------+-------+
|       Property        | Value |
+-----------------------+-------+
|   backup_gigabytes    | 1000  |
|       backups         |  10   |
|      gigabytes        | 1000  |
|    gigabytes_LUKS     |  -1   |
| per_volume_gigabytes  |  -1   |
|      snapshots        |  10   |
|    snapshots_LUKS     |  -1   |
|       volumes         |  10   |
|     volumes_LUKS      |  -1   |
+-----------------------+-------+
```

The results show the current usage of the demo project's quota:

```
$ cinder quota-usage 90829e88e94a4a39b9860ac61183e98d
+-----------------------+--------+----------+-------+
|         Type          | In_use | Reserved | Limit |
+-----------------------+--------+----------+-------+
|   backup_gigabytes    |   0    |    0     | 1000  |
|       backups         |   0    |    0     |  10   |
|      gigabytes        |   0    |    0     | 1000  |
|    gigabytes_LUKS     |   0    |    0     |  -1   |
| per_volume_gigabytes  |   0    |    0     |  -1   |
|      snapshots        |   0    |    0     |  10   |
|    snapshots_LUKS     |   0    |    0     |  -1   |
|       volumes         |   0    |    0     |  10   |
|     volumes_LUKS      |   0    |    0     |  -1   |
+-----------------------+--------+----------+-------+
```

To update Cinder service quotas for an existing project, you need a quota name and the suggested number:

```
$ cinder quota-update --snapshots 17 90829e88e94a4a39b9860ac61183e98d
+-----------------------+-------+
|       Property        | Value |
+-----------------------+-------+
|   backup_gigabytes    | 1000  |
|       backups         |  10   |
|      gigabytes        | 1000  |
|   gigabytes_LUKS      |  -1   |
| per_volume_gigabytes  |  -1   |
|      snapshots        |  17   |
|    snapshots_LUKS     |  -1   |
|       volumes         |  10   |
|     volumes_LUKS      |  -1   |
+-----------------------+-------+
```

For removing all quotas for the project use the quota-delete command:

```
$ cinder quota-delete 90829e88e94a4a39b9860ac61183e98d
```

Back Up and Restore Volumes and Snapshots

The cinder command can create a whole volume backup or incremental backup (starting from the Liberty release). You can restore a volume from a backup if the backup's associated metadata exist in the Cinder database. You can also export metadata if you are concerned about a database crush.

First, you need to know the volume ID. You can use the cinder list command to find this. Next, you can enter the command:

```
$ cinder backup-create 78680241-7928-41d5-b9bc-f2f82dad7bba
+-----------+--------------------------------------+
| Property  |                Value                 |
+-----------+--------------------------------------+
|    id     | 4dc8c496-85f1-438f-9eb7-56fb2aa04503 |
|   name    |                 None                 |
| volume_id | 78680241-7928-41d5-b9bc-f2f82dad7bba |
+-----------+--------------------------------------+
```

It is possible to check the status of existing backups using the command:

```
$ cinder backup-list
+--------------+------------+-----------+------+------+--------------+----------------+
|      ID      | Volume ID  |  Status   | Name | Size | Object Count |   Container    |
+--------------+------------+-----------+------+------+--------------+----------------+
| 4dc8c496-..  | 78680241-..| available |  -   |  1   |      22      | volumes_backup |
+--------------+------------+-----------+------+------+--------------+----------------+
```

All backups go to the Swift Object Storage by default. You can check the volumes_backup container and objects inside this container:

```
$ swift list
volumes_backup
$ swift list volumes_backup
volume_78680241-7928-41d5-b9bc-f2f82dad7bba/20160424152627/az_nova_backup_4dc8c496-..-00001
...
volume_78680241-7928-41d5-b9bc-f2f82dad7bba/20160424152627/az_nova_backup_4dc8c496-..-00021
volume_78680241-7928-41d5-b9bc-f2f82dad7bba/20160424152627/az_nova_backup_4dc8c496-.._
metadata
volume_78680241-7928-41d5-b9bc-f2f82dad7bba/20160424152627/az_nova_backup_4dc8c496-.._
sha256file
```

Restoration of an existing backup is similar to the backup procedure:

```
$ cinder backup-restore 4dc8c496-85f1-438f-9eb7-56fb2aa04503
+-------------+----------------------------------------------------+
|  Property   |                       Value                        |
+-------------+----------------------------------------------------+
|  backup_id  |        4dc8c496-85f1-438f-9eb7-56fb2aa04503        |
|  volume_id  |        7cf64dd4-4e35-455e-9b15-f2ad75b6e78b        |
| volume_name | restore_backup_4dc8c496-85f1-438f-9eb7-56fb2aa04503 |
+-------------+----------------------------------------------------+
```

With the option --volume you can choose the name or ID of the volume to which you wish to restore your backup to. By default, a new volume will be created:

```
$ cinder list
+------------+---------+----------------+----+-----------+--------+-----------+------------+
|     ID     |Status   |Name            |Size|Volume Type|Bootable|Multiattach|Attached to |
+------------+---------+----------------+----+-----------+--------+-----------+------------+
| 78680241-..|available| apresstest1    |1   |-          |false   |  False    |            |
| 7cf64dd4-..|available| restore_backup |1   |-          |false   |  False    |            |
|            |         |    _4dc8c496.. |    |           |        |           |            |
+------------+---------+----------------+----+-----------+--------+-----------+------------+
```

As mentioned earlier, you can export the metadata of a volume backup. To do so, you will need to run this command as an admin user:

```
$ source keystonerc_admin
```

```
$ cinder backup-export 4dc8c496-85f1-438f-9eb7-56fb2aa04503
+----------------+-------------------------------------------------------------+
|    Property    |                            Value                            |
+----------------+-------------------------------------------------------------+
| backup_service |                cinder.backup.drivers.swift                  |
|   backup_url   | eyJzdGFOdXMiOiAihaWxhYmxlIiwgImRpc3BsYXlfbmFtZSI6IG51bGwsICJhdmGFiaWxp |
|                |                             ...                             |
+----------------+-------------------------------------------------------------+
```

To import backup metadata, run the following command:

```
$ cinder backup-import eyJzdGFOdXMiOiAihaWxhYmxlIiwgI.....
```

Manage Volume Snapshots

Using volume snapshots is another way to create a back up of an existing volume. Volume snapshots provide a way to obtain a nondisruptive copy of the volume. Snapshot will be stored in Cinder's back-end storage system, as opposed to Swift Object Storage in cases of backups. In the default installation LVM will take care of creating snapshots. Do not confuse Cinder snapshots with Nova snapshots. You can use snapshot when the volume is in use by a VM, but from a consistency point of view, it is best if the volume is not connected to an instance when the snapshot is taken. It is possible to create new volumes from snapshots.

Let's look at some examples of how to work with Cinder snapshots. First, you need to know the volume ID that will be used:

```
$ cinder list
+--------------------+----------+----------+----+------+--------+----------+---------------+
|ID                  |Status    |Name      |Size|Volume|Bootable|Multiattach| Attached to   |
|                    |          |          |    |Type  |        |          |               |
+--------------------+----------+----------+----+------+--------+----------+---------------+
| 78680241-7928-41d5-|available |apresstest1|1  |-     |false   |False     |               |
| b9bc-f2f82dad7bba  |          |          |    |      |        |          |               |
+--------------------+----------+----------+----+------+--------+----------+---------------+
```

Next, you can enter a command to create a snapshot:

```
$ cinder snapshot-create --display-name apresstest1_snap1 78680241-7928-41d5-b9bc-
f2f82dad7bba
+-------------+-------------------------------------------+
|  Property   |                   Value                   |
+-------------+-------------------------------------------+
| created_at  |        2016-04-25T16:06:04.676842         |
| description |                   None                    |
|     id      |   393a436d-3112-425f-8faf-ca14e3db3092    |
|  metadata   |                    {}                     |
|    name     |             apresstest1_snap1             |
|    size     |                     1                     |
|   status    |                 creating                  |
|  volume_id  |   78680241-7928-41d5-b9bc-f2f82dad7bba    |
+-------------+-------------------------------------------+
```

Then you should make sure that a snapshot was created:

```
$ cinder snapshot-list
+--------------------+--------------------+-----------+-------------------+------+
|ID                  |Volume ID           | Status    |       Name        | Size |
+--------------------+--------------------+-----------+-------------------+------+
| 393a436d-3112-425f-| 78680241-7928-41d5-| available | apresstest1_snap1 |  1   |
  8faf-ca14e3db3092    b9bc-f2f82dad7bba                                         |
+--------------------+--------------------+-----------+-------------------+------+
```

And now knowing the snapshot ID, you can show the details of the snapshot:

```
$ cinder snapshot-show 393a436d-3112-425f-8faf-ca14e3db3092
+-------------------------------------------+--------------------------------------+
|                 Property                  |                Value                 |
+-------------------------------------------+--------------------------------------+
|                created_at                 |      2016-04-25T16:06:04.000000       |
|                description                |                 None                 |
|                    id                     | 393a436d-3112-425f-8faf-ca14e3db3092 |
|                 metadata                  |                  {}                  |
|                   name                    |          apresstest1_snap1           |
|  os-extended-snapshot-attributes:progress |                 100%                 |
| os-extended-snapshot-attributes:project_id |   1542af2b20d349d29710d8c4019ba202   |
|                   size                    |                  1                   |
|                  status                   |              available               |
|                 volume_id                 | 78680241-7928-41d5-b9bc-f2f82dad7bba |
+-------------------------------------------+--------------------------------------+
```

At the end, you can create a new volume from the snapshot. As a part of the creation process, you can specify a new volume size in gigabytes:

```
# cinder create --display-name apresstest2_from_snap1 --snapshot-id 393a436d-3112-425f-8faf-
ca14e3db3092 1
+-----------------------------------+--------------------------------------+
|             Property              |                Value                 |
+-----------------------------------+--------------------------------------+
|            attachments            |                  []                  |
|         availability_zone         |                 nova                 |
|             bootable              |                false                 |
|         consistencygroup_id       |                 None                 |
|            created_at             |      2016-04-25T19:10:40.000000       |
|            description            |                 None                 |
|             encrypted             |                False                 |
|                id                 | 027c2640-8f96-4024-8a42-5265b263e32c |
|             metadata              |                  {}                  |
|            multiattach            |                False                 |
|               name                |        apresstest2_from_snap1        |
|      os-vol-tenant-attr:tenant_id |   1542af2b20d349d29710d8c4019ba202   |
|    os-volume-replication:driver_data |               None                 |
| os-volume-replication:extended_status |             None                 |
|        replication_status         |               disabled               |
```

```
|              size              |                     1                     |
|           snapshot_id          |   393a436d-3112-425f-8faf-ca14e3db3092    |
|          source_volid          |                    None                   |
|             status             |                  creating                 |
|             user_id            |      ec92590f7ff84887ab9c0329f5ce850c     |
|           volume_type          |                    None                   |
+--------------------------------+-------------------------------------------+
```

You can also delete the snapshot if needed:

```
$ cinder snapshot-delete 393a436d-3112-425f-8faf-ca14e3db3092
```

Figure 9-5 shows the Volume Snapshots tab in the Horizon web user interface.

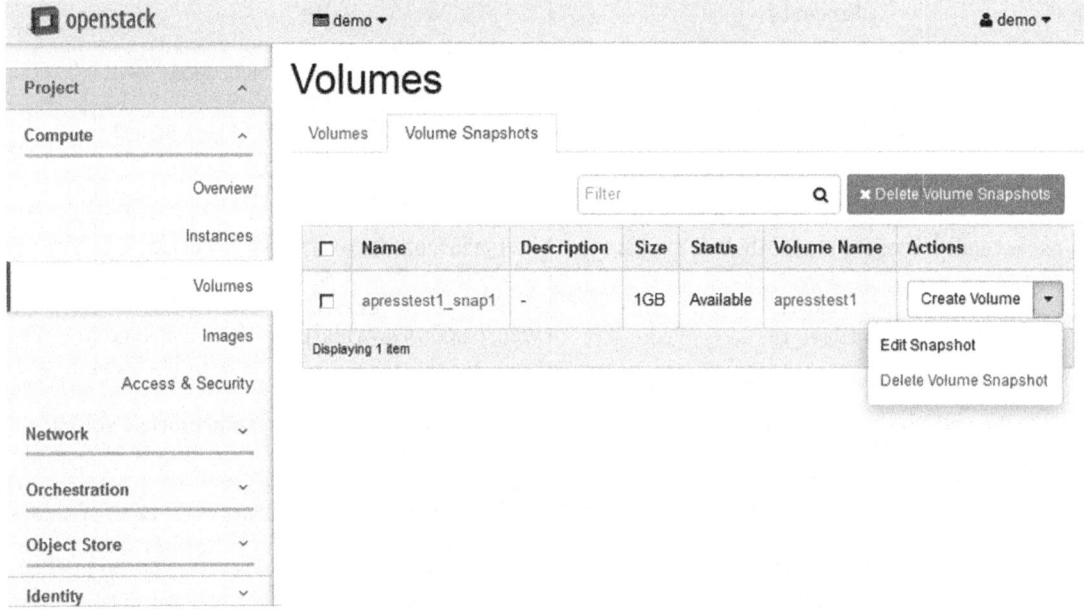

Figure 9-5. *Working with snapshots in Horizon web interface view*

Manage Volumes Encryption

OpenStack supports two options for volume encryption. One of them is called the static shared secret, and the other is with support of the new Barbican OpenStack Key Manager Service. The easiest way to set up volume encryption is to use the static secret. The disadvantage of this method is that if shared secret is compromised, then all volumes will be compromised. To use the static shared secret-based encryption you need to add one common section to all configuration files: /etc/nova/nova.conf and /etc/cinder/cinder.conf:

```
[keymgr]
fixed_key = my_fixed_key_value
```

After that you need to restart the correspondent services. Everything is ready now so you can create the new Cinder LUKS (Linux Unified Key Setup) volume type. LUKS specifies a platform-independent disk format for use in encryption tools. The reference implementation is based on the cryptsetup GNU/Linux tool with the dm-crypt back end.

```
$ source keystonerc_admin
$ cinder type-create LUKS
+----------------------------------------+------+-------------+-----------+
|                  ID                    | Name | Description | Is_Public |
+----------------------------------------+------+-------------+-----------+
| 6e565bfa-a16a-4bc5-9bfe-1ec54969ec81   | LUKS |      -      |    True   |
+----------------------------------------+------+-------------+-----------+
```

Now you can mark the LUKS volume type as encrypted and provide the necessary details such as cipher and key size:

```
$ cinder encryption-type-create --cipher aes-xts-plain64 --key_size 512 --control_location
front-end LUKS nova.encryptors.luks.LuksEncryptor
+------------------------+---------------------+-----------+----------+-------------------+
|Volume Type ID          |Provider             |Cipher     | Key Size | Control Location  |
+------------------------+---------------------+-----------+----------+-------------------+
| 6e565bfa-a16a-4bc5-    |nova.encryptors.luks |aes-xts-   |512       |front-end          |
|  9bfe-1ec54969ec81     |  LuksEncryptor      |plain64    |          |                   |
+------------------------+---------------------+-----------+----------+-------------------+
```

The corresponding screenshot of the admin web UI is shown in Figure 9-6.

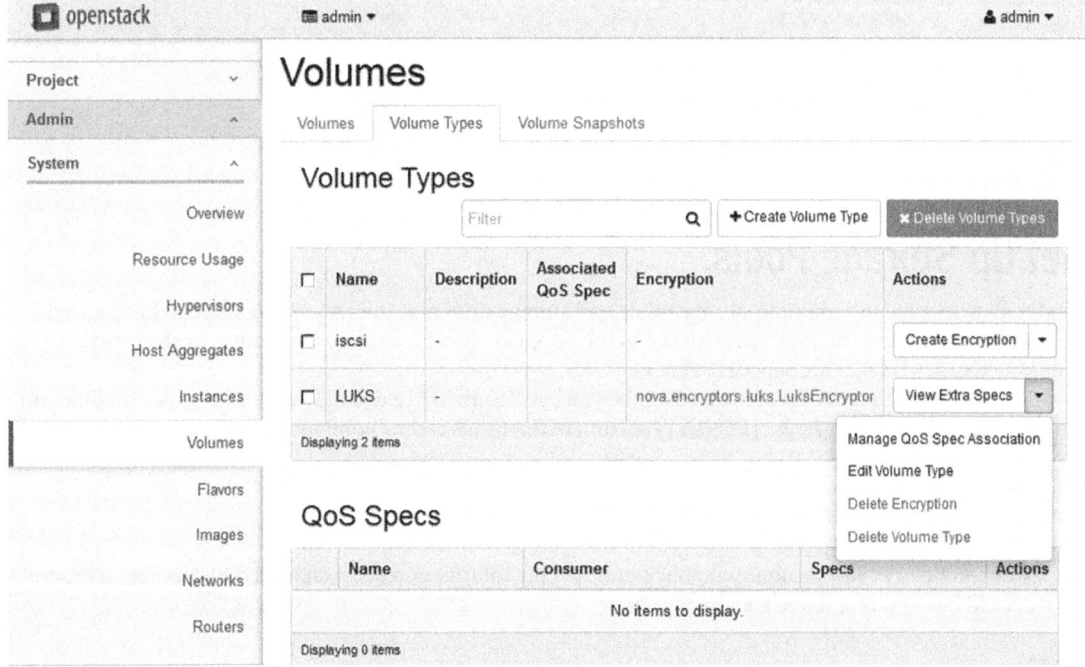

Figure 9-6. *Volume Types tab in the Horizon web interface view*

Now you can create the encrypted volume:

```
$ cinder create --display-name volEncr --volume-type LUKS 1
+---------------------------------+------------------------------------------+
|            Property             |                  Value                   |
+---------------------------------+------------------------------------------+
|           attachments           |                    []                    |
|        availability_zone        |                   nova                   |
|            bootable             |                  false                   |
|       consistencygroup_id       |                   None                   |
|           created_at            |         2016-04-25T19:36:51.000000        |
|           description           |                   None                   |
|            encrypted            |                   True                   |
|               id                |   d681fc68-8034-416d-9f46-b521c9c40b8e   |
|            metadata             |                    {}                    |
|        migration_status         |                   None                   |
|           multiattach           |                  False                   |
|              name               |                 volEncr                  |
|       os-vol-host-attr:host     |                   None                   |
|    os-vol-mig-status-attr:migstat |                 None                   |
|   os-vol-mig-status-attr:name_id |                 None                   |
|     os-vol-tenant-attr:tenant_id |      560a3e76bdc64ea2bee9316038b12793   |
|  os-volume-replication:driver_data |               None                   |
| os-volume-replication:extended_status |            None                   |
|        replication_status       |                 disabled                 |
|              size               |                    1                     |
|           snapshot_id           |                   None                   |
|           source_volid          |                   None                   |
|             status              |                 creating                 |
|             user_id             |      15b05be5765b49698bd2c890399bb8ae    |
|           volume_type           |                   LUKS                   |
+---------------------------------+------------------------------------------+
```

Set Up Storage Pools

Cinder allows you to use multiple storage pools and storage drivers at the same time. You can find the list, which contains more than 50 storage drivers, at the Support Matrix web page for Cinder (https://wiki. openstack.org/wiki/CinderSupportMatrix).

You need to enumerate all of the back ends when you want to use two or many back ends with different or the same type of drivers in the [DEFAULT] section of the cinder.conf configuration file:

```
[DEFAULT]
enabled_backends = lvmA, lvmB, nfsA
```

Now you need to add sections with back-end specific information for each back end. Here is an example for two LVM back ends and one NFS back end:

```
[lvmA]
volume_group=cinder-volumes-1
```

```
volume_driver=cinder.volume.drivers.lvm.LVMISCSIDriver
volume_backend_name=LVM
[lvmB]
volume_group=cinder-volumes-2
volume_driver=cinder.volume.drivers.lvm.LVMISCSIDriver
volume_backend_name=LVM
[nfsA]
nfs_shares_config=/etc/cinder/shares.txt
volume_driver=cinder.volume.drivers.nfs.NfsDriver
volume_backend_name=NFS
```

If you want to give the user the right to choose on which back end their volumes are created, then a volume type must be defined by the admin:

```
$ source ~/keystonerc_admin
$ cinder type-create lvm1
$ cinder type-create lvm2
$ cinder type-create nfs1
$ cinder type-key lvm1 set volume_backend_name=lvmA
$ cinder type-key lvm2 set volume_backend_name=lvmB
$ cinder type-key nfs1 set volume_backend_name=nfsA
```

Review Questions

1. How many cinder-volume services exist in a typical installation?

   A. One.

   B. At least three.

   C. One per storage back end.

   D. One per database instance.

2. What parameter in the configuration file defines the public Identity API endpoint?

   A. auth_uri

   B. auth_ure

   C. auth_url

   D. auth_url_public

3. How can you create a volume with a name test and the size 1GB?

   A. openstack volume create test 1

   B. cinder create --name test

   C. openstack volumes create --size 1 test

   D. cinder create --display-name test 1

4. What is the Linux LVM partition number?

   A.   82

   B.   8e

   C.   83

   D.   1F

5. How does Cinder back up differ from snapshot (choose two)?

   A.   Back up is stored in Glance.

   B.   Back up is stored in Swift.

   C.   Back up can't be incremental.

   D.   Back up can be incremental.

Answers to Review Questions

1. C

2. A

3. D

4. B

5. B and D

CHAPTER 10

■ ■ ■

Orchestration of OpenStack

This chapter covers 8% of the Certified OpenStack Administrator exam requirements.

Architecture and Components of Heat

The last but certainly not the least service covered in this book is OpenStack Orchestration (Heat). This is the orchestration service: "One ring to rule them all." The main purpose of the service is to manage the entire lifecycle of the infrastructure and applications within OpenStack clouds. For orchestration, Heat uses templates that describe instances, networks, volumes, etc. Heat can also rule scale-in/scale-out scenarios with Ceilometer's help.

Two formats of templates can be used with OpenStack Orchestration:

- **HOT (Heat Orchestration Template)**: OpenStack-native YAML-based template format.

- **CFT (AWS CloudFormation Template)**: Compatible with AWS CloudFormation (http://aws.amazon.com/cloudformation/) JSON-based template format. You can use a lot of templates designed for AWS. A good starting point for research is https://aws.amazon.com/cloudformation/aws-cloudformation-templates/.

The OpenStack Orchestration architecture is shown in Figure 10-1. Heat consists of several services that are implemented as GNU/Linux daemons and CLI commands:

- **heat-api**: Accepts an OpenStack-native REST API call for template processing. After receiving API calls, heat-api processes them by sending them to the heat-engine via the AMQP protocol.

- **heat-api-cfn**: This is a CloudFormation API service. It is similar to heat-api by function.

- **heat-engine:** The main service of Heat. The engine does all the work of orchestrating, launching templates, and providing feedback to the client.

- **heat-api-cloudwatch**: An additional minimal implementation of AWS CloudWatch–compatible service (https://aws.amazon.com/cloudwatch/). It is primarily required to enable metric collection for high availability and autoscaling functionality.

- **heat**: The CLI tool that communicates with the heat-api.

© Andrey Markelov 2016
A. Markelov, *Certified OpenStack Administrator Study Guide*, DOI 10.1007/978-1-4842-2125-9_10

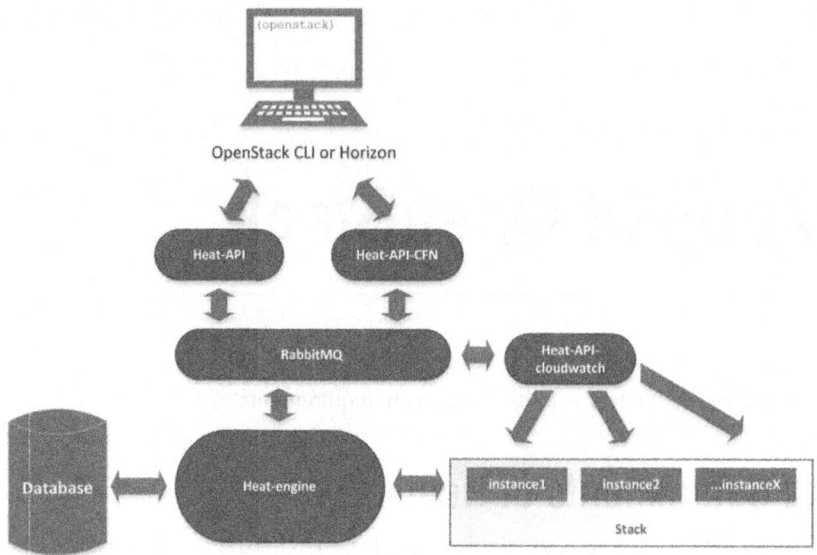

Figure 10-1. *Architecture of the OpenStack Orchestration sevice*

Introducing the Heat OpenStack Template

The input information for Heat is a template that describes the stack. Stack is the branch of OpenStack resources that creates an application. Applications can consist of several instances and networks. HOT (Heat OpenStack Template) was originally introduced in the Icehouse release and it acts as a primary standard for Heat.

Have a look at Figure 10-2, where the structure of the HOT is shown. The template is divided into four parts. The first part is a template header. It consists of the HOT version and an optional description for the OpenStack operator. In Table 10-1 you can find the most recent versions of HOT.

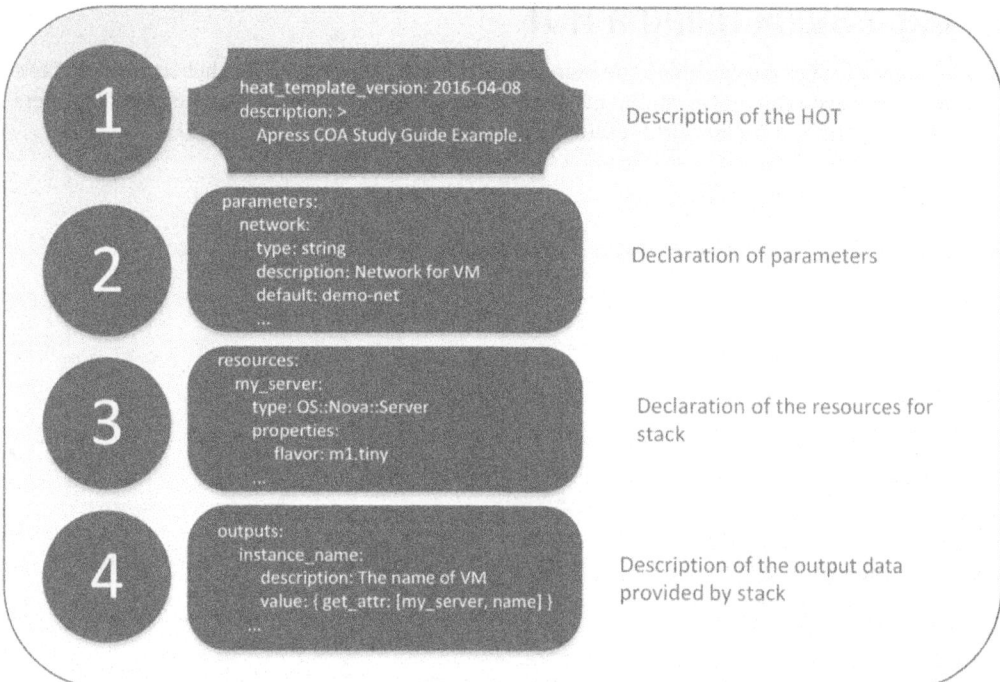

Figure 10-2. *Example of the Heat OpenStack Template (HOT) format*

Table 10-1. *OpenStack Heat OpenStack Templates Versions*

Series	HOT Version
Icehouse	heat_template_version: 2013-05-23
Juno	heat_template_version: 2014-10-16
Kilo	heat_template_version: 2015-03-30
Liberty	heat_template_version: 2015-10-15
Mitaka	heat_template_version: 2016-04-08

The second optional section is the parameters. This section allows you to customize the deployment and specify the input parameters that have to be provided when instantiating the template.

The third section is always mandatory. It starts from general resources and defines actual resources that make up a stack. There are more than 100 resource types that can be defined here. You can find a full description of HOT at the OpenStack documentation project site (http://docs.openstack.org/developer/heat/template_guide/index.html). There should be at least one resource definition in this section.

The last section defines the output parameters that should be available to the user after a stack has been created. These output parameters are available from CLI and in the Horizon web client.

Launching a Stack Using a HOT

To be a little bit more specific, you can check the examples of templates at https://github.com/openstack/heat-templates/. There you can find examples of templates that demonstrate core Heat functionality. Here is a listing of a slightly modified "hello world" example from this repository:

```
heat_template_version: 2014-10-16
description: >
  Apress Certified OpenStack Administrator Study Guide.
  One VM Example

parameters:
  network:
    type: string
    description: Network for VM
    default: demo-net
  image:
    type: string
    description: Cirros Image for VM
    default: cirros-0.3.4-x86_64

resources:
  my_server:
    type: OS::Nova::Server
    properties:
      flavor: m1.tiny
      key_name: mykey
      networks:
      - network: { get_param: network }
      image: { get_param: image }
      user_data: |
        #!/bin/sh
        echo "Instance started :)"
      user_data_format: RAW

outputs:
  instance_name:
    description: The name of VM
    value: { get_attr: [my_server, name] }
  private_ip:
    description: The private IP of VM
    value: { get_attr: [ my_server, first_address ] }
```

The example consists of all four main parts of the template. There are two parameters defined: network and image. They have default values, but you can redefine them at the time of stack launching. The only described resource type OS::Nova::Server in this stack is my_server. By the way, you can find descriptions of all the resource types in the Horizon web interface. The results of this example are shown in Figure 10-3. Probably the most interesting part of the definition is the example of how to run a specific script at the time of starting the instance. And at the end of the template the name of the virtual machine and IP output are defined.

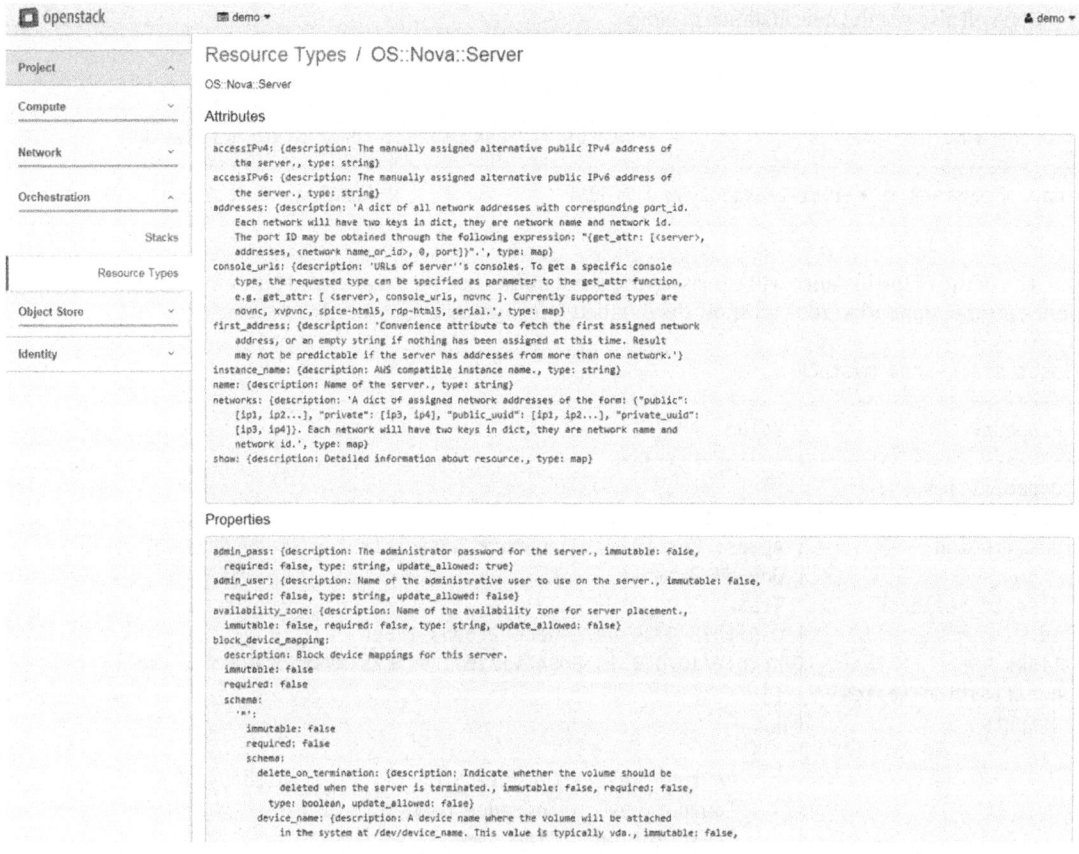

***Figure 10-3.** Example of the resource types' description in Horizon*

Now you can start the stack either in Horizon or in command line. If you choose Horizon, then go to Orchestration ➤ Stacks and click the "Launch Stack" button. You can use the -P option for defining parameters if you choose to use the command line:

```
$ heat stack-create -f Hello-World.yml -P network=private -P image=cirros-raw mystack
+------------------------+------------+---------------------+---------------------+--------------+
| id                     | stack_name | stack_status        | creation_time       | updated_time |
+------------------------+------------+---------------------+---------------------+--------------+
| 035ffd78-9739-4a7d-..  | mystack    | CREATE_IN_PROGRESS  | 2016-06-25T07:34:49 | None         |
+------------------------+------------+---------------------+---------------------+--------------+
```

Then you can issue the `heat stacl-list` command to make sure the stack creation is completed:

```
$ heat stack-list
+---------------------------+------------+----------------+---------------------+--------------+
| id                        | stack_name | stack_status   | creation_time       | updated_time |
+---------------------------+------------+----------------+---------------------+--------------+
| 035ffd78-9739-4a7d-98cc.. | mystack    | CREATE_COMPLETE| 2016-06-25T07:34:4  | None         |
+---------------------------+------------+----------------+---------------------+--------------+
```

123

You will also see the new instance in Nova:

```
$ nova list
+------+--------------------------------+--------+------------+-------------+------------------+
| ID   | Name                           | Status | Task State | Power State | Networks         |
+------+--------------------------------+--------+------------+-------------+------------------+
| dd.. | mystack-my_server-2z4b42d2y5w  | ACTIVE | -          | Running     | private=10.0.0.4 |
+------+--------------------------------+--------+------------+-------------+------------------+
```

The name of the instance will consist of the stack name, instance name, and automatically generated alpha-number appendix. You can show the detailed information about running the stack:

```
$ heat stack-show mystack
+----------------------+----------------------------------------------------------------+
| Property             | Value                                                          |
+----------------------+----------------------------------------------------------------+
| capabilities         | []                                                             |
| creation_time        | 2016-06-25T07:34:49                                            |
| description          | Apress Certified OpenStack Administrator Study Guide.          |
|                      | One VM Example                                                 |
| disable_rollback     | True                                                           |
| id                   | 035ffd78-9739-4a7d-98cc-3f6eb35f16ed                           |
| links                | http://10.0.2.15:8004/v1/16../stacks/mystack/035f.. (self)     |
| notification_topics  | []                                                             |
| outputs              | [                                                              |
|                      |   {                                                            |
|                      |     "output_value": "mystack-my_server-2z4b42d2y5wo",          |
|                      |     "output_key": "instance_name",                             |
|                      |     "description": "The name of VM"                            |
|                      |   },                                                           |
|                      |   {                                                            |
|                      |     "output_value": "10.0.0.4",                                |
|                      |     "output_key": "private_ip",                                |
|                      |     "description": "The private IP of VM"                      |
|                      |   }                                                            |
|                      | ]                                                              |
| parameters           | {                                                              |
|                      |     "OS::project_id": "16f44d2a075a4139a2a5425a42f1b447",       |
|                      |     "image": "cirros-raw",                                     |
|                      |     "OS::stack_id": "035ffd78-9739-4a7d-98cc-3f6eb35f16ed",     |
|                      |     "OS::stack_name": "mystack",                               |
|                      |     "network": "private"                                       |
|                      | }                                                              |
```

```
| parent                 | None                                              |
| stack_name             | mystack                                           |
| stack_owner            | None                                              |
| stack_status           | CREATE_COMPLETE                                   |
| stack_status_reason    | Stack CREATE completed successfully               |
| stack_user_project_id  | 769b289c72bf412fbe33cded5e89ab89                  |
| tags                   | null                                              |
| template_description   | Apress Certified OpenStack Administrator Study Guide. |
|                        | One VM Example                                    |
| timeout_mins           | None                                              |
| updated_time           | None                                              |
+------------------------+---------------------------------------------------+
```

This same information is also available inside the Horizon web interface (see Figure 10-4).

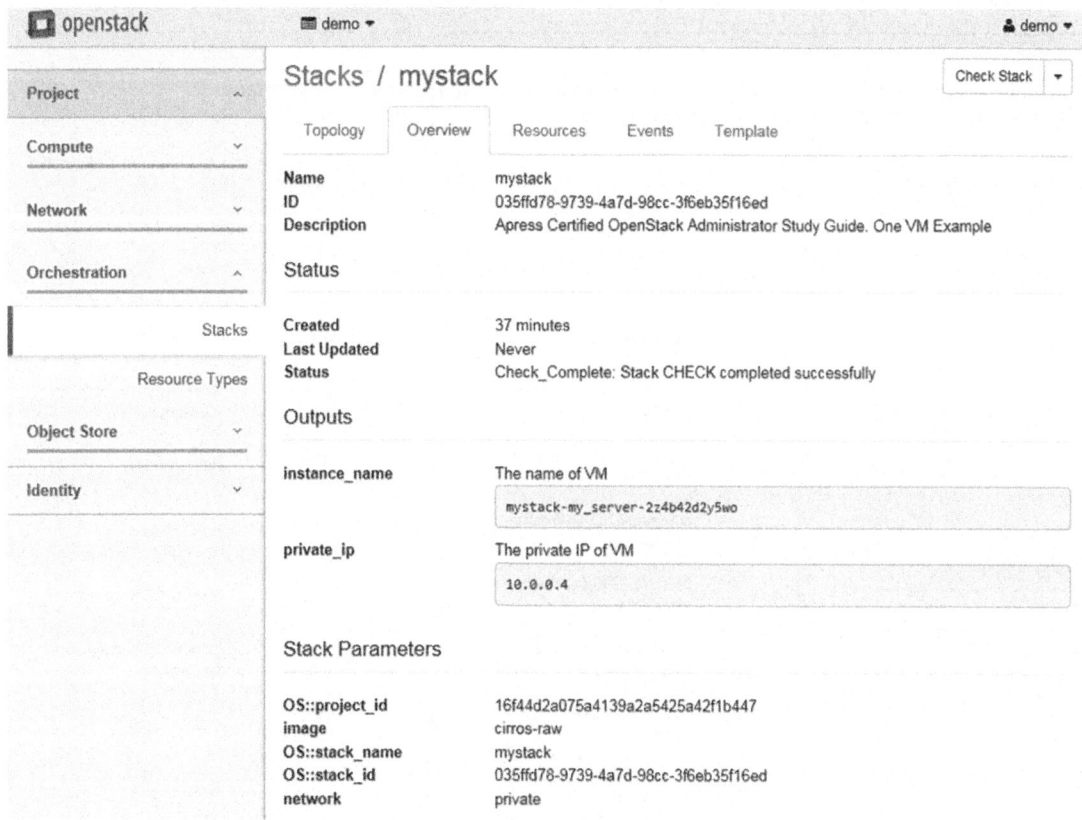

Figure 10-4. *Example of the stack details in the Horizon web interface*

Using Heat CLI and Dashboard

Let's examine the most common operations with stacks. If you troubleshoot the stack and want to see what happens with the resources, the heat event-list command will be very useful:

```
$ heat event-list mystack
+----------------+--------+----------------------+---------------------+----------------------+
| resource_name  | id     | resource_status_reason | resource_status     | event_time           |
+----------------+--------+----------------------+---------------------+----------------------+
| mystack        | 911..  | Stack CREATE started   | CREATE_IN_PROGRESS  | 2016-06-25T07:34:50  |
| my_server      | dd1..  | state changed          | CREATE_IN_PROGRESS  | 2016-06-25T07:34:51  |
| my_server      | 480..  | state changed          | CREATE_COMPLETE     | 2016-06-25T07:35:07  |
| mystack        | 0d8..  | Stack CREATE completed | CREATE_COMPLETE     | 2016-06-25T07:35:07  |
| mystack        | 855..  | Stack CHECK started    | CHECK_IN_PROGRESS   | 2016-06-25T08:03:55  |
| my_server      | 4d3..  | state changed          | CHECK_IN_PROGRESS   | 2016-06-25T08:03:55  |
| mystack        | c99..  | Stack SUSPEND started  | SUSPEND_IN_PROGRESS | 2016-06-25T10:53:45  |
+----------------+--------+----------------------+---------------------+----------------------+
```

In Figure 10-5 you can see how the list of events looks in the Horizon web interface.

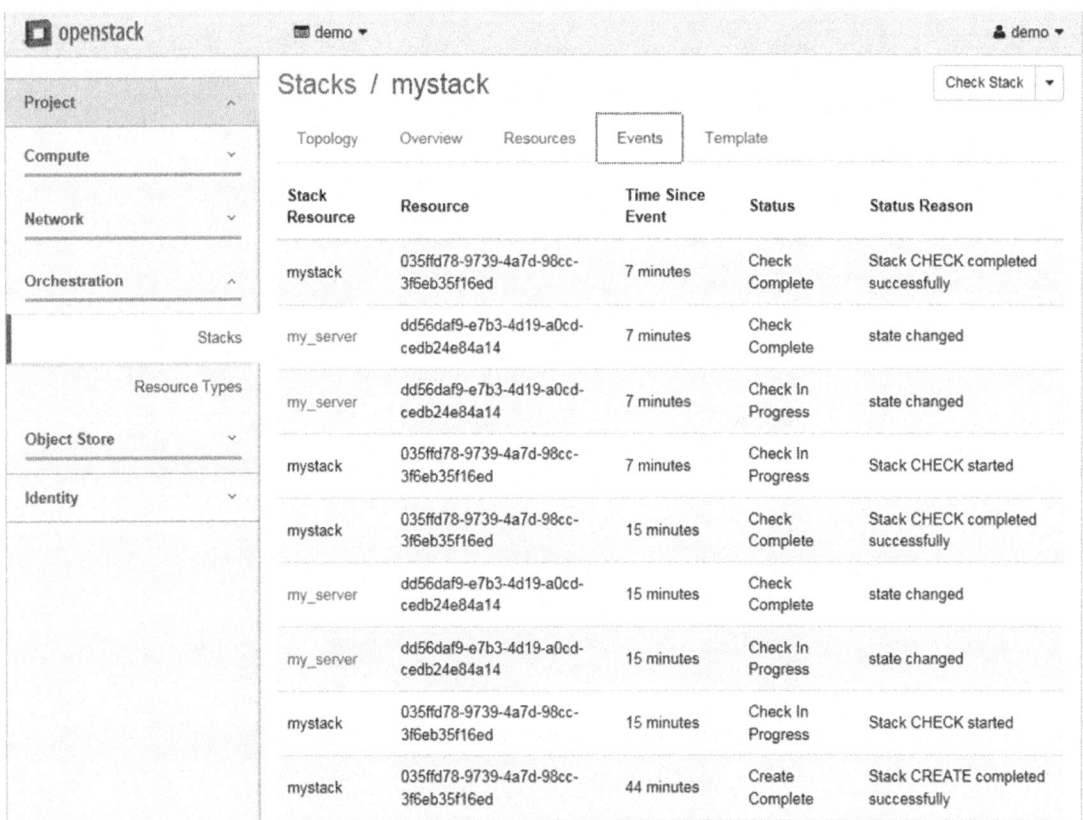

Figure 10-5. *Example of the stack events list in the Horizon web interface*

As the owner of the stack, you can suspend and resume your stacks again:

```
$ heat action-suspend mystack
+---------------------------+------------+----------------+---------------------+--------------+
| id                        | stack_name | stack_status   | creation_time       | updated_time |
+---------------------------+------------+----------------+---------------------+--------------+
| 035ffd78-9739-4a7d-98cc.. | mystack    | CHECK_COMPLETE | 2016-06-25T07:34:49 | None         |
+---------------------------+------------+----------------+---------------------+--------------+
$ heat action-resume mystack
+---------------------------+------------+------------------+---------------------+--------------+
| id                        | stack_name | stack_status     | creation_time       | updated_time |
+---------------------------+------------+------------------+---------------------+--------------+
| 035ffd78-9739-4a7d-98..   | mystack    | SUSPEND_COMPLETE | 2016-06-25T07:34:49 | None         |
+---------------------------+------------+------------------+---------------------+--------------+
```

With Horizon and CLI, it is possible to see the resources of your stack:

```
$ heat resource-list mystack
+---------------+-----------------+-----------------+-----------------+---------------------+
| resource_name | physical_res_id | resource_type   | resource_status | updated_time        |
+---------------+-----------------+-----------------+-----------------+---------------------+
| my_server     | dd56daf9-e7b3-..| OS::Nova::Server| RESUME_COMPLETE | 2016-06-25T07:34:50 |
+---------------+-----------------+-----------------+-----------------+---------------------+
```

If you prefer to work with Horizon, you can see the same information. An example of the stack resources in Horizon is shown in Figure 10-6.

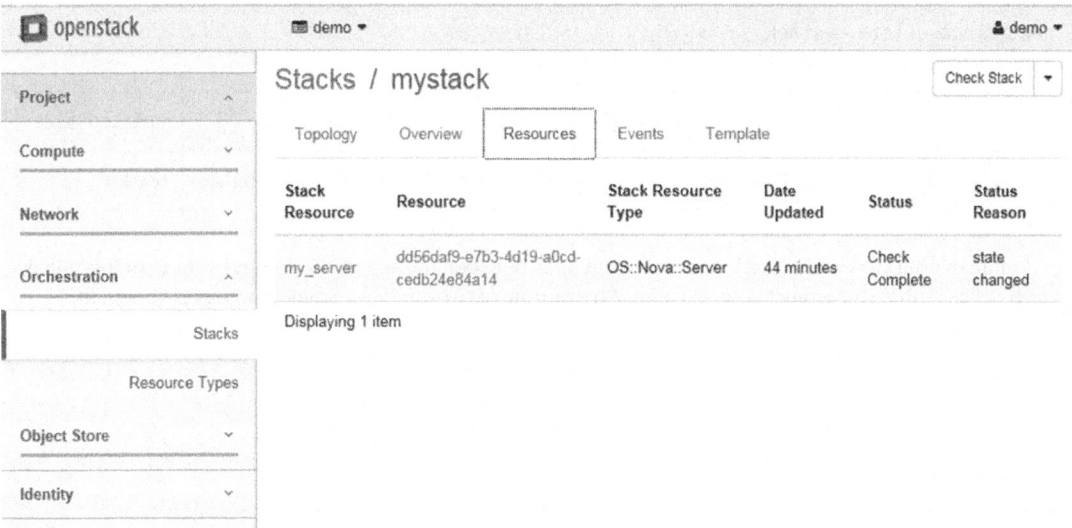

Figure 10-6. *Example of the stack resources as shown in the Horizon web interface*

As mentioned earlier, heat stack-show will show you the information of all the stacks' properties including output. You can use another command if you want to see output only:

```
$ heat output-list mystack
+---------------+----------------------+
| output_key    | description          |
+---------------+----------------------+
| instance_name | The name of VM       |
| private_ip    | The private IP of VM |
+---------------+----------------------+
```

Also you can see the template using the command:

```
$ heat template-show mystack
```

If you update the text of the template file, you may also want to update a stack. To update an existing stack from a modified template file, run the following command:

```
$ heat stack-update -f Hello-World.yml -P network=private -P image=cirros-raw mystack
+------+------------+-----------------+---------------------+--------------+
| id   | stack_name | stack_status    | creation_time       | updated_time |
+------+------------+-----------------+---------------------+--------------+
| 6b.. | mystack    | CREATE_COMPLETE | 2016-06-25T12:42:50 | None         |
+------+------------+-----------------+---------------------+--------------+
```

Some resources are updated in place, while others are replaced with new resources. At the end you can also delete a stack:

```
$ heat stack-delete mystack
Are you sure you want to delete this stack(s) [y/N]? y
+-----------------------+------------+-----------------+---------------------+--------------+
| id                    | stack_name | stack_status    | creation_time       | updated_time |
+-----------------------+------------+-----------------+---------------------+--------------+
| 035ffd78-9739-4a7d-98.. | mystack  | RESUME_COMPLETE | 2016-06-25T07:34:49 | None         |
+-----------------------+------------+-----------------+---------------------+--------------+
```

For an overall view of the stack resources and links between them, the "Topology" subtab of the "Stack Details" page within the project is very useful. An example of two-instance stack topology is shown in Figure 10-7.

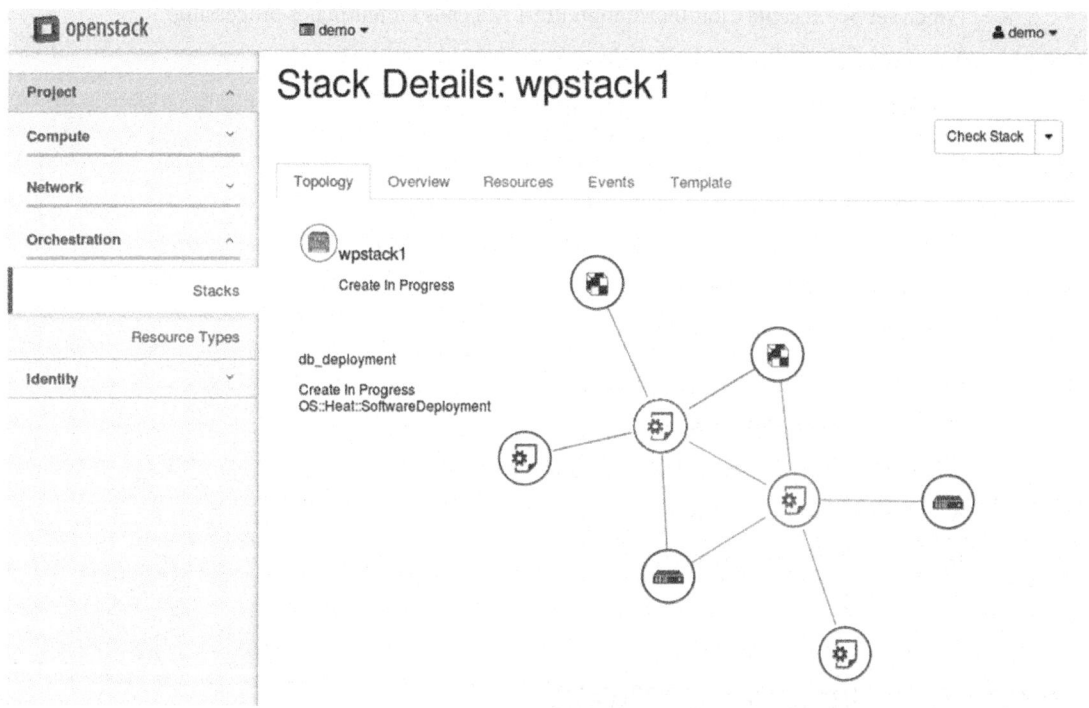

Figure 10-7. *Example of the stack topology.*

Review Questions

1. How can the status of the running stack be checked?

   A. heat event-list mystack

   B. heat stack-show mystack

   C. heat stack-check mystack

   D. heat template-show mystack

2. How can you run a stack (choose all applicable)?

   A. heat stack-create -f Hello-World.yml -P network=private -P image=cirros stack

   B. heat stack-create -f Hello-World.yml -P network=192.168.0.0/24 -P image=cirros stack

   C. heat stack-create -f Hello-World.yml -P network=private stack

   D. heat stack-create -f Hello-World.yml -P image=cirros stack

3. Which service accepts CloudFormation REST API calls for templates processing?

    A. heat-api-cloudwatch

    B. heat-cfn

    C. heat-api-cfn

    D. heat-api

4. How would you see the stack output (choose all applicable)?

    A. heat output-list mystack

    B. heat output-show mystack

    C. heat stack-show mystack

    D. heat stack-list mystack

5. Is it possible to update a stack?

    A. Yes, only when stack is suspended.

    B. Yes, you can update running stack.

    C. No.

Answers to Review Questions

1. B

2. A, C, D

3. C

4. A, C

5. B

CHAPTER 11

Troubleshooting

This chapter covers 13% of the Certified OpenStack Administrator exam requirements. Please note that backing up OpenStack instances is discussed in Chapter 9 and analyzing storage status is discussed in Chapters 4, 8, and 9.

The Main Principles of Troubleshooting

Usually troubleshooting of OpenStack is not straightforward because it consists of a lot of separate projects that work with one another in different combinations. That is why the discussion of troubleshooting is left until the end of this book. You need to know the previous material before you learn the troubleshooting techniques.

First, you should be aware of the concerns about generic debugging. Always make a backup copy of your configuration file before you begin changing it. Next, it is very important to make only one change at a time. And at the end, do not forget to revert your configuration files to the original if any test is unsuccessful.

OpenStack troubleshooting techniques depend to a certain extent on general GNU/Linux troubleshooting skills. That discussion is outside the scope of this book. However, Table 11-1 briefly summarizes the main GNU/Linux troubleshooting utilities.

Table 11-1. *Basic GNU/Linux Troubleshooting Commands*

GNU/Linux Command	Useful Options and Example
ps: Report list of the current processes	To see every process on the system use the aux option. It can be useful with the grep command for searching exact processes or you can use pgrep.

`# ps aux | grep cinder`
 	
`cinder    1006  1.0  1.8 468280 74316 ?        Ss   11:49   2:36`
`/usr/bin/python2 /usr/bin/cinder-api --config-file`
`/usr/share/cinder/cinder-dist.conf --config-file`
`/etc/cinder/cinder.conf --logfile /var/log/cinder/api.log`	

top: Show dynamic view of the system processes. Unlike the ps output, this command continuously refreshes the view	You can use interactive keystrokes in the top environment. ? - help, q - quit, l - toggles for load header line, t - toggles for threads header line, m - toggles for memory header line, u - filter process for user name, M - sorts process listing by memory usage in descending order, P - sorts process listing by processor utilization in descending order, k - kill a process.

(continued)

© Andrey Markelov 2016

A. Markelov, *Certified OpenStack Administrator Study Guide*, DOI 10.1007/978-1-4842-2125-9_11

Table 11-1. (*continued*)

GNU/Linux Command	Useful Options and Example
df: Report file system disk space usage	Usually df is used with the -h option that means human readable format (e.g., 1K 234M 2G)

```
# df -h
Filesystem                Size   Used   Avail   Use%   Mounted on
/dev/mapper/linux-root    50G    8.8G   42G     18%    /
/dev/mapper/linux-home    56G    33M    56G     1%     /home
/dev/sda1                 497M   133M   364M    27%    /boot
```

du: Estimate file space usage	The same -h option as in df is often used.

```
# du -h /var/lib/glance/images/
13M     /var/lib/glance/images/
```

ip: Show/manipulate routing, devices, policy routing, and tunnels	The most common subcommands are show - for displaying IP information, route - for showing routing information.

```
# ip addr show enp0s3
2: enp0s3: <BROADCAST,MULTICAST,UP,LOWER_UP> mtu 1500 qdisc pfifo_fast state UP qlen 1000
link/ether 08:00:27:41:05:a6 brd ff:ff:ff:ff:ff:ff
inet 10.0.2.15/8 brd 10.255.255.255 scope global enp0s3
valid_lft forever preferred_lft forever
inet6 fe80::a00:27ff:fe41:5a6/64 scope link
valid_lft forever preferred_lft forever
```

ss and netstat: Utilities to investigate sockets	The ss command is similar to the netstat command and it is used to display socket statistics. They have similar options. Options are -t - show TCP sockets, -u - show UDP sockets, -a - show listening and established sockets, -p - show process using the sockets.

```
# ss -ta
State   Recv-Q  Send-Q Local   Address:Port              Peer Address:Port
LISTEN  0       128             *:8776                         *:*
LISTEN  0       128             *:25672                        *:*
LISTEN  0       128             *:8777                         *:*
LISTEN  0       128     10.0.2.15:27017                        *:*
LISTEN  0       64      10.0.2.15:rsync                        *:*
LISTEN  0       50              *:mysql                        *:*
```

find: Search for files in a directory hierarchy	There are many options for the find utility: -name - find by name, -iname - like -name, but the match is case insensitive, -group and -user - find file that belongs to group or user, -type with f or d to find only files or directories.

```
# find /etc -name swift*
/etc/swift
/etc/swift/swift.conf
/etc/logrotate.d/openstack-swift
```

■ **Note**   Traditionally, network interfaces are enumerated as etho,1,2... In some modern Linux distributions, the default naming behavior can differ. The names of interfaces can be based on device topology, type, and firmware. For example, the ethernet interface on PCI slot 0 and port number 3 can be named enpos3.

How to Check the OpenStack Version

It is always good to know which version of OpenStack environment you are working with. Before the Liberty version, all projects except Swift had a version based on the year and month. Starting with Liberty, all components have a traditional version structure X.Y.Z., where X is always the same in one release.

Here is an example for Mitaka:

```
# keystone-manage --version
9.0.0
# nova-manage --version
13.0.0
```

And here is an example of the old-fashioned version convention used in OpenStack Kilo:

```
# keystone-manage --version
2015.1.0
# nova-manage --version
2015.1.0
```

Also you can find the version on the System Information tab in the Admin menu at the right corner of the page bottom. In Table 11-2, several of the latest OpenStack releases are listed.

Table 11-2. *OpenStack Releases*

Series	Releases	Initial Release Date
Juno	2014.2	October 16, 2014
Kilo	2015.1	April 30, 2015
Liberty	Nova 12.0; Keystone 8.0; Neutron 7.0; Swift 2.4	October 15, 2015
Mitaka	Nova 13.0; Keystone 9.0; Neutron 8.0; Swift 2.6	April 7, 2016
Newton	Nova 14.0; Keystone 10.0; Neutron 9.0; Swift 2.8	October 6, 2016 (planned)

Where to Find and How to Analyze Log Files

Usually in GNU/Linux systems log files are persistently stored in the /var/log directory. Here is an example of this directory's content from the OpenStack controller node:

```
# ls /var/log --group-directories-first -F
anaconda/    nova/          cron-20160524.gz    secure
audit/       openvswitch/   dmesg               secure-20160410.gz
ceilometer/  ppp/           dmesg.old           secure-20160417.gz
cinder/      puppet/        grubby              secure-20160426.gz
```

glance/	rabbitmq/	lastlog	secure-20160524.gz
glusterfs/	redis/	maillog	spooler
heat/	swift/	maillog-20160410.gz	spooler-20160410.gz
horizon/	tuned/	maillog-20160417.gz	spooler-20160417.gz
httpd/	boot.log	maillog-20160426.gz	spooler-20160426.gz
keystone/	btmp	maillog-20160524.gz	spooler-20160524.gz
libvirt/	btmp-20160524.gz	messages	tallylog
mariadb/	cron	messages-20160410.gz	wpa_supplicant.log
mongodb/	cron-20160410.gz	messages-20160417.gz	wtmp
nagios/	cron-20160417.gz	messages-20160426.gz	yum.log
neutron/	cron-20160426.gz	messages-20160524.gz	

As you see, parts of the content are directories and other parts are files. If one of the services has more than one log file, usually such logs are placed in their own subdirectory. For example, the /var/log/glance/ directory contains two files: api.log and registry.log. The first is the log for the glance-api service and the second is for the glance-registry. You can also see that part of the files' names have -YYYYMMDD at the end of the name and they are compressed by the Gzip tool. The utility logrotate renames, rotates, and compresses old logs. Instructions for logrotate are stored in the /etc/logrotate.d/ directory and /etc/ logrotate.conf contains the configuration file.

The logging subsystem of GNU/Linux is based on the Syslog protocol. In modern distributions the rsyslog daemon sorts and stores syslog messages in files under the /var/log directory. There are some well-known system-wide log files:

- messages: Most of the syslog messages are stored in this file.

- secure: All authentication-related and security messages are stored here.

- cron: The log file related to periodically executed jobs.

In general all syslog messages are categorized by a type and a priority. Priority can be from 0 (system is unusable) up to 7 (debug-level message). The type can be mail, cron, authpriv, etc. The RULES section of the configuration file /etc/rsyslog.conf contains directives that define where log messages are saved. The rules consist of the type, dot symbol, priority, and destination. Here is part of a default configuration file with rules:

```
#### RULES ####

# Log all kernel messages to the console.
# Logging much else clutters up the screen.
#kern.*                                     /dev/console

# Log anything (except mail) of level info or higher.
# Don't log private authentication messages!
*.info;mail.none;authpriv.none;cron.none   /var/log/messages

# The authpriv file has restricted access.
authpriv.*                                  /var/log/secure

# Log all the mail messages in one place.
mail.*                                      -/var/log/maillog
```

```
# Log cron stuff
cron.*                                              /var/log/cron

# Everybody gets emergency messages
*.emerg                                             :omusrmsg:*

# Save news errors of level crit and higher in a special file.
uucp,news.crit                                      /var/log/spooler
```

All log entries in log files are managed by the rsyslog and stored in a standard format:

```
Jun  5 13:26:32 test-host nova-compute: 2016-06-01 13:26:32.020 2156 INFO nova.compute.
manager [req-06e94777-d6cb-4093-bfc4-d48ad918e4e8 - - - - -] [instance: 653 ced0c-d50b-413a-
bc09-c3103b149aaf] VM Resumed (Lifecycle Event)
```

The first part of the message is the timestamp, then the name of the host, then the name of the program that sends the message, and the last part is a message.

For real-time log monitoring, a command `tail -f /var/log/logfilename` can be very useful. This command prints the last ten lines of a log and continues to output new lines as they are added to this log file.

Back Up the Database Used by an OpenStack Instance

In most common cases, all OpenStack databases are on one MariaDB server. It is very easy to create a database back up then:

```
# mysqldump --opt --all-databases > /tmp/all-openstack.sql
```

■ **Tip**   The `mysqldump` command will ask you for a password. You can avoid this by adding the –p option with the password, for example: –p apress.

If you only want to back up a single database, you can run:

```
# mysqldump --opt neutron > /tmp/neutron.sql
```

To list all database names you can use `mysql` CLI:

```
# mysql
Welcome to the MariaDB monitor.  Commands end with ; or \g.
Your MariaDB connection id is 42
Server version: 5.5.40-MariaDB-wsrep MariaDB Server, wsrep_25.11.r4026

Copyright (c) 2000, 2015, Oracle, MariaDB Corporation Ab and others.

Type 'help;' or '\h' for help. Type '\c' to clear the current input statement.
```

```
MariaDB [(none)]> show databases;
+--------------------+
| Database           |
+--------------------+
| information_schema |
| cinder             |
| glance             |
| heat               |
| keystone           |
| mysql              |
| neutron            |
| nova               |
| performance_schema |
| test               |
+--------------------+
10 rows in set (0.00 sec)
```

Analyze Host/Guest OS and Instance Status

The easiest way to check the status of OpenStack components like hosts and instances is by using the Horizon web client. The most general view of the cloud is found on the Overview tab on the System menu. If you are searching for the information about the Hypervisors you need to use the third tab named Hypervisors. Both tabs are shown, respectively, in Figures 11-1 and 11-2.

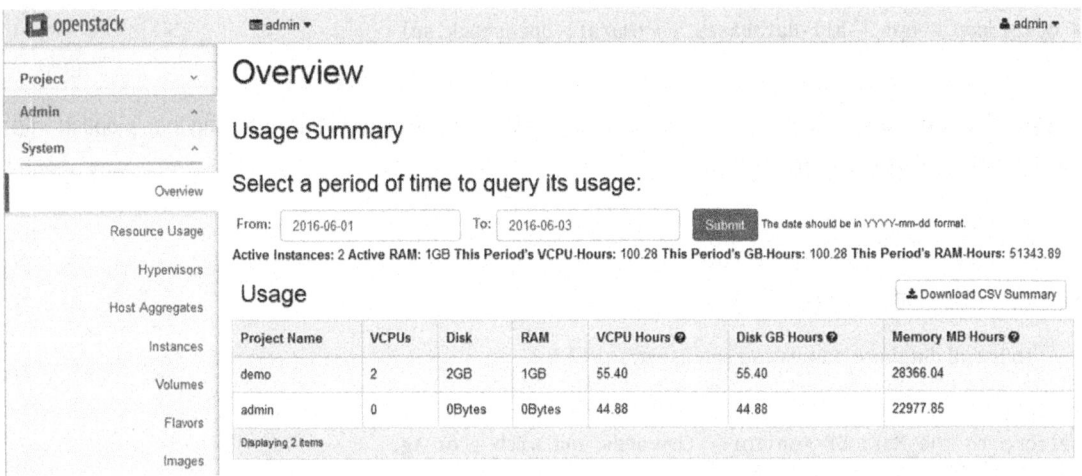

Figure 11-1. *OpenStack usage summary*

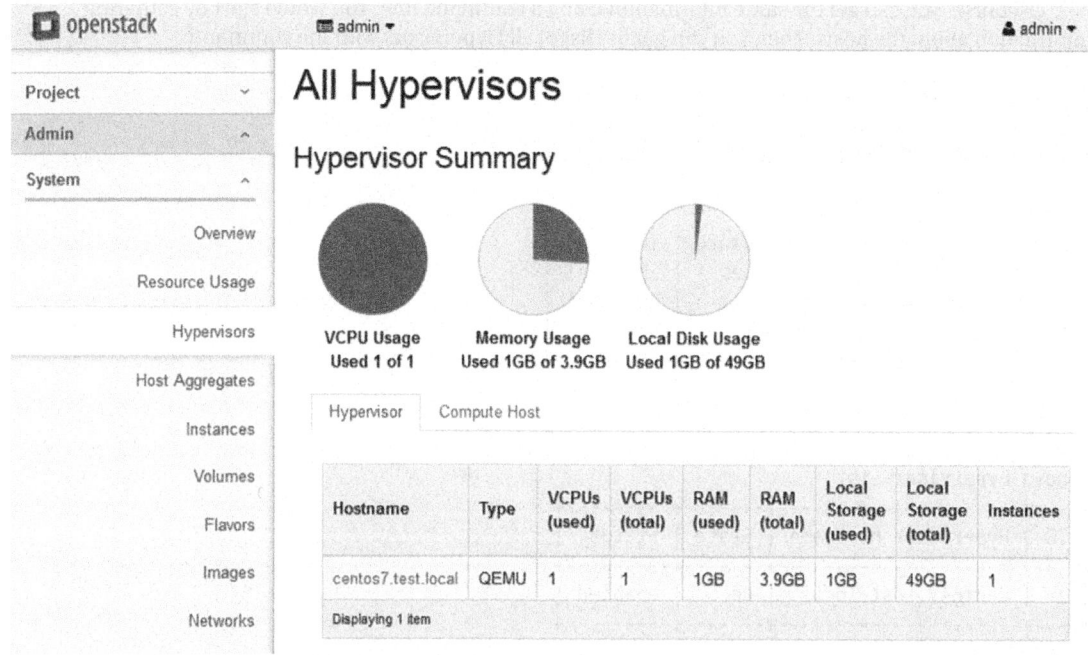

Figure 11-2. *Hypervisor usage summary*

Usually users can find their instances in the Project menu. Almost all instances can be viewed by the administrator on the Instances tab of the System menu. Figure 11-3 shows an example of the Instances page.

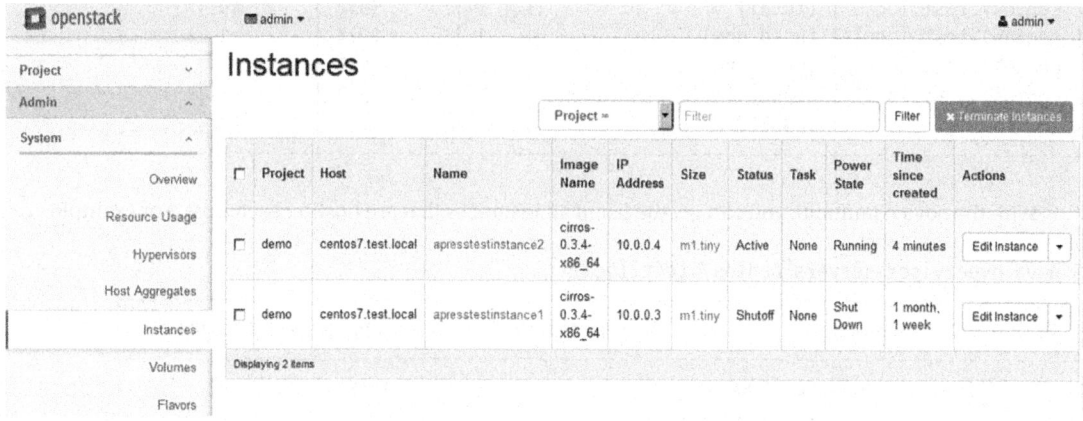

Figure 11-3. *All instances summary.*

Of course, you can get the same information using a command line. You would start by gathering information about the hosts. Then you can get the list of all Hypervisors with the command:

```
$ openstack host list
+--------------------+-------------+----------+
| Host Name          | Service     | Zone     |
+--------------------+-------------+----------+
| centos7.test.local | cert        | internal |
| centos7.test.local | consoleauth | internal |
| centos7.test.local | scheduler   | internal |
| centos7.test.local | conductor   | internal |
| centos7.test.local | compute     | nova     |
+--------------------+-------------+----------+
```

or

```
$ nova hypervisor-list
+----+---------------------+-------+---------+
| ID | Hypervisor hostname | State | Status  |
+----+---------------------+-------+---------+
| 1  | centos7.test.local  | up    | enabled |
+----+---------------------+-------+---------+
```

If you want to get more information about specific host, the openstack host show command may help:

```
$ openstack host show centos7.test.local
+--------------------+------------------------+-----+-----------+---------+
| Host               | Project                | CPU | Memory MB | Disk GB |
+--------------------+------------------------+-----+-----------+---------+
| centos7.test.local | (total)                | 1   | 3952      | 49      |
| centos7.test.local | (used_now)             | 1   | 1024      | 1       |
| centos7.test.local | (used_max)             | 1   | 512       | 1       |
| centos7.test.local | ae8d3e3f5cff4a959f1ae1c| 1   | 512       | 1       |
|                    | fe9e80d6d              |     |           |         |
+--------------------+------------------------+-----+-----------+---------+
```

With the nova command, you can get the list of all instances that are hosting each host. For example:

```
$ nova hypervisor-servers centos7.test.local
+--------------+--------------------+-----------------+-------------------------+
| ID           | Name               | Hypervisor ID   | Hypervisor Hostname     |
+--------------+--------------------+-----------------+-------------------------+
| c0b91a3c-... | instance-00000001  | 1               | centos7.test.local      |
+--------------+--------------------+-----------------+-------------------------+
```

For the same purpose you can search through the Nova database:

```
$ nova-manage vm list | grep active
test-vm    centos7.test.local m1.tiny    active       2016-06-06 10:05:59+00:00
039daa2e-6b3e-4e31-b1da-ab3e6feb8b30
ae8d3e3f5cff4a959f1ae1cfe9e80d6d    a1bec1d6dfcd4e3bb61c522bb319c266 None          0
```

138

Also, to print the list of virtual machines, you could use the openstack command:

```
$ openstack server list
+-------------------------------+---------+--------+---------------------+
| ID                            | Name    | Status | Networks            |
+-------------------------------+---------+--------+---------------------+
| c0b91a3c-                     | test-vm | ACTIVE | public=172.24.4.227 |
| dfc1-4187-9577-95737bff95ac   |         |        |                     |
+-------------------------------+---------+--------+---------------------+
```

If you want to get all information regarding a specific instance, use the command:

```
$ openstack server show test-vm
+---------------------------------+-------------------------------------------+
| Field                           | Value                                     |
+---------------------------------+-------------------------------------------+
| OS-DCF:diskConfig               | MANUAL                                    |
| OS-EXT-AZ:availability_zone     | nova                                      |
| OS-EXT-SRV-ATTR:host            | centos7.test.local                        |
| OS-EXT-SRV-ATTR:hypervisor_hostname | centos7.test.local                    |
| OS-EXT-SRV-ATTR:instance_name   | instance-00000001                         |
| OS-EXT-STS:power_state          | 1                                         |
| OS-EXT-STS:task_state           | None                                      |
| OS-EXT-STS:vm_state             | active                                    |
| OS-SRV-USG:launched_at          | 2016-06-13T10:05:59.000000                |
| OS-SRV-USG:terminated_at        | None                                      |
| addresses                       | public=172.24.4.227                       |
| config_drive                    |                                           |
| created                         | 2016-06-13T10:05:45Z                      |
| flavor                          | m1.tiny (1)                               |
| hostId                          | 5e43e36184f81f18ea7d89b122091b6a78194..   |
| id                              | c0b91a3c-dfc1-4187-9577-95737bff95ac      |
| image                           | cirros-raw (039daa2e-6b3e-4e31-b1da-a..)  |
| key_name                        | None                                      |
| name                            | test-vm                                   |
| os-extended-volumes:volumes_attached | []                                   |
| progress                        | 0                                         |
| project_id                      | ae8d3e3f5cff4a959f1ae1cfe9e80d6d          |
| properties                      |                                           |
| security_groups                 | [{u'name': u'default'}]                   |
| status                          | ACTIVE                                    |
| updated                         | 2016-06-14T10:06:00Z                      |
| user_id                         | a1bec1d6dfcd4e3bb61c522bb319c266          |
+---------------------------------+-------------------------------------------+
```

Analyze Messaging Servers

As mentioned earlier, a messaging server is used by almost all OpenStack services. Nowadays the most common messaging server for OpenStack is RabbitMQ. Alternatives for RabbitMQ are Qpid and ZeroMQ. For transmitting information between OpenStack services, these servers use AMQP (Advanced Message Queuing Protocol). I will briefly describe the functions of RabbitMQ here.

For checking the RabbitMQ status, you can use the command:

```
# rabbitmqctl status
Status of node rabbit@centos7 ...
[{pid,972},
 {running_applications,[{rabbit,"RabbitMQ","3.3.5"},
                        {os_mon,"CPO  CXC 138 46","2.2.14"},
                        {xmerl,"XML parser","1.3.6"},
                        {mnesia,"MNESIA  CXC 138 12","4.11"},
                        {sasl,"SASL  CXC 138 11","2.3.4"},
                        {stdlib,"ERTS  CXC 138 10","1.19.4"},
                        {kernel,"ERTS  CXC 138 10","2.16.4"}]},
 {os,{unix,linux}},
 {erlang_version,"Erlang R16B03-1 (erts-5.10.4) [source] [64-bit] [async-threads:30] [hipe]
[kernel-poll:true]\n"},
 {memory,[{total,211601864},
          {connection_procs,2653544},
          {queue_procs,1273056},
          {plugins,0},
          {other_proc,13363136},
          {mnesia,363184},
          {mgmt_db,0},
          {msg_index,86264},
          {other_ets,916560},
          {binary,170846960},
          {code,16700042},
          {atom,602729},
          {other_system,4796389}]},
 {alarms,[]},
 {listeners,[{clustering,25672,"::"},{amqp,5672,"::"}]},
 {vm_memory_high_watermark,0.4},
 {vm_memory_limit,1657934643},
 {disk_free_limit,50000000},
 {disk_free,50450022400},
 {file_descriptors,[{total_limit,16284},
                    {total_used,68},
                    {sockets_limit,14653},
                    {sockets_used,66}]},
 {processes,[{limit,1048576},{used,794}]},
 {run_queue,0},
 {uptime,9767}]
...done.
```

To list all users, use would use the command:

```
# rabbitmqctl list_users
Listing users ...
guest    [administrator]
...done.
```

As you see in this demo environment, there is only one user guest with administrator rights. All OpenStack services use that particular user for sending and receiving messages. To check whether you can find RabbitMQ settings in the services config files:

```
rpc_backend = rabbit
rabbit_host = 10.0.2.15
rabbit_port = 5672
rabbit_userid = guest
rabbit_password = guest
```

This is a common part of most configuration files, like /etc/cinder/cinder.conf, /etc/nova/nova. conf, /etc/neutron/neutron.conf, etc. For managing and monitoring the RabbitMQ server, you can activate the graphical web console:

```
# /usr/lib/rabbitmq/bin/rabbitmq-plugins enable rabbitmq_management
The following plugins have been enabled:
  mochiweb
  webmachine
  rabbitmq_web_dispatch
  amqp_client
  rabbitmq_management_agent
  rabbitmq_management
Plugin configuration has changed. Restart RabbitMQ for changes to take effect.
# systemctl restart rabbitmq-server.service
```

Then open the web browser and point it to http://name-of-server:15672 on the RabbitMQ server host. A screenshot of the console is shown in Figure 11-4. As you saw before, the login name is guest and the password is also guest by default.

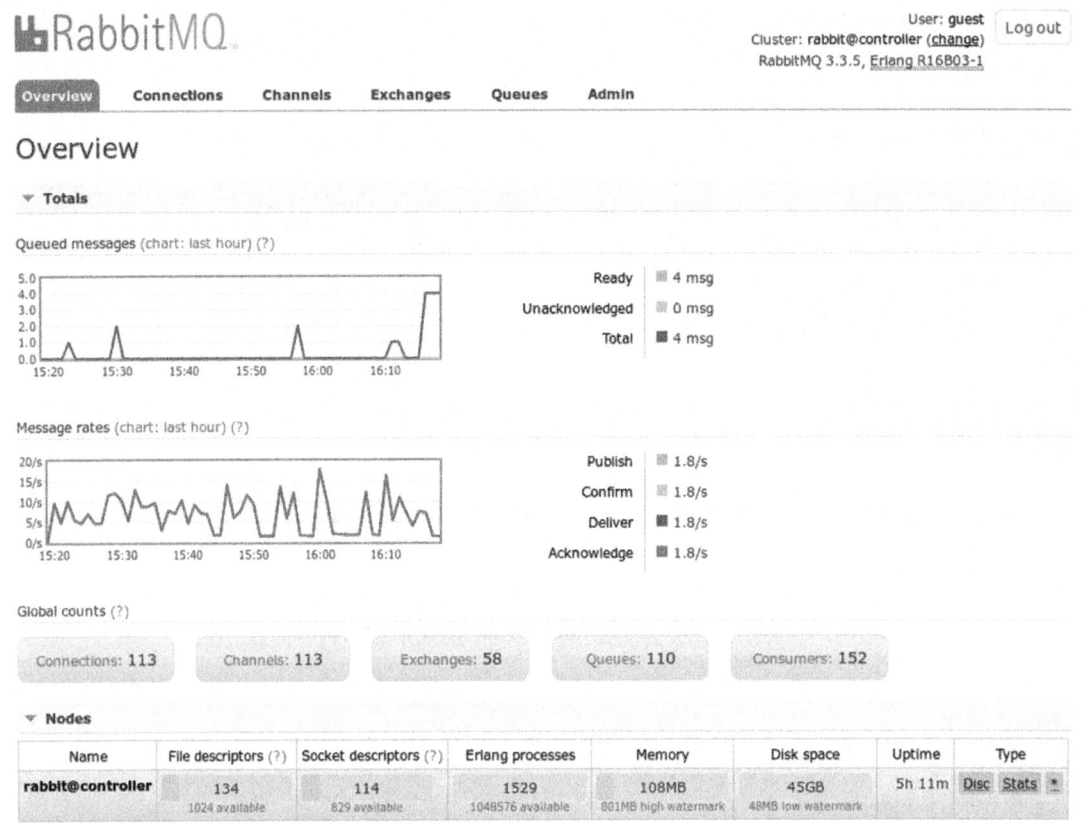

Figure 11-4. *RabbitMQ web plug-in*

Analyze Network Status

First, you can check the list of processes that build up Neutron service:

```
# pgrep -l neutron
971 neutron-meterin
984 neutron-server
988 neutron-metadat
1731 neutron-l3-agen
1732 neutron-openvsw
1734 neutron-dhcp-ag
1825 neutron-rootwra
2164 neutron-ns-meta
```

The exact list of processes can be different and depends on the host configuration. As you know, Neutron works through a lot of agents or plug-ins. In Horizon, the status of these plug-ins is listed on the Network Agents tab of the System Information view, as shown in Figure 11-5.

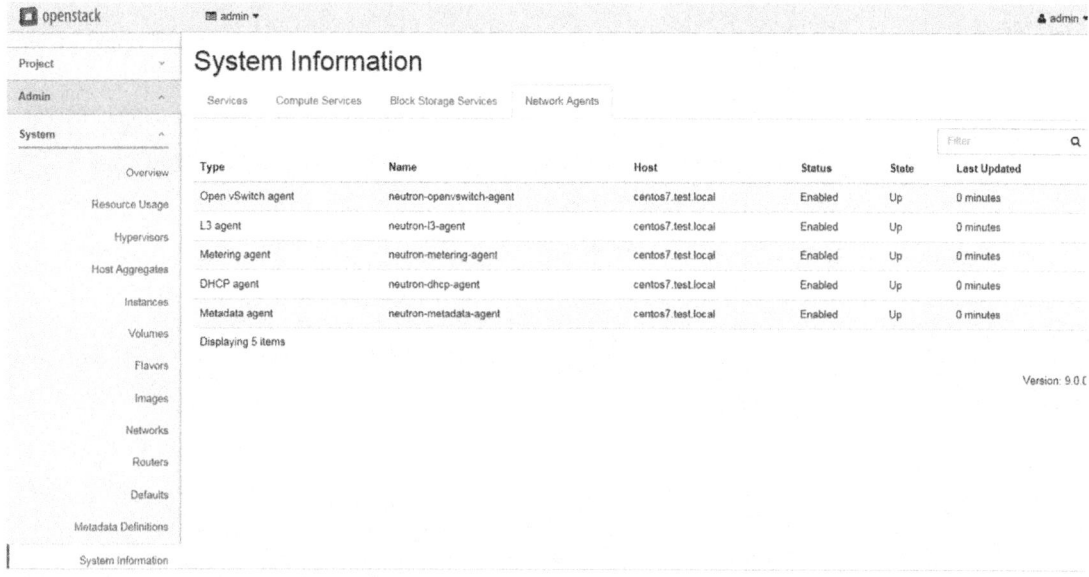

Figure 11-5. *OpenStack Neutron agents list*

At the command line, the same information can be retrieved by using the neutron command:

```
$ neutron agent-list
+------+--------------+--------+----------------+-----+--------------+----------------------+
| id   |agent_type    |host    |availability_zone|alive|admin_state_up |binary                |
+------+--------------+--------+----------------+-----+--------------+----------------------+
| 384..|Open vSwitch  |centos7 |                | :-) | True         |neutron-openvswitch-  |
|      | agent        |        |                |     |              | agent                |
| 665..|L3 agent      |centos7 |nova            | :-) | True         |neutron-l3-agent      |
| 7c4..|Metering agent|centos7 |                | :-) | True         |neutron-metering-agent|
| 82b..|DHCP agent    |centos7 |nova            | :-) | True         |neutron-dhcp-agent    |
| 9b8..|Metadata agent|centos7 |                | :-) | True         |neutron-metadata-agent|
+------+--------------+--------+----------------+-----+--------------+----------------------+
```

Neutron has its own log file for each agent:

```
ls /var/log/neutron/
dhcp-agent.log   metadata-agent.log   neutron-ns-metadata-proxy-621d3f89-4db4-4a4d-b6b1-
724ed5de8575.log  ovs-cleanup.log
l3-agent.log     metering-agent.log   openvswitch-agent.log
```

Let's look at the virtual networks part of OpenStack configuration. And again, you can explore them in Horizon, as shown at Figure 11-6, or you can use a command line:

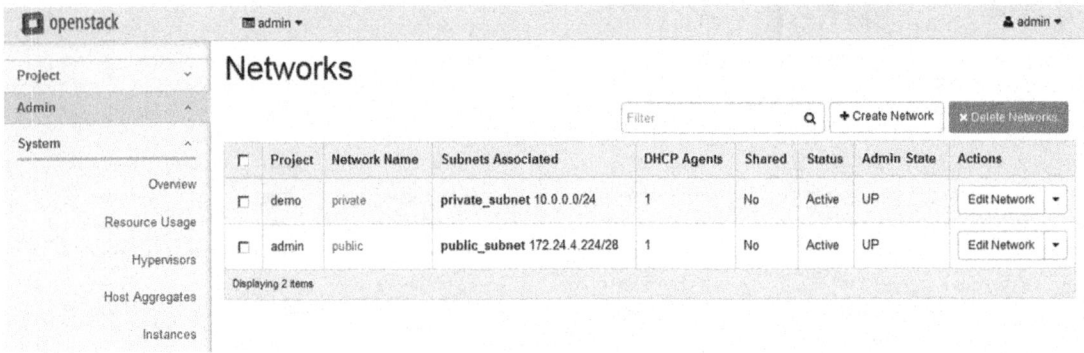

Figure 11-6. *OpenStack networks page*

```
$ openstack network list
+--------------------------------------+---------+--------------------------------------+
| ID                                   | Name    | Subnets                              |
+--------------------------------------+---------+--------------------------------------+
| e9021784-0309-4b5c-95de-6227bf18b5b8 | private | 0d9241d8-8a70-48f1-92d7-90a580e7823b |
| c9ac2cd3-f4fd-4fab-b24a-10145c40bd52 | public  | ffc30ff0-75a0-4a27-bfe5-4d5511d58e0e |
+--------------------------------------+---------+--------------------------------------+
```

For getting more information on a specific network, you can click a network name. The relevant screenshot to show this is Figure 11-7. If you prefer CLI, you would use the command:

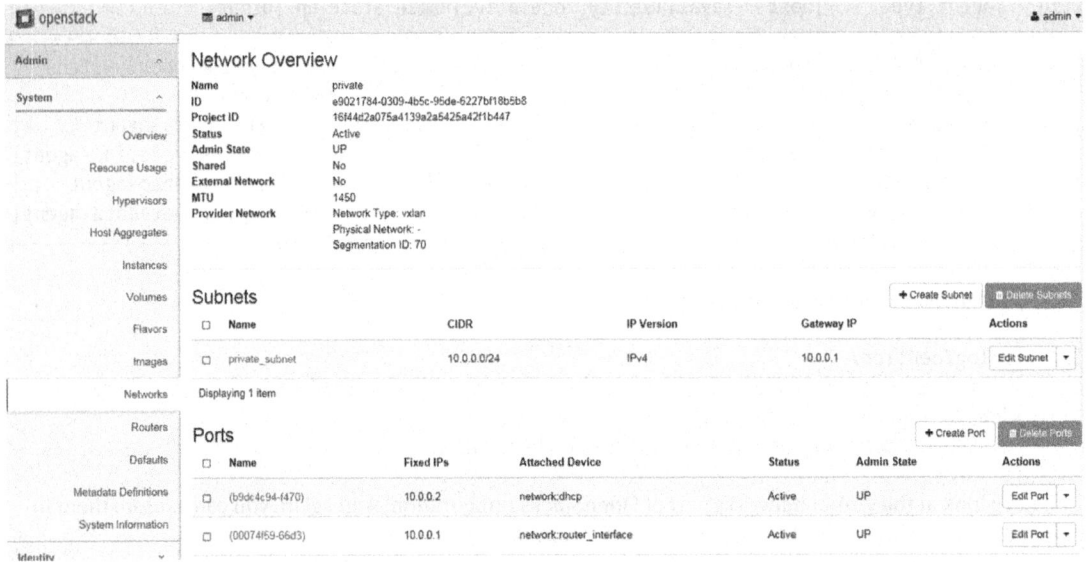

Figure 11-7. *Network overview details*

```
$ openstack network show private
+-----------------------------+--------------------------------------+
| Field                       | Value                                |
+-----------------------------+--------------------------------------+
| admin_state_up              | UP                                   |
| availability_zone_hints     |                                      |
| availability_zones          | nova                                 |
| created_at                  | 2016-06-13T09:37:41                  |
| description                 |                                      |
| id                          | e9021784-0309-4b5c-95de-6227bf18b5b8 |
| ipv4_address_scope          | None                                 |
| ipv6_address_scope          | None                                 |
| mtu                         | 1450                                 |
| name                        | private                              |
| project_id                  | 16f44d2a075a4139a2a5425a42f1b447     |
| provider:network_type       | vxlan                                |
| provider:physical_network   | None                                 |
| provider:segmentation_id    | 70                                   |
| router_external             | Internal                             |
| shared                      | False                                |
| status                      | ACTIVE                               |
| subnets                     | 0d9241d8-8a70-48f1-92d7-90a580e7823b |
| tags                        | []                                   |
| updated_at                  | 2016-06-14T09:37:41                  |
+-----------------------------+--------------------------------------+
```

In the previous command you could use the network name, in this case private, or the network ID. Figure 11-8 provides the list of virtual routers.

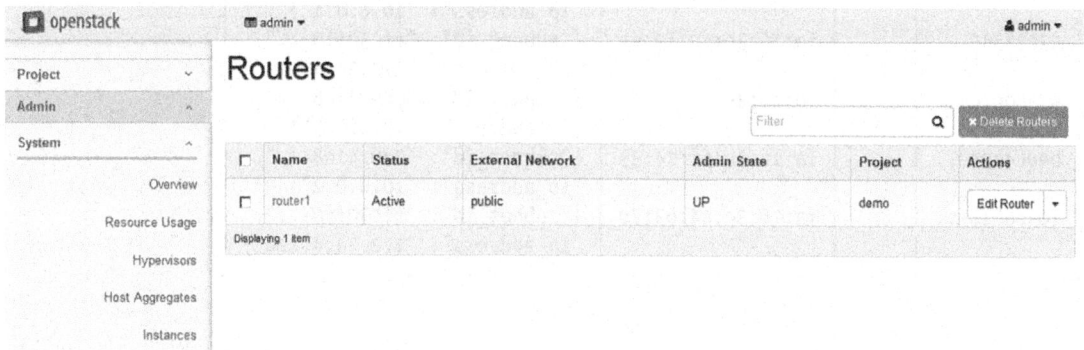

Figure 11-8. *OpenStack routers*

The corresponding CLI command to find the list of routers is:

```
$ openstack router list
+-------------+---------+--------+-------+-------------+-------+---------+
| ID          | Name    | Status | State | Distributed | HA    | Project |
+-------------+---------+--------+-------+-------------+-------+---------+
| 621d3f89-.. | router1 | ACTIVE | UP    | False       | False | 16f44.. |
+-------------+---------+--------+-------+-------------+-------+---------+
```

```
$ openstack router show router1
+-------------------------+-------------------------------------------------------------+
| Field                   | Value                                                       |
+-------------------------+-------------------------------------------------------------+
| admin_state_up          | UP                                                          |
| availability_zone_hints |                                                             |
| availability_zones      | nova                                                        |
| description             |                                                             |
| distributed             | False                                                       |
| external_gateway_info   | {"network_id": "c9ac2cd3-f4fd-4fab-b24a-10145c40bd52",      |
|                         | "enable_snat": true, "external_fixed_ips":                  |
|                         | [{"subnet_id": "ffc30ff0-75a0-4a27-bfe5-4d5511d58e0e",      |
|                         | "ip_address": "172.24.4.226"}]}                             |
| ha                      | False                                                       |
| id                      | 621d3f89-4db4-4a4d-b6b1-724ed5de8575                        |
| name                    | router1                                                     |
| routes                  | []                                                          |
| status                  | ACTIVE                                                      |
| tenant_id               | 16f44d2a075a4139a2a5425a42f1b447                            |
+-------------------------+-------------------------------------------------------------+
```

For enumerating the list of ports, use the neutron command. Using the command openstack port show would show the details of the port by port ID:

```
$ neutron port-list
+-------------+------+-------------------+------------------------------+
| id          | name | mac_address       | fixed_ips                    |
+-------------+------+-------------------+------------------------------+
| 00074f59-.. |      | fa:16:3e:cb:16:0d | {"subnet_id": "0d9241d8-..", |
|             |      |                   | "ip_address": "10.0.0.1"}    |
| 52126845-.. |      | fa:16:3e:ce:f9:ea | {"subnet_id": "ffc30ff0-..", |
|             |      |                   | "ip_address": "172.24.4.227"}|
| 97380c2c-.. |      | fa:16:3e:4d:35:ff | {"subnet_id": "0d9241d8-..", |
|             |      |                   | "ip_address": "10.0.0.3"}    |
| b9dc4c94-.. |      | fa:16:3e:6f:14:33 | {"subnet_id": "0d9241d8-..", |
|             |      |                   | "ip_address": "10.0.0.2"}    |
| f03eec13-.. |      | fa:16:3e:44:63:70 | {"subnet_id": "ffc30ff0-..", |
|             |      |                   | "ip_address": "172.24.4.226"}|
+-------------+------+-------------------+------------------------------+
```

```
$ openstack port show 00074f59-66d3-48ec-9585-9e88d24b5ac1
+---------------------+---------------------------------------------+
| Field               | Value                                       |
+---------------------+---------------------------------------------+
| admin_state_up      | UP                                          |
| allowed_address_pairs |                                           |
| binding_host_id     | centos7.test.local                          |
| binding_profile     |                                             |
| binding_vif_details | ovs_hybrid_plug='True', port_filter='True'  |
| binding_vif_type    | ovs                                         |
| binding_vnic_type   | normal                                      |
| created_at          | 2016-06-12T09:37:52                         |
| description         |                                             |
| device_id           | 621d3f89-4db4-4a4d-b6b1-724ed5de8575        |
| device_owner        | network:router_interface                    |
| dns_name            | None                                        |
| extra_dhcp_opts     |                                             |
| fixed_ips           | ip_address='10.0.0.1', subnet_id='0d9241..' |
| id                  | 00074f59-66d3-48ec-9585-9e88d24b5ac1        |
| mac_address         | fa:16:3e:cb:16:0d                           |
| name                |                                             |
| network_id          | e9021784-0309-4b5c-95de-6227bf18b5b8        |
| project_id          | 16f44d2a075a4139a2a5425a42f1b447            |
| security_groups     |                                             |
| status              | ACTIVE                                      |
| updated_at          | 2016-06-13T09:22:58                         |
+---------------------+---------------------------------------------+
```

■ **Note** For real-world network problems and troubleshooting, the utility plotnetcfg can be useful. It creates a network configuration diagram that can be visualized with the help of the dot utility. For more information, check the project web site (https://github.com/jbenc/plotnetcfg).

For a project-level network overview, the Network Topology tab is probably the best place to look. Figure 11-9 shows an example of the information provided on that page.

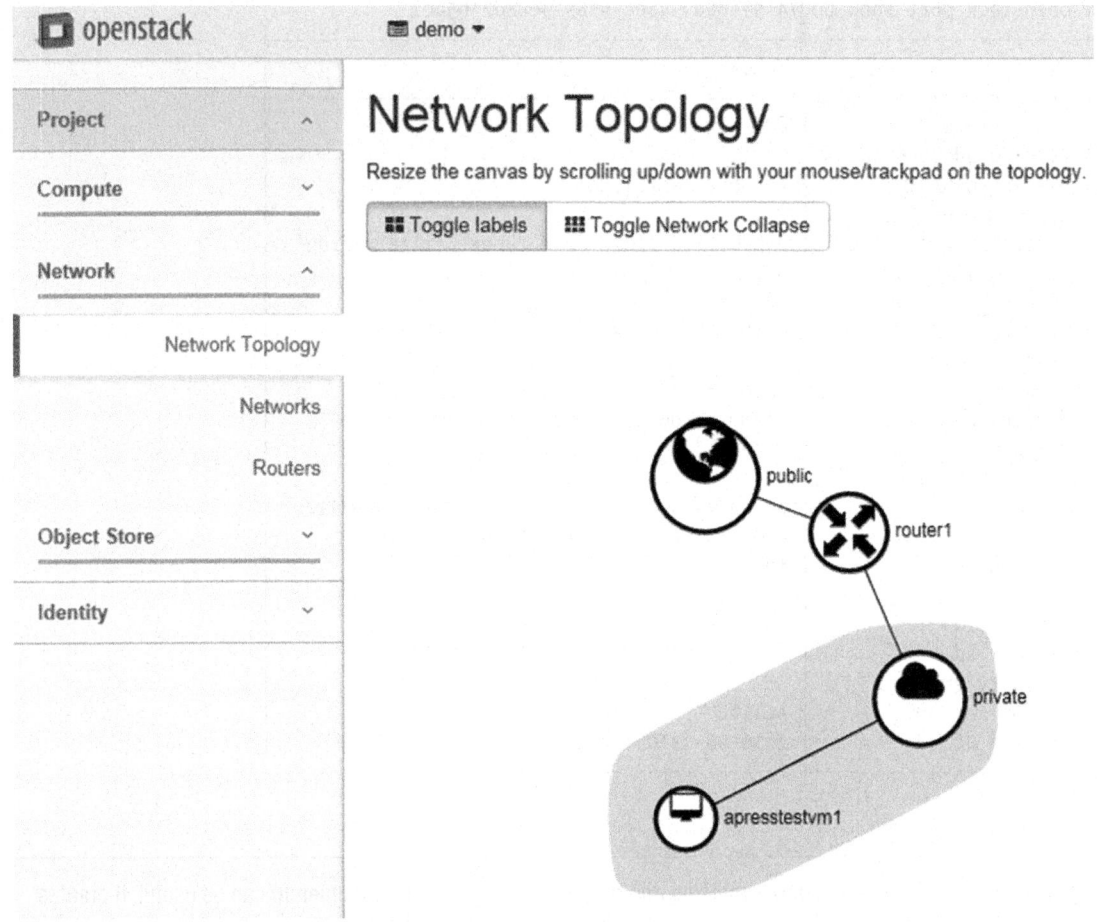

Figure 11-9. *Project Network Topology tab*

Digest the OpenStack Environment

As mentioned earlier, all OpenStack services are deployed as GNU/Linux daemons. Part of these services is represented as a single daemon and part of them consists of two or more services. The best place to start looking for the services status is on the System Information tab on the Admin menu, as shown in Figure 11-10.

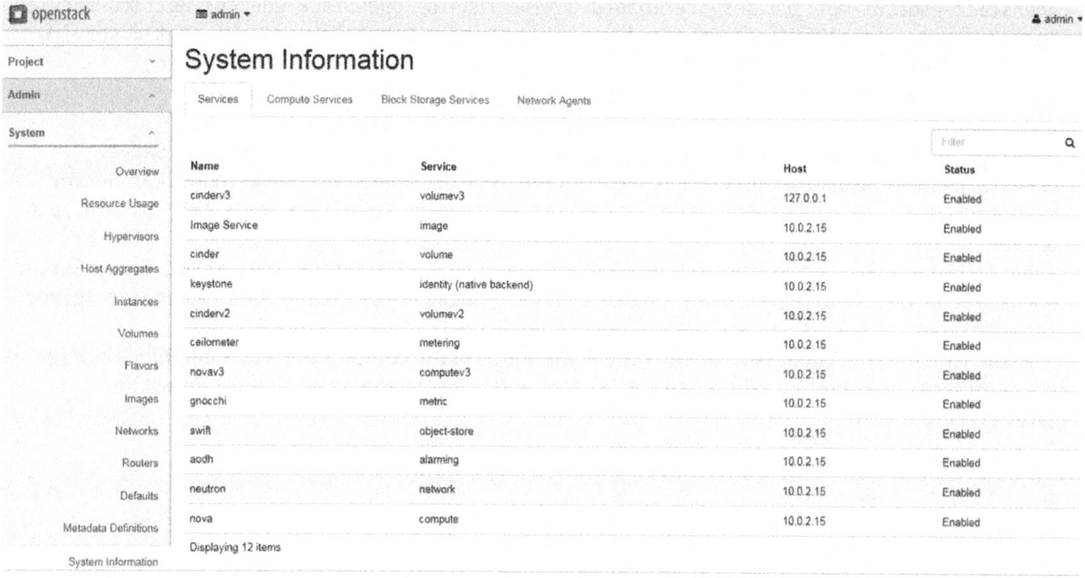
openstack
admin
admin
Project
Admin
System
Overview
Resource Usage
Hypervisors
Host Aggregates
Instances
Volumes
Flavors
Images
Networks
Routers
Defaults
Metadata Definitions
System Information
System Information
Services
Compute Services
Block Storage Services
Network Agents
Filter
Name
Service
Host
Status
cinderv3
volumev3
127.0.0.1
Enabled
Image Service
image
10.0.2.15
Enabled
cinder
volume
10.0.2.15
Enabled
keystone
identity (native backend)
10.0.2.15
Enabled
cinderv2
volumev2
10.0.2.15
Enabled
ceilometer
metering
10.0.2.15
Enabled
novav3
computev3
10.0.2.15
Enabled
gnocchi
metric
10.0.2.15
Enabled
swift
object-store
10.0.2.15
Enabled
aodh
alarming
10.0.2.15
Enabled
neutron
network
10.0.2.15
Enabled
nova
compute
10.0.2.15
Enabled
Displaying 12 items

Figure 11-10. *OpenStack services information*

As you can see, all of the services' information with their status is shown. To do the same thing with a command line for this demo environment based on CentOS 7, you can use the systemctl command:

```
[root@centos7 ~]# systemctl | grep openstack
  openstack-aodh-evaluator.service loaded active running OpenStack Alarm evaluator service
  openstack-aodh-listener.service  loaded active running OpenStack Alarm listener service
  openstack-aodh-notifier.service  loaded active running OpenStack Alarm notifier service
  openstack-ceilometer-central.service loaded active running OpenStack ceilometer central
  agent
  openstack-ceilometer-collector.service loaded active running OpenStack ceilometer
  collection service
  openstack-ceilometer-compute.service loaded active running OpenStack ceilometer compute
  agent
  openstack-ceilometer-notification.service loaded active running OpenStack ceilometer
  notification agent
  openstack-cinder-api.service loaded active running OpenStack Cinder API Server
  openstack-cinder-backup.service loaded active running OpenStack Cinder Backup Server
  openstack-cinder-scheduler.service loaded active running OpenStack Cinder Scheduler Server
  openstack-cinder-volume.service loaded active running OpenStack Cinder Volume Server
  openstack-glance-api.service loaded active running OpenStack Image Service (code-named
  Glance) API server
  openstack-glance-registry.service loaded active running OpenStack Image Service (code-
  named Glance) Registry server
```

```
openstack-gnocchi-metricd.service loaded active running OpenStack gnocchi metricd service
openstack-gnocchi-statsd.service loaded active running OpenStack gnocchi statsd service
openstack-losetup.service loaded active exited Setup cinder-volume loop device
openstack-nova-api.service loaded active running OpenStack Nova API Server
openstack-nova-cert.service loaded active running OpenStack Nova Cert Server
openstack-nova-compute.service loaded active running OpenStack Nova Compute Server
openstack-nova-conductor.service loaded active running OpenStack Nova Conductor Server
openstack-nova-consoleauth.service loaded active running OpenStack Nova VNC console auth
Server
openstack-nova-novncproxy.service loaded active running OpenStack Nova NoVNC Proxy Server
openstack-nova-scheduler.service loaded active running   OpenStack Nova Scheduler Server
```

In the Horizon web client you can also check the status of the computer services and block storage services on separate subtabs on the System Information tab. Respective examples are shown on Figures 11-11 and 11-12.

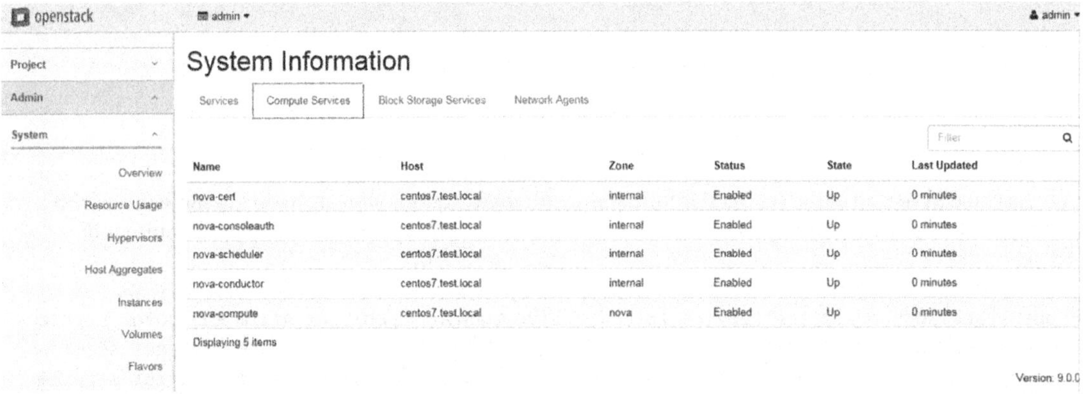

Figure 11-11. *OpenStack compute services*

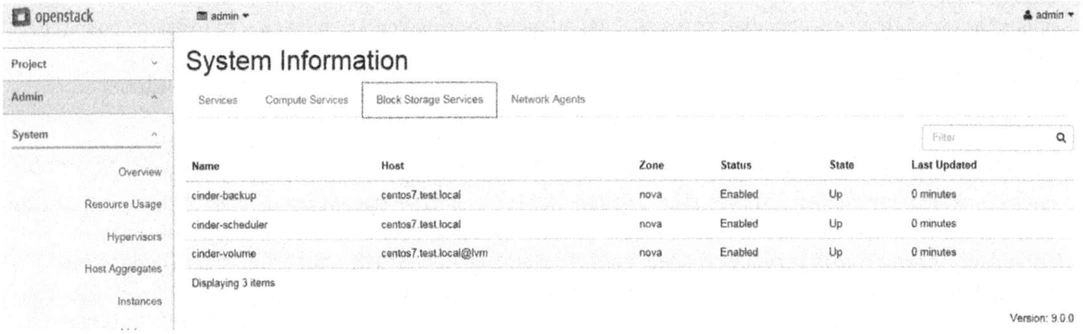

Figure 11-12. *OpenStack block storage services*

Review Questions

1. How would you search for the Identity Service configuration files in a configuration directory hierarchy?

   A. find /etc -name keystone*

   B. find /etc --name heat*

   C. find /var --name keystone*

   D. find / --name heat*

2. Where would you find all of the messages from Cinder service (choose all applicable)?

   A. /var/log/messages

   B. /var/log/cinder/api.log

   C. /var/log/cinder/scheduler.log

   D. /var/log/cinder/backup.log

3. How would you back up all the OpenStack databases?

   A. mysqlbackup --opt --all-db > /tmp/all-openstack.sql

   B. mysqlbackup --opt --all-databases > /tmp/all-openstack.sql

   C. mysqldump --opt --all-db > /tmp/all-openstack.sql

   D. mysqldump --opt --all-databases > /tmp/all-openstack.sql

4. How would you enumerate all the computer hosts (choose all applicable)?

   A. openstack hypervisor list

   B. openstack host list

   C. nova host-enumerate

   D. nova hypervisor-list

5. How would you get a list of all virtual machines?

   A. openstack vm list

   B. openstack server list

   C. openstack host list

   D. openstack instance list

6. How would you check the status of the RabbitMQ messaging server?

   A. rabbitmqctl stat

   B. rabbitmq status

   C. rabbitmqctl status

   D. rabbitmq state

7. How would you check the status of the Neutron agents?

    A. neutron agent-list

    B. neutron plugin-list

    C. openstack agent list

    D. openstack network list

8. How would you get the details of a given router?

    A. neutron router list router

    B. neutron router show router

    C. openstack router list router

    D. openstack router show router

Answers to Review Questions

1. A

2. A, B, C, D

3. D

4. B, D

5. B

6. C

7. A

8. D

CHAPTER 12

■ ■ ■

Conclusion

If you've read this far and understand what was presented, you are close to being ready to take the Certified OpenStack Administrator exam. The next step should be studying the official OpenStack documentation at `http://docs.openstack.org`, which includes the following:

- Install Guides for three GNU/Linux distributions: SUSE Linux, CentOS/RHEL, and Ubuntu

- Administrator Guide

- Operations Guide

- Security Guide

- Virtual Machine Image Guide

- Architecture Design Guide

- Networking Guide

- Configuration Reference

- API Complete References

In the Linux world, there's the "Linux From Scratch (LFS)" project. It is the guide on how to build your own GNU/Linux installation from nothing to a working instance. In general it is not suitable for production but used for learning purposes only. Installation guides at the OpenStack web site are like "OpenStack From Scratch." These materials are very useful for learning. You will build your own cloud step by step, configuration file by configuration file. It is highly recommended to follow these guides at least once without any automation tools.

The next valuable source of information is mailing lists. Check out `https://wiki.openstack.org/wiki/Mailing_Lists`. This archive engine for mailing lists has an internal search ability, so before asking a question, look there at previous conversations. Most of the interesting lists are called Operators, for cloud operator's discussions, and Announcements, for project's announcements.

OpenStack project has its own blog and RSS feed named "Planet OpenStack" at `http://planet.openstack.org/`. Planet OpenStack is a collection of thoughts from the developers and other key players of the OpenStack projects. This project consists of more than 200 blogs.

Also I can recommend the online magazine by the OpenStack marketing team, available at `http://superuser.openstack.org`. The OpenStack Foundation created the *Superuser* publication to facilitate knowledge sharing and collaborative problem solving among individuals who are running OpenStack clouds and the cloud-based infrastructure, across all industries.

More documentation is produced by specific OpenStack vendors, which is vendor specific and describes a particular distribution.

© Andrey Markelov 2016
A. Markelov, *Certified OpenStack Administrator Study Guide*, DOI 10.1007/978-1-4842-2125-9_12

Documentation for Mirantis OpenStack has lots of guides at https://docs.mirantis.com/. They also have the brilliant "OpenStack: Unlocked" newsletter mailing list with tons of information. You can subscribe to it at https://content.mirantis.com/openstack-unlocked-newsletter-landing-page.html. Mirantis also regularly runs webinars. Its landing page is https://www.mirantis.com/openstack-webinars/ including recordings of previous webinars.

Full Red Hat documentation, including knowledge base and reference architectures, is available only for customers, but base product documentation is open and can be downloaded at https://access.redhat.com/documentation/en/. Choose Red Hat OpenStack Platform from the landing page and you can access documentation online or download it in EPUB or PDF format.

For your convenience, I have included lists of OpenStack supporting services and the network ports used by OpenStack, respectively, in Tables 12-1 and 12-2.

Table 12-1. *OpenStack and Supporting Services*

Service	Description
rabbitmq-server	RabbitMQ: AMQP message broker.
mariadb	MariaDB: One of most popular database servers. Used by most of OpenStack services.
glance-api	Glance API: Gives access to Image Service REST API.
glance-registry	Glance Registry: Stores the metadata about images.
cinder-api	Cinder API: Gives access to Block storage service REST API.
cinder-scheduler	Cinder Scheduler: Selects the optimal storage provider node on which to create the volume.
cinder-volume	Cinder Volume: Responds to read and write requests sent to the Block Storage service to maintain a state. It can interact with a variety of storage providers through a driver architecture.
cinder-backup	Cinder Backup: Provides backup volumes of any type to a backup storage provider.
nova-api	Nova API: Accepts and responds to end-user compute API calls.
nova-scheduler	Nova Scheduler: Takes a virtual machine instance request from the queue and determines on which compute server host it runs.
nova-conductor	Nova Scheduler: Mediates interactions between the nova-compute service and the database.
nova-consoleauth	Nova Console Authorization: Authorizes tokens for users that console proxies provide.
nova-novncproxy	Nova noVNC Proxy: Provides a proxy for accessing running instances through a VNC connection.
nova-compute	Nova Compute: A worker daemon that creates and terminates virtual machine instances through Hypervisor APIs.
mongodb	NoSQL database used for Ceilometer service.
ceilometer-api	Ceilometer API: Runs on one or more central management servers to provide data access from the data store.
ceilometer-collector	Ceilometer Collector: Runs on a central management server and dispatches collected telemetry data to a data store or external consumer.

(continued)

Table 12-1. (*continued*)

Service	Description
ceilometer-notification	Ceilometer Notification: Runs on a central management server and consumes messages from the message queue to build event and metering data.
ceilometer-central	Ceilometer Central: Runs on a central management server to poll for resource utilization statistics for resources not tied to instances or compute nodes.
ceilometer-compute	Ceilometer Compute: Runs on each compute node and polls for resource utilization statistics.
httpd	Apache web-server: Used for Horizon and for Keystone.
heat-engine	Heat Engine: Orchestrates the launching of templates and provides events back to the API consumer.
heat-api	Heat API: An OpenStack-native REST API that processes API requests by sending them to the Heat engine over the Remote Procedure Call.
heat-api-cfn	Heat API for Cloud Formation: An AWS Query API that is compatible with AWS CloudFormation. It processes API requests by sending them to the Heat engine over RPC.
neutron-server	Neutron Server: Accepts and routes API requests to the appropriate OpenStack networking plug-in for action.
neutron-l3-agent	Neutron l3 Agent: Agent for routing and NAT service.
neutron-dhcp-agent	Neutron DHCP Agent: With the help of dnsmasq processes, it provides DHCP service for instances.
neutron-metadata-agent	Neutron Metadata Agent: Works with Nova to provide metadata information into running instances.
openvswitch	Open vSwitch: OpenSource implementation of a distributed virtual multilayer switch.
neutron-openvswitch-agent	Neutron Open vSwitch Agent: Works with neutron-server and sends through message broker commands to OVS.
openstack-swift-proxy	OpenStack Swift Proxy: Accepts OpenStack Object Storage API and raw HTTP requests to upload files, modifies metadata, and creates containers.
openstack-swift-account	OpenStack Swift Account: Manages accounts defined with Object Storage.
openstack-swift-container	OpenStack Swift Container: Manages the mapping of containers or folders, within Object Storage.
openstack-swift-object	OpenStack Swift Object: Manages actual objects, such as files, on the storage nodes.

Table 12-2. *Network Ports Used by OpenStack*

Service	Port Number
Keystone: admins API endpoint	35357
Keystone: public API endpoint	5000
Glance endpoint	9292
Glance Registry	9191
Cinder block storage and iSCSI target	8776, 3260
Compute Service (Nova)	8774
Nova API	8773, 8775
Access to instances by VNC protocol	5900-5999
VNC proxy for browser access	6080
HTML5 proxy for browser access	6082
Swift object storage and rsync	8080, 6000, 6001, 6002, 873
Heat orchestration service	8004
Neutron network service	9696
Ceilometer telemetry	8777
RabbitMQ AMQP message broker	5672
MariaDB database	3306

Here at the end of this book, I would like to thank all of you readers. I hope you have found it interesting and useful and enjoyed the reading as much as I enjoyed writing it.

Index

© Andrey Markelov 2016
A. Markelov, *Certified OpensStack Administrator Study Guide*, DOI 10.1007/978-1-4842-2125-9

Get the eBook for only $5!

Why limit yourself?

Now you can take the weightless companion with you wherever you go and access your content on your PC, phone, tablet, or reader.

Since you've purchased this print book, we're happy to offer you the eBook in all 3 formats for just $5.

Convenient and fully searchable, the PDF version enables you to easily find and copy code—or perform examples by quickly toggling between instructions and applications. The MOBI format is ideal for your Kindle, while the ePUB can be utilized on a variety of mobile devices.

To learn more, go to www.apress.com/companion or contact support@apress.com.

CPSIA information can be obtained
at www.ICGtesting.com
Printed in the USA
LVOW02s0545130317
526920LV00019B/107/P